LANGUAGE AND LANGUAGE LEARNING

The Prague School of Linguistics and Language Teaching

LANGUAGE AND LANGUAGE LEARNING

General Editors: RONALD MACKIN *and* PETER STREVENS

1 Henry Sweet *The Practical Study of Languages*
2 J. R. Firth *The Tongues of Men* and *Speech*
3 Randolph Quirk and A. H. Smith *The Teaching of English*
4 Neile Osman *Modern English*
5 H. E. Palmer *The Principles of Language-Study*
6 N. E. Enkvist, J. Spencer and M. Gregory *Linguistics and Style*
7 H. E. Palmer *Curso Internacional de Inglés*
8 J. C. Catford *A Linguistic Theory of Translation*
9 Peter Strevens *Papers in Language and Language Teaching*
10 David Abercrombie *Studies in Phonetics and Linguistics*
11 *Five Inaugural Lectures* edited by Peter Strevens
12 Axel Wijk *Rules of Pronunciation for the English Language*
13 L. A. Hill *Selected Articles on the Teaching of English as a Foreign Language*
14 H. H. Stern *Foreign Languages in Primary Education*
15 Peter Ladefoged *Three Areas of Experimental Phonetics*
16 A. S. Hayes *Language Laboratory Facilities*
17 *Modern Language Teaching* edited by Hans Jalling
18 H. E. Palmer *The Scientific Study and Teaching of Languages*
19 *A Functional Language Examination* edited by H. S. Otter
20 J. Dakin, B. Tiffen and H. Widdowson *Language in Education*
21 *Language Testing Symposium* edited by Alan Davies
22 H. E. Palmer and Sir Vere Redman *This Language-Learning Business*
23 *An Annotated Bibliography of Modern Language Teaching: Books and Articles 1946–67* compiled by Janet O. Robinson
24 *Languages and the Young School Child* edited by H. H. Stern
25 *Prosodic Analysis* edited by F. R. Palmer
26 Edward M. Stack *The Language Laboratory and Modern Language Teaching: Third edition*
27 *The Prague School of Linguistics and Language Teaching* edited by V. Fried
28 *The Indispensable Foundation: a selection of the writings of Henry Sweet* edited by E. J. A. Henderson
29 J. B. Pride *The Social Meaning of Language*
30 W. H. Mittins *et al* *Attitudes to English Usage*
31 *Chomsky: Selected Readings* edited by J. P. B. Allen and P. van Buren
32 *Active Methods and Modern Aids in Foreign Language Teaching* edited by R. Filipovic

The Prague School of Linguistics and Language Teaching

Edited by V. FRIED

London
OXFORD UNIVERSITY PRESS
1972

Oxford University Press, Ely House, London W.1

GLASGOW NEW YORK TORONTO MELBOURNE WELLINGTON
CAPE TOWN SALISBURY IBADAN NAIROBI LUSAKA ADDIS ABABA
BOMBAY CALCUTTA MADRAS KARACHI LAHORE DACCA
KUALA LUMPUR SINGAPORE HONG KONG TOKYO

PRINTED IN GREAT BRITAIN BY HEADLEY BROTHERS LTD.
109 KINGSWAY LONDON WC2 AND ASHFORD KENT

Contents

To my great teachers, colleagues and friends
of the Czechoslovak linguistic community
past and present.

V.F.

Editor's Introduction

Vilém Fried

The linguistic sciences have been much in vogue during the past twenty years and their popularity seems unlikely to diminish. I have the impression that many of the culturally advanced countries have become more language conscious in the last two decades than ever before in their history. It would, no doubt, be an interesting subject of sociolinguistic investigation to analyse the cause of this social phenomenon in our time. With this constantly growing interest in both pure and applied linguistics, more attention is being paid to the history of its development; those interested in modern linguistic research and in its findings are also keen to learn about the beginnings of present-day linguistic science, in particular of structural linguistics, which is the label usually given to linguistic thought in this century. As a rule, three blends of early linguistic structuralism are mentioned: American (Bloomfieldian) Descriptivism, Danish (Hjelmslevian) Glossematics, and the Functional Linguistics of the Prague School. All three blends originated practically simultaneously in the nineteen-twenties and thirties. The Prague School of Linguistics has been mainly identified with the concept of the phoneme and the development of the phonological theory from the earliest books on modern linguistics:

> I have inserted a short account of the aims and methods of a new school of linguistics centred in Prague. The phonologists, as they are called, are working on a new theory of speech sounds . . . it is one of the most promising movements in present-day linguistics, for it opens up the prospect of a functional treatment of speech sounds.
>
> (L. R. Palmer, *Introduction to Modern Linguistics*. London, 1936, p. vii)

to one of the more recent of numerous publications on linguistics, R. H. Robins' *Short History of Linguistics* (London, 1967). This author speaks about the contribution of the Prague School mainly in connexion with phoneme theory and mentions, like so many other authors of similar books, the works of Prince Nikolaj Trubetskoy (especially his *Grundzüge der Phonologie*) and those of Roman Jakobson; at the same time, Robins admits that, especially since 1945, a number of contributions to other areas of linguistics (syntactic studies, stylistics, comparative typology, etc.) have been made by Czech linguists (204–6).

One of the aims of this volume of collected papers by Czechoslovak linguists is to prove that the range of functional linguistic studies pursued by members of the Prague School from the very start of its existence has been much wider than is generally assumed; the main reason for the lack of this information in other parts of the world is certainly due to the fact that most of these contributions were written in Czech or Slovak and were therefore inaccessible to speakers of non-Slavic languages. While we do not want to diminish in the least the great role played by what may be called the Russian group of scholars who were members of the Prague School, it is necessary to state that they were far out-numbered by their Czech and Slovak colleagues. Czech scholars like V. Mathesius, B. Trnka, B. Havránek, J. Mukařovský, J. Vachek and many others have indeed been both initiators and equally original followers of the new methods in linguistic research according to the functional and structural principles of language analysis. It is largely due to the unceasing efforts of Professor Josef Vachek that the general picture of the Linguistic School of Prague in English-speaking countries is now a very different one from that characterized by the quotations from Palmer and Robins above. Vachek has published three important books on the Prague School: *The Linguistic School of Prague* (1966), *A Prague School Reader in Linguistics* (1964), and *Dictionnaire de linguistique de l'École de Prague* (1966). In addition to these, in 1964 he published two particularly relevant articles: 'Prague phonological studies today' and, together with F. Daneš, 'Prague studies in structural grammar today'. Another important source of information is P. L. Garvin's *Prague School Reader in Esthetics, Literary Structure and Style* (1964) (cf. all these items in the bibliographical survey at the close of Vachek's contribution to this volume, pp. 25–28). The present book reveals one further dimension of the efforts of the Prague Linguistic School which has not yet been generally acknowledged outside Czechoslovakia: members of the Prague School and those who continue to work according to its principles have always been interested in the practical application of their linguistic theory, especially in the sphere of language teaching.

Let us recall briefly the history of what is today generally called the Prague School of Linguistics. Its beginning may be dated by the first meeting of the Cercle Linguistique de Prague on 6 October 1926. Its first chairman was Vilém Mathesius, Professor of English Language and Literature at the Caroline University of Prague. The members of the committee were B. Havránek, R. Jakobson, J. Mukařovský, F. Slotty, F. Trávníček, and B. Trnka. Its membership was not very large but included both Czechoslovak and foreign scholars, linguists and literary scientists. Among the members we find the names of V. Brøndal, P. Bogatyrev, H. Becker, D. Čyževskyj, L. Tesniére, N. Trubetzkoy, A. V. Isačenko, J. Rypka, J. Vachek, Z. Vančura and R. Wellek. The first common task which faced the members of the Circle was the formulation of collective theses to be presented to the First International Congress of Slavists in Prague in the summer of 1929. These theses were later published in Volume I of the *Travaux du Cercle linguistique de Prague* (1929). It was through the eight volumes of these *Travaux*, which were published until 1939, that the Prague School became known abroad. In 1930, on the initiative of the Circle, the first international phonological conference was convened in Prague in preparation for the International Linguistic Congress in Geneva in 1931. From then onwards the members of the Prague Circle prepared joint theses for several other international linguistic gatherings. It is worth noting here that in the prospectus to the First International Congress of Phonetic Sciences in Amsterdam in 1932 the term *L'école de Prague* was used for the first time. The activities of the Prague Circle were not confined to problems of general linguistic theory and its elaboration at international meetings but were also directed home: the members of the Circle applied the idea of functional interpretation of linguistic data to Modern Czech and Slovak usage in particular. They defended the usage of modern standard Czech against those who wanted to preserve as standard usage forms of expression which corresponded to a historical concept of the Czech language, thereby disregarding its living force as manifested in the works of good contemporary Czech authors (e.g. Karel Čapek), in the style of serious newspapers and periodicals, and above all in educated standard spoken Czech. The collection of papers by members of the Prague Circle so often mentioned in the footnotes to contributions to this volume, *Standard Czech and the Cultivation of Good Language* (1932) represents a milestone in the interpretation of Modern Czech. While the international activities of the members of the Prague School were abruptly interrupted by the outbreak of World War II and the tragic consequences of the Nazi occupation, it was on the home front that their influence continued. Many valuable papers were written by members of the Circle in wartime, but were published only in Czech or Slovak. They may chiefly be found in the Circle's periodical *Slovo a Slovesnost* ('Language and Literature') which was launched in 1935 and which continues to appear. The contributors to this volume refer to many papers published in this journal in the course of the past thirty years. Since the war the community of Czech and Slovak linguists who showed an active interest in modern linguistics and who therefore readily subscribed to the ideas of the Prague School has significantly grown in number. It was the Sixth International Congress of Linguists in Paris in 1948 to which members of the Circle for the last time presented collective answers to the questions formulated by the organizers, and the *Cercle linguistique de Prague* formally ceased to exist in 1950. It has at present two successors. This is due to the reorganization of scientific activities in Czechoslovakia after 1950 in connexion with the foundation of the Czechoslovak Academy of Sciences. The *Linguistic Association* comprises mainly specialists in general linguistics, in phonetics, in Slavic languages, and in Czech and Slovak linguistics, while the Group for Functional Linguistics at the *Circle of Modern Philologists* represents linguists in the field of English, Germanic and Romance languages. These organizations are not only active in Prague, but have several branches in many parts of the country (Bratislava, Brno, Olomouc, etc.). In the 'sixties Czechoslovak linguists again felt the need to publish collected volumes of those papers written in one of the world languages as evidence of the continuity—though far more broadly-based than before—of the Linguistic School of Prague. Bi-annually, since 1964, a new series has appeared, *Travaux de Linguistique de Prague*, which, together with another bi-annual publication, *Prague Studies in Mathematical Linguistics*, gives a fair picture of what the notion of 'the Prague Linguistic School' means today. The Slovak structural linguists published the *Recueil linguistique de Bratislava* in 1947, and a second volume was published in 1969. Further volumes will appear at regular intervals.

I should like to enumerate briefly the main topics of linguistic research which have interested the members of the Prague School and which could be called characteristic of the Prague School. Phonology, including historical phonology, holds first place. While this was the predominant field of interest before the war,[1] in post-war years it somehow receded into the background. It is not for this reason, however, that no paper dealing with a phonological problem proper has been included in this volume, but because its application in foreign language teaching has always been most evident, as e.g. Pierre Delattre pointed out in 1962. We have, however, included one

[1] A new revised edition of the classic monograph by B. Trnka, *A Phonological Analysis of Present-Day Standard English* (1935) has recently appeared in Japan (Tokyo, 1966).

paper, that by Jan Firbas, which deals in part with the problems of intonation from a structural point of view. Another typical topic—or perhaps rather a methodological approach to research—is the analytical confrontation of language data in unrelated or related languages. It may come as a surprise that we have not included in this volume an article that directly discusses this topic, the practical application of which in the foreign language teaching and learning process is undoubtedly of great importance. Our careful readers will, however, not fail to find that in the majority of contributions the method of analytical confrontation or comparison (we prefer this term to that of 'contrastive linguistics') has been applied and its results have been exploited. May I refer those readers who would like a fuller account of the principles of this method of analytical confrontation of two languages and its application to foreign language teaching to my own contribution to *Modern Language Teaching* (Vol. 17 of this Language and Language Learning series) entitled 'Comparative Linguistic Analysis in Language Teaching' (1968, pp. 38–46). (The papers in this volume were presented to the ninth Congress of the *Fédération Internationale des Professeurs de Langues Vivantes.*) This method of approach leads to linguistic characterology and typology of languages and the conclusions made in numerous papers included in the present volume are of this nature (e.g. the nominal character of present-day English or French). After the war more interest was shown in structural morphology. K. Bareš's paper indicates how this topic has been treated. Many more followers of the present-day Prague School have been interested in structural syntax, and several papers included here discuss some aspects of structural syntax in connexion with stylistic problems (see for example E. Beneš's paper). Another subject of linguistic research in which members of the Prague School have made pioneering contributions is the functional distinction of the written and spoken norms in one and the same language. Several papers in this volume further elaborate this distinction (e.g. V. Barnet). The interest in the study of word-order and its varying functions in different languages appeared in the writings of the members of the Prague School almost before it had been formally established. These studies led to profound analyses of the functional sentence perspective, to the evaluation of the theme-rheme relations in sentence types of various languages. We have, therefore, included a special paper on this subject by J. Firbas, who is an acknowledged expert in this field of research. Being members of a Slav speaking nation the members of the Prague School were naturally always interested in the problems of verbal aspect. The contribution of J. Šabršula is entirely devoted to this subject. Finally, the problem of style as a linguistic phenomenon has been of great interest to the members of the Prague School from its earliest times. A great many papers and discussions among the members of the Prague School have been devoted to outlining the notions of functional style, technical language, the language of science, terminology, literary language, poetic language, spoken language, etc. Here I think more has been done by the Prague School than has been generally realized outside Czechoslovakia and we have included eight papers that deal with problems of functional style (or register, as British linguists prefer to call this linguistic phenomenon) because it is in this field that the most profitable conclusions for the application of linguistic theory to language teaching can be made.

This brief enumeration of the main topics of interest in the linguistic research pursued by the Prague School may also serve as an explanation for the arrangement of the articles in this volume. Professor Vachek's paper discusses Prague School linguistics in general. The papers by V. Barnet, A. Menšíková and I. Poldauf indicate how some principles of the Prague theory of functional linguistics are of direct relevance to language teaching and learning theory. The papers by J. Firbas and by J. Šabršula each deal with one specific linguistic problem. J. Dubský's paper is meant as an introduction to the papers that follow, as it gives a general outline of the Prague concept of functional style and of the way in which this notion has developed in the writings of the Prague School. The papers that follow deal with the morphology and syntax of technical and scientific writing, with the specific stylistic features of dialogue, prose fiction, with problems of terminology, and with the style of technical language, especially the language of commerce.

Practically without exception, all papers included in this volume show how linguistic theory can be applied to language teaching in theory and practice; this principle has been inherent in Prague linguistic theory from its very beginning. In 1929, the founder of the Prague Linguistic Circle, Professor Vilém Mathesius, addressed a national conference of grammar school teachers in Prague and read a paper entitled 'Functional Linguistics'. In it he said, 'Every truly great idea must find practical application and have practical consequences'. Foreign language teaching has had of necessity a long tradition in Czechoslovakia because of its situation in the very heart of Europe with extensive frontiers which separate it from four linguistically distinct countries. The country of John Amos Comenius has always had a ready and open mind for new and better and more efficient methods of foreign language teaching and learning and the new concepts of the Linguistic School of Prague therefore fell on fertile ground. The theory could not have been restricted to the teaching of only one language. The chief representatives of the Prague School both now and in the past are Anglicists and Slavicists. It is therefore only natural that the impact of Prague linguistics was most felt in the teaching of English and Russian to Czechs and Slovaks. (After World War II Russian became the first foreign language in the Czechoslovak school system.) Of the contributions to this volume, six discuss problems of English, three of Russian, two of French and one of German, but at least two papers refer to phenomena in more than one language.

Foreign language teaching has not been the only practical concern of the members of the Prague School. Two nations—the Czech and Slovak, that for centuries had been nationally oppressed and yet preserved their national tongues because of the enlightened work of village teachers, peasant autodidacts and others who instilled in the people a love of their own native tongue—have never ceased to relish their native language. The national rebirth in the nineteenth century was inseparably linked with the revival of the two languages which quickly achieved a high literary standard once again. Hence both academic philologists and practising teachers, and the Czech and Slovak bourgeoisie at large, had always devoted the greatest attention to the proper teaching of the mother tongue. The strong democratic ideas in language cultivation, which were upheld on scientific grounds by the members of the Prague School, had also found their way into the classroom and greatly influenced the concept of the teaching of the mother tongue in schools of all levels. No paper dealing with this topic has been included in this volume because it would necessarily have to deal with linguistic examples from Czech or Slovak which, no doubt, are quite unfamiliar to most readers. May I only briefly state that practically all modern textbooks of Czech and Slovak used in Czechoslovak schools at present are definitely marked by the ideas of Prague linguistic theory.

Finally a few words about the contributors to this volume. Professor Josef Vachek, Ph.D., now senior research worker in linguistics in the Institute of the Czech language of the Czechoslovak Academy of Sciences, is so closely linked with the history of the Prague School of Linguistics that he needs no further introduction. Ivan Poldauf, Ph.D., is Professor of English Language in the Faculty of Philosophy of the Caroline University of Prague. He is also editor-in-chief of the journal *Cizí jazyky ve škole* (Foreign Languages in School). Vladimír Barnet, Ph.D., Associate Professor of Russian Language, is head of the department of East Slavonic languages in the Faculty of Philosophy of the Caroline University of Prague; his collaborators are Mrs Irena Camutaliová, Ph.D., and Mrs Květa Koževniková, Ph.D., lecturers in Russian in the same department; the three are part of a team that has developed the concept of audio-lingual teaching of Russian at university level. Jan Firbas, Ph.D., is Associate Professor of English Language and Head of the department of English and American studies in the Faculty of Philosophy of Brno University. Jan Šabršula, Ph.D., is Professor of Romance Philology in the Faculty of Philosophy of the Caroline University of Prague. Miss Antonie Menšíková is lecturer in practical French in the same faculty. Josef Dubský, Ph.D., is Assistant Professor of Spanish Language and head of the department of Romance languages at the College of Economics in Prague, and Josef Pytelka, Ph.D., is Assistant Professor of English Language and head of the department of English at the same school. Karel Bareš, Ph.D., is Assistant Professor of English Language at the University of 17th November in Prague. Rostislav Kocourek, Ph.D., is Assistant Professor in the department of Romance Languages, Dalhousie University, Nova Scotia. Eduard Beneš, Ph.D., is a research worker in German in the Institute of Language and Literature of the Czechoslovak Academy of Sciences in Prague. Miroslav Renský, Ph.D., is Professor of English at Brooklyn College, City University of New York.

The Editor is Associate Professor of Linguistics Applied to Language Teaching in the Faculty of Philosophy of the Caroline University of Prague, and head of the department of non-Slavonic languages in the same faculty; from 1936–39 he was student assistant to the late Professor Vilém Mathesius; 1945 he was also on the staff of the English Department of the Caroline University. From January 1969–March 1970 he was visiting professor for English as a second language in the English department of the University of California, in Los Angeles. At present he is Reader in Linguistics at Portsmouth Polytechnic.

I apologize in advance for a certain degree of repetition and overlapping in the papers, but this has been a necessary shortcoming. Each author was obliged to develop his particular theme from selected principles of Prague linguistic theory, and this common denominator will be evident. There has been no attempt to cross reference each of the fourteen contributions. The observant reader will also find repetition in bibliographical notes attached to each paper. Here the authors quoted many papers that were written in Czech or Slovak. The bibliographical list (pp. 25–28) following J. Vachek's paper, however, contains the most essential information about publications referring to the Prague School of Linguistics; practically all the items quoted there originally appeared in a world language or in translation.

Bibliographical note. All the papers except one in this book were originally submitted in English and have not been translated either by the editor or the publishers.

LIST OF ABBREVIATIONS

AUC Acta universitatis Carolinae (Prague)
BSE Brno Studies in English
CJvŠ Cizí jazyky ve škole (Foreign Languages in Schools)
ČMF Časopis pro moderní filologii (Journal for Modern Philology)
ČsR Československá rusistika (Czechoslovak Russian Studies)
IF Indoeuropäische Forschungen
Lg Language
OUPB Opera Universitatis Purkynianae Brunensis
PGB Beiträge zur Geschichte der deutschen Sprache u. Literatur Hrgg. von H. Paul u. W. Braune
PP Philologica Pragensia
PSE Prague Studies in English
PSRE Prague School Reader in Esthetics, Literary Structure and Style
PSRL Prague School Reader in Linguistics
SaS Slovo a slovesnost (Word and Literature), Journal of the Prague Linguistic Circle, founded in 1935
SPFFBU Sborník prací filosofické fakulty brněnské universitatis (Collected Volume of Papers of the Faculty of Philosophy of Brno University)
SČJK Spisovná čeština a jazyková kultura (Volume of papers on Standard Czech and the Culture of Language) Prague 1932
SJMP Sborník jazykovedných a metodických prací (Volume of Papers on Linguistics and FL Teaching Methods)
SW R. Jakobson: Selected Writings I (The Hague, 1960)
TCLP Travaux de Cercle linguistique de Prague, (volumes published from 1929 to 1939 in Prague)
TLP Travaux linguistiques de Prague (bi-annual collected volumes founded in 1964)
ZÚOŠ Zprávy ústavu obchodního školství (Reports of the Institute for Commercial Education)

1 The Linguistic Theory of the Prague School

Josef Vachek

I. A great deal has already been written in the last ten years[1] about the basic importance of the ideas of the Early Prague Linguistic Group for the post-1930 development of general linguistic theory. We may therefore confine ourselves in the present paper to singling out some of the more important aspects of the Prague theory, those which constitute its major contribution to the general linguistic thinking of the late 'twenties and early 'thirties, the period in which the Prague theory was globally formulated for the first time. Some of these aspects reveal the Prague reaction to the Neogrammarian approach, at that time still prevailing in world linguistics, others have a wider significance. In addition, we want to comment briefly on the present-day Prague conception of language, as this conception has organically developed from that of the Early Prague group, as can be seen from some of the recent Prague publications, dating from the mid-sixties.[2] Moreover, we want to point out and explain how the Prague theory has proved capable of solving many linguistic problems of everyday life. Right at the outset it should be stated that, unlike many other linguistic currents, the Prague group has never confined its attention to theoretical problems alone, and has always been opposed to research in linguistic theory done exclusively for theory's sake. On the contrary, the Prague group has always been noted for its systematic effort to derive practical consequences from its theoretical findings: this will also be demonstrated by most of the papers included in the present volume.

When historical linguists discuss the achievements and merits of the Early Prague Group, three points are usually emphasized: the first,

[1] See, e.g. V. A. Zvegincev 1964; M. M. Guchman and V. V. Jarceva (ed.) 1964; J. Vachek 1966a.

[2] See especially the two series of linguistic contributions appearing in Prague since 1964, i.e. *TLP* 1 (1964), 2 (1966), and 3 (1968), and *Prague Studies in Mathematical Linguistics* 1 (1966) and 2 (1967).

the most obvious but not the most essential, is the vindication of the synchronistic approach to facts of language; the second is the stress laid by the Prague scholars on the prevailingly systemic character of language; finally, the third, in the present writer's opinion the most essential of all, is the emphasis put on the function performed by language in the given language community. Each of the three points will be briefly discussed here.

As is commonly known, the Neogrammarian conception of language approved only of the historical linguistic research. Hermann Paul, the foremost theoretician of the group, even went so far as to stamp non-historical analysis of language as unscientific.[1] It should be most emphatically stressed that the Prague linguists have never neglected historical research; they made a point, however, of stressing that non-historical, synchronistic study is also fully justified, the more so that, unlike historical study, it can draw upon complete and easily controllable materials of investigation. This dictum may now read as common-place, almost banal truth, but when the founder of the Prague group, V. Mathesius, first formulated it in 1911,[2] that is, some fifteen years before the formation of the Prague Linguistic Circle, the organizing centre of the group, and five years before F. de Saussure's famous *Cours de linguistique générale* was to appear in print, it sounded almost revolutionary. Admittedly, some isolated voices had declared the necessity of synchronistic research into language before Mathesius (among them, especially, the names of W. von Humboldt, G. v.d. Gabelentz, and J. Baudouin de Courtenay should be mentioned, as Mathesius himself used to quote their writings among the sources that had helped him to formulate his own conception of language). But Mathesius went farther than most of them: he insisted on the possibility, and necessity, of applying to contemporary languages, whether genetically related or not, what he called the method of analytical comparison. In present-day linguistics, roughly the same approach characterizes the so-called contrastive (or, confrontational) method; it deserves to be noted that while the latter was only to emerge, in Western linguistics, in the 'fifties, Mathesius's first attempt at the application of this approach goes back to as early as 1928 and that, from then on until his death in the mid-forties, he was systematically availing himself of the contrastive method with the professed aim of arriving at what he called 'the linguistic characterology' of concrete

[1] H. Paul, p. 19.

[2] V. Mathesius 1911, p. 3 et pass

languages, especially of Modern English and Modern Czech.[1] This kind of research concentrated on those features of the examined language which stand out as particularly characteristic and typical of it. Thus, for example, in confronting ModE and ModCz, one finds the former characterized by a marked trend to nominal predications, while the predications of the latter language are predominantly verbal (compare, for example, ModE *we take our breakfast*, where the semantically most essential element is expressed by a noun, and its ModCz equivalent *snídáme*, which is the finite verb form of the first person plural with no trace of a nominal element).

While the justification of the synchronistic approach of the Prague group had had a native organic basis which only was to be later confirmed and intensified by the contributions of the Russian members of the group, the systemic and structural conception of language may be regarded as the specific contribution of the Russian scholars R. Jakobson and N. S. Trubetzkoy to Prague linguistic ideology. It was mainly Jakobson who, as early as in the late 'twenties, insisted on the fact that no element of any language system can be properly evaluated if viewed in isolation: its correct assessment can only be obtained if its relationship is established to all other elements co-existing with it in that same language system. Jakobson also pointed out that the evolution of language can only be duly interpreted if it is conceived of as an evolution of a systemic whole within which the relations of the elements composing it are often reshaped and/or replaced by other relations, the main aim of such changes being to maintain (or, as the case may be, to restore) the balance of the given language system.[2] It will be easily seen that in this highly important point the Prague conception again showed a radical departure from the Neogrammarian tradition which, as a rule, was intent on the observation and study of some isolated language element through the history of the given language, without considering the question of whether the relationship of such an element to its partners in the system remained unchanged or whether it was subject to minor or major shifts or alterations.

The third point typical of the Prague conception of language (and, as has already been noted, probably the most important of the three) is the functional approach to the facts of language.[3] It was rooted both

[1] In his lifetime, Mathesius only published a long series of papers comparing, from the indicated point-of-view, the said two languages. A more synthetizing view of his approach to the linguistic characterology of English can be obtained from his university course, published posthumously, sixteen years after his death (Mathesius 1961).

[2] On this point, see R. Jakobson 1929, p. 13f.

[3] See R. Jacobson (1963); K. Horálek; P. Novák and P. Sgall; R. Meyerstein.

in the Czech and in the Russian linguistic tradition but the Early Prague Group was to work it out in detail and to apply it most consistently to language phenomena of all kinds. This approach visualizes language as a tool performing a number of essential functions or tasks in the community using it. The most outstanding (and most obvious) among these tasks is undoubtedly the communicative function, serving the needs and wants of the mutual understanding of individual members of the given language community. There are, however, some elements of the language system which clearly serve more specific purposes. Such are, for example, archaisms like ModE *thou*, *kine*, etc., which go farther than common communication: they also constitute signals of a somewhat unusual and solemn approach to the treated extralingual reality. It is also well known that poetic language is characterized by some specific patterns of organization of language elements which, besides communicating some content, are also intent on the way in which this content is being communicated (such are, for example, various patterns of rhythm, repetition of some specific combinations of sounds, use of lexical and/or phraseological units otherwise not employed in usual communication, etc., etc.). Moreover, it is also pointed out that even in those utterances which serve the purpose of ordinary, aesthetically uncharged communication, important differentiations can be established according to whether, for example, the speaker confines himself to a simple, matter-of-fact announcement, or analyses the communicated content in a more detailed manner, pointing out the inner connections of the facts of the extra lingual reality referred to: in the former case the syntactic make-up of the communication is simpler than in the latter, and the selection of the lexical units will be done in a more casual way in the former case, and with regard to finer semantic shades of such units in the latter case.

Clearly, in all the above-described instances the use of language is prompted by the speaker's approach to the extra lingual reality reflected in his act of communication or, briefly, by the meaning to which his act of communication is seen to refer. It should be noted that this regard for meaning has been justly considered one of the characteristic features of the Prague linguistic approach, differentiating it from some other structurally orientated linguistic currents which deliberately disregard problems of meaning (especially the post-Bloomfieldian Northern American approach, currently denoted as that of the Yale linguistic group). It is worth recalling that an eminent Soviet specialist even goes so far as to regard this functionalist approach as a specific feature of the Prague linguistic group.[1] It certainly constitutes one of its most essential features: the facts adduced in the preceding paragraph reveal clearly enough that it was exactly this feature which was to enable the Prague group to tackle the basic problems of stylistics; later on, it will be shown that the functionalist approach makes the Prague group also capable of contributing, in a not insignificant way, to the solution of some questions of language teaching, which is the primary concern of the present volume.

II. Even today, after World War II, bearing in mind the preceding discussion, the three points constitute the fundamental elements of what might be called the neo-Prague approach, which is more or less typical of virtually all Czechoslovak linguistic effort. Some aspects of this approach, however, have become particularly stressed and developed in the post-1950 period, although in principle they must undoubtedly have been present in the pre-war Prague conception. First and foremost, we should like to draw the reader's attention to the conception of language not as a uniform, closed system, but as an open (that is, not fully balanced) system of sub-systems, all of which are mutually interdependent. Such sub-systems are constituted by what is usually termed the levels of language, such as phonological, morphological, syntactic, lexical, etc. An important consequence of the interdependence of such sub-systems is that a change incurred by one of them may cause some other change in one or more other sub-systems of that same language. It was commonly acknowledged years ago that, e.g., the morphological change by which the Late Old English 'synthetic' declension of nouns came to be reshaped into the Middle English 'analytical' declension (and which itself had had a phonological motivation, as the weakening and ultimate loss of inflectional endings had been due to the operation in Germanic languages of strong dynamic stress) very naturally had some consequences on the syntactic level of Middle English and Early Modern English, inasmuch as the originally 'free' word-order of the OE sentence was to become much more fixed in ME, and especially in EModE.[2] It may be ascertained, however, that the impulse to such 'chain reactions' need not necessarily have its source at the phonological level, but that, on the contrary, some phonological change (or, as the case may be, the non-occurrence of some imminent phonological change) may be motivated by the

[1] V. A. Zvegincev, in his survey of the history of linguistics of the nineteenth and twentieth centuries, gives the chapter on the Prague group a very characteristic heading, 'Funkcional'naja lingvistika' (p. 121).

[2] Some interesting aspects of the process were pointed out by J. Šimko.

needs and wants of some higher language level, especially morphological and lexical.

An interesting example of such interdependence (which is by no means 'mixing of levels', as is sometimes asserted—the levels preserve their relative autonomy despite their mutual interdependence) may be discovered in the development of English, compared with that of some Slavonic languages (such as Russian or Czech). In the latter languages, the loss of the final 'weak' vowels ь̮, ъ̮ caused a devoicing of the originally voiced paired consonant phonemes that had preceded such vowels, so that words like *plod*ъ 'fruit'—*plot*ъ 'fence' turned homonyms, both being, from then on, pronounced as [plɔt]. The physiological motivation of the devoicing process is too obvious to necessitate any detailed explanation or justification. The more surprising is the fact that in the course of the development of English, in situations fairly analogous to the above-noted Slavonic ones, no such merger of voiced and voiceless paired consonants occurred, so that word-pairs like *plod—plot*, *rib—rip*, *ridge—rich*, etc., have not become homophonous and continue to be kept apart by the phonemic differences of the final elements of the members of each pair. The preservation of the consonantal opposition was made possible by an interesting process of phonemic re-evaluation: the opposed phonemes are no longer evaluated as 'voiced' *versus* 'voiceless' but as 'lax' *versus* 'tense'. The new opposition, originally a mere concomitant factor to the opposition of voice, came to be raised to the status of an opposition that is functionally relevant.

Very naturally, one is faced here with the question as to why the phonic development in the two languages went different ways. In one of our earlier papers[1] we have shown that the general situation on the 'higher' language levels in ModCz was such as to admit the increase of homophonous word-pairs (such as *plod—plot*) by the operation of the above-described devoicing process. The members of such new ModCz homophonous pairs, that is to say, could only be kept apart with the help of the sentence context, and the ModCz sentence context is perfectly able to perform the function of distinguishing them because it has not been charged too heavily with other distinguishing functions (grammatical or lexical). Contrary to this, in ModE there are many distinguishing functions the sentence context must perform—it is commonly known that, e.g., the cases of nouns are regularly differentiated by sentence context alone, and even word-classes are very frequently identified only thanks to the sentence context (this fact

[1] See J. Vachek 1961.

underlies the notorious phenomenon of ModE conversion).[1] Under these circumstances, it is obvious that any additional charging of the ModE sentence context with some further differentiating functions would not be thought wise. In other words, the overcharged ModE sentence context could hardly take on the additional task of distinguishing from one another members of word-pairs like *plod—plot*, *rib—rip*, *ridge—rich*, if such members were to become homophonous. Thus it would seem necessary to preserve the phonological differentiation of the members of such word-pairs, and as such differentiation in terms of voice did not, on physiological grounds, prove feasible, the only acceptable solution has proved to be the phonological re-evaluation of the given phonic difference in terms of the opposition 'lax': 'tense'.

So much has had to be said about the mutual interdependence of the sub-systems found within the system of language. Some comment is also needed on the open character of the language system, a point which in recent years has been increasingly worked out by Czechoslovak linguists building on the pre-war Prague tradition,[2] though, of course the fact itself did not escape the pre-war pioneers of the Prague approach. The above-noted Jakobsonian thesis of 1929, implying that no language ever constitutes a perfectly balanced system, also necessarily implies that any language system, at any moment of its existence, contains some structural deficiences (features which some American linguists like C. F. Hockett and K. L. Pike sometimes denote by the term 'fuzzy points'; the Prague people prefer to speak here rather of peripheral elements of the system of language, which are opposed to its central elements). As an example of such a peripheral element on the phonological level of ModE may be adduced the phoneme /h/ which in the standard language is only maintained by force of tradition, while in the popular dialects, unhampered by traditional factors, it has been discarded from their phonological systems (see J. Vachek, 1964b, Ch. II).

The existence of structural deficiences does not, as is sometimes feared, detract from the convincingness of the structural approach to language; it is perfectly compatible with the conception of the language system viewed as a dynamic structure. That language has exactly this type of structure, not a static one, is clearly shown by the universal phenomenon of language development—as a matter of fact, a static structure would be wholly unable to develop because the absence of 'fuzzy points' in it would imply the lack of inner tension responsible

[1] Most recently, conversion phenomena were discussed by S. Potter, 1966.

[2] See especially the central theme of the second volume of the post-war Prague series *TLP* (the volume bears the title 'Les problèmes du centre et de la périphérie du système de la langue'), 1966.

for its dynamism. Moreover, it should be realized that the unbalanced, dynamic character of the system of language is a necessary consequence of the communicative function of language. It is a commonplace fact that the extra lingual reality in and about which the language users communicate is becoming ever more complicated and that the language system must again and again be adapted to this increasing complexity if it is to be functionally adequate to the needs and wants of the reality to be communicated. This is particularly evident on the lexical level which has to be increasingly enriched by new items, denoting the newly emerging facts of technological and social reality, if it is to cope with its communicative tasks satisfactorily (needless to say, the same level also gets rid of those items which no longer refer to any element of the extralingual reality, or at least shifts such lexical items to the periphery of the lexical sub-system of the language). Similar processes might be ascertained on other language levels, even if less conspicuously than on the lexical level. The fact that the complexity of the extra-lingual reality is increasing incessantly clearly reveals that no language can ever be regarded as fully up to its tasks and, for this reason too, can never be regarded as fully balanced.

It may be useful to point out that it is exactly this conception of language as an open, dynamic system which makes it eminently suited for the analysis of standard languages, research into which has often been neglected by most existing currents of linguistic theory (including the Neogrammarians). The Prague group may indeed claim to have been the first to work out, mainly in the writings of B. Havránek (1932, 1936, 1962), a fully consistent functionalist theory of the standard language and of the cultivation of language in general. (On these points, see J. Dubský's paper in the present volume.) The working out of such a theory is based, among other things, on the postulate of 'elastic stability' which, according to V. Mathesius (1932) should be fulfilled by any standard language. The attribute 'elastic' (as opposed to 'rigid') duly respects the dynamic nature of the language system, while the reference to the 'stability' of the standard language pays tribute to its genuinely systemic character, to the fact that for the members of the language community using it the literary standard does constitute a kind of stable norm, guaranteeing not only the fact of mutual understanding of all its users but also the existence of identical literary aesthetic values valid for the whole of this community. It deserves to be mentioned that in the Anglo-American linguistic literature problems of the standard language and of the cultivation of language in general have only very recently been discovered as topics worthy of serious theoretical investigation (see particularly P. S. Ray, (1963), P. L. Garvin and M. Mathiot, 1956), more than two decades after their first theoretical treatment by the theoreticians of the Prague linguistic group.

III. The functionalist and structuralist approach also enabled the Prague linguistic group to gain a deeper insight into the manner in which concrete utterances are being construed in everyday life. V. Mathesius has given new sense to the traditional distinction of grammatical and psychological subject (and to the analogous distinction of the two kinds of predicates) by replacing its psychologistic terms with those based on the functional linguistic approach. He envisaged, that is to say, the sentence-utterance from the viewpoint of the information conveyed by it, and so found that, as a rule, it consists of two basic parts. The first of them, now usually called the theme, refers to a fact (or facts) already known from the preceding context or to facts taken for granted, and so does not (or does only slightly) contribute to the information transmitted by the given sentence-utterance. The other part, now usually called the rheme, contains the essential information transmitted by the given sentence-utterance and so substantially enriches the listener's knowledge. This distinction, again formulated by Mathesius as early as in the early 'thirties, may remind an Anglo-American reader of the opposition of 'topic' and 'comment' which was to be formulated by some American scholars some two decades later. In Mathesius's conception this distinction has proved to be a valuable tool for contrasting sentence structures in various languages and for establishing some hitherto unknown specific features of their syntax and stylistics,[1] J. Firbas's paper in the present volume discusses these problems in detail.

The Prague approach to language has also been helpful in throwing some new light on the way in which language is employed for emotive purposes. In attacking this problem, Prague linguists availed themselves of K. Bühler's notorious model of the functions of language.[2] As is commonly known, this model distinguishes three basic functions of language (or rather, of speech utterances by which language is being implemented), viz. the function of expression ('Ausdrucks-' or 'Kundgabefunktion'), the function of appeal ('Appellfunktion') and the function of reference ('Darstellungsfunktion'). While the task of the last-mentioned is to convey the factual content reflecting the

[1] See J. Firbas: Comparative Word-order Studies.
[2] See K. Bühler's monograph Sprachtheorie (1934).

communicated extra lingual reality, the first two functions serve the emotive purposes: the function of expression characterizes the speaker as distinct from other speakers, while the function of appeal (by some termed the 'conative' function) is directed at the listener who is to be influenced by the given utterance. Very frequently such influencing consists in transmitting to the listener some emotive evaluation (whether positive or negative) of the communicated content, with the more or less obvious intention of evoking analogous emotive evaluation on the part of the listener. The interesting point is that in studying concrete utterances from the indicated viewpoint one invariably finds that the language used for the purpose of signalling the emotive approach is precisely that which has not been utilized for purely communicative non-emotive purposes (i.e. for the purposes of the function of reference). As a concrete specimen of such use of language means may be adduced by the well-known French '*accent d'insistance*', placed on the initial syllable of a polysyllabic word, while the word-stress uncharged with the emotive function and serving purely communicative purposes invariably lies on the last syllable of such a word (and, of course, may be wholly suppressed for rhythmical or intonational reasons). On the grammatical level, the use in ModE of the feminine pronoun in referring to nouns denoting inanimate objects (the usual reference to which is provided by the neuter pronoun) may also be evaluated as a signal of strong, positive emotional feeling—see instances like *My poor little car, she had a breakdown*, or *I'll take her down* (speaking of a plane), etc.[1] It is hardly necessary to stress the importance of this 'complementary distribution' of the use of language means both for the theory of style and for concrete stylistic instruction (as is well known, problems of style, and also those of the poetic language, closely allied to them, were the subject of close examination in the pre-war Prague group).[2]

If the idea of the above-mentioned 'complementary distribution' of devices of language is thought out consistently, it cannot but lead to the conclusion that the stylistic differentiation of language is due to the differences of the approach of language users to what is essentially one and the same extralingual reality. The differences of approach are effected by making an adequate selection of the existing language means (an adequate sub-code, if one prefers that term), the selection which appears to be indicated for the given specific purpose. Thus,

[1] More comment on this use of the pronoun may be found in J. Vachek 1964a.
[2] Cf. especially the work done, before the war, by J. Mukařovský, a foremost Czech aesthetician and literary scholar.

for example, an account of one and the same trip will use different language means according to whether the speaker describing it is, for example, addressing a close friend, a person superior to him or her, or writing about it in an essay to be published in some periodical. The differences involved in the process of selection will be concerned with virtually all language levels—lexical and syntactic, as well as morphological and phonological.[1]

IV. In full conformity with the above-sketched Prague conception of the stylistic differentiation of language is also the Prague approach to questions of speech correctness and of the cultivation of language in general. To what has already been said in passing on this subject some interesting details should be added on the approach to this problem by Prague pre-functionalist linguistics of the early 'thirties. At that time, the predominant conception of correct speech had been a historically biased one: only those lexical and phraseological elements could have been evaluated as correct which could have claimed continuous existence in the language for at least four centuries—a more recent emergence of a word or a phrase was regarded as a weighty argument for its inadequacy and inability to rank as 'correct'. Opposed to this historicism, the Prague linguistic group urged that functional adequacy should be the main criterion by which the correctness of a word or a phrase is to be gauged. If a word or a phrase is functionally needed in the language and if it has managed to take firm root in the practice of language users, it has demonstrated its functional adequacy and must be evaluated as a 'correct' element of the given language. Even foreignisms (such as Czech words and phrases coined on foreign, especially German, models) should be regarded as functionally adequate if they have been accepted by the language community and if in the current use of that community there is no native element equally well qualified that might be capable of replacing them. Obviously, this view introduced a consistently functionalist approach of the problem, an approach which ultimately was to prevail in Czech and Slovak theory of speech standardization as well as in the practice corresponding to it. (Incidentally, this approach has been endorsed, in the post-war period, by a number of scholars of international renown who had tackled these and allied problems, e.g. the late A. Sommerfelt, E. Haugen, and P. L. Garvin.)

Closely connected with the above-discussed stylistic differentiation

[1] For more information see B. Havránek 1932, and J. Dubský's paper in the present volume.

is also the differentiation in language of the synchronically domestic and synchronically foreign elements. Admittedly, the use of the latter may have a specific stylistic value (as a rule, their use signals either an elevated, 'highbrow' approach, or points to a highly specialized subject matter, tending to raise the context above the level of simple, non-specialized communication). It should, however, be emphatically stressed with V. Mathesius (1934) that synchronic foreignisms should not be identified with diachronic foreignisms, i.e. with words of etymologically foreign origin. As is well known, in the course of language development, it not infrequently happens that an originally foreign word becomes adapted to the regularities of the native word-stock to such a degree as to become, from the purely synchronistic viewpoint, indistinguishable from synchronically domestic words. As examples of such adaptation may be adduced ModE words like *fine*, *beef*, *sport*, etc., which a linguistically unschooled English speaker would hardly suspect of being of French origin.

For the synchronistic classification of lexical items into domestic and foreign only those features of lexical items are really essential which are strictly synchronistic and can be identified by an unsophisticated speaker of the language concerned. Signals of synchronically foreign character may be found at various levels of language, mainly of course at the level of phonology and grammar. As examples of the former in ModE may be mentioned the nasalized vowel phonemes, frequently found in loans taken from French and still evaluated as foreignisms (see instances like *restaurant*, *feuilleton*, etc.); among the latter, e.g., the formation of plural forms like *bacilli* from sg. *bacillus, crises* from *crisis*, etc.

That the synchronistic distinction of domestic and foreign elements is based on realities of language and is not a mere fancy of a linguist's abstractive capacity, is proved by interesting facts recorded in their time by V. Mathesius (1929) and N. S. Trubetzkoy (1939). Both these scholars point out that sometimes the synchronically foreign evaluation of this or that word may be underlined by the (etymologically unjustified) addition of a phonological feature exclusively characteristic of synchronically foreign lexical units. Thus, e.g., Trubetzkoy shows that the ModGerman word *Telephon*, already identified as synchronically foreign owing to its oxytonic stress, is often heard in Vienna to be pronounced not with final /-on/, but with the nasal vowel /õ/, which in ModGer, as in ModE, clearly signals the synchronically foreign lexical elements. Similarly, as shown by Mathesius, native speakers of Czech often replace, in the substandard pronunciation of synchronically foreign words, the phoneme /k/ by /g/, which again in Czech is an obvious foreignism (e.g. words like *cirkus* 'circus', *balkón* 'balcony' may be heard in the forms /cirgus/, /balgo:n/. It is hardly necessary to stress that without a clear distinction of synchronically domestic and foreign elements[1] no description of a language can be considered complete. The fact that in some cases the line separating the two categories may not be very easy to draw—and possibly in some specific instances may not be ascertainable at all—is a different matter, resulting from the very existence of peripheral phenomena of language, which, as noted above, has been duly stressed by the Prague linguistic group. It should only be added that the differentiation discussed in this paragraph is not a mere theoretical affair but also has practical significance: it cannot be neglected either by the translator or by the teacher of a foreign language if he is to transmit its stylistic values adequately to his reader or pupil.

V. It is only natural that the reader of the present volume will be most interested in the question of whether the Prague linguistic group has ever been engaged in the problems connected with language teaching, especially in teaching foreign languages. The answer to this question is, of course, decidely positive. Already in their 1929 theses, which constituted, as it were, a blueprint of their theory, and which were presented by them to the First International Congress of Slavists, problems of language teaching were considered.[2] The scholars who drafted the theses had already shown (or were to show later on) in their own writings or practical textbooks how they wanted their theoretical principles to be concretely applied—see especially the grammar and exercise-book of Czech as a native language, compiled by B. Havránek and his colleagues, L. V. Kopeckij's textbooks of Russian for the Czechs, a number of textbooks of English by B. Trnka and some other authors, etc. V. Mathesius himself, by specialization an Anglicist, demonstrated in a series of broadcast lectures how the confrontational method can be applied to the teaching of English.[3] Other members of the Prague group who in the 'forties worked in this field were K. Roubíček, K. Hais, J. Vachek and others. The new functionalist approach, based on the confrontational method, was to

[1] The difference of phonological regularities obtaining between synchronically domestic and synchronically foreign words was to be noticed, outside the Prague group, only fifteen years after Mathesius's paper was published (cf. C. C. Fries—K. L. Pike).

[2] The theses were published in French in TCLP1 (1929), partly reprinted in PSRL. Russian version see Kondrasev; Italian transl. See Garroni.

[3] These lectures appeared in print (Mathesius 1936); on Mathesius's example, J. Nosil, compiled an analogous book for Modern German.

prove particularly useful in the research and teaching of the language of commerce (on this subject see especially Z. Vančura 1936). After World War II, work on the application of Prague linguistic principles to language teaching was continued by members of the younger generation of scholars. Among them the name of the Anglicist L. Cejp, who died at a very early age, deserves to be singled out; many of Havránek's and Kopeckij's pupils have applied the contrastive method to the study of Russian and to its teaching in the Czech schools, and analogous work in problems of Modern English, German and French has also yielded a number of interesting results. (It will be observed that many of the Prague workers in this and adjacent fields have contributed to the present volume.)[1]

As has already been mentioned, the theory and practice of language teaching based on Prague linguistic principles makes full use of the contrastive (confrontational) method which was worked out by V. Mathesius in the late 'twenties. The advantage of that method lies in the possibility it offers of comparing any two languages, whether generically related or not, and, on top of this, two different stages of one and the same language. In effecting such comparison, common background (the '*tertium comparationis*') is constituted by the communicative needs and wants to be expressed, which are roughly analogous in all language communities. Then, of course, the different ways in which the compared languages express these needs and wants are mutually compared to make the specific features of the given languages (the 'linguistic characterology' of each of them, to use Mathesius's term) stand out as clearly as possible.

In language teaching, the instructor using the contrastive method makes a point of stressing, in the taught foreign language, not only those of its features which are identical or parallel in it with the corresponding features of the pupil's mother tongue, but also, and particularly, those features in which the two languages are found to differ. The theoretical rules to be utilized in the process of teaching have to be simple and always derived from typical specimens of living speech. In the formulation of such rules the experience gained by the adherents of the generative grammar may be of some use (still, to make the generative method the basis of the whole teaching process would hardly be profitable, in view of the complexity and high abstraction of many such rules). Both the inductive and the deductive method should be used in the process of teaching and should complement one another.

[1] For a more detailed account see the article by V. Fried (1965).

It is hardly necessary to stress that of course the theory underlying the contrastive approach should itself by no means become the subject of teaching. On the other hand, the factual basis of this approach is so solid that, if reasonably applied, the approach can result in a considerable rationalization of the process of teaching. Supplying this solid ground for the teaching process is the undeniable fact that any pupil does possess adequate command of his own mother tongue which he is able to use in the more or less differentiated situations he faces in his daily life, i.e. in roughly the same situations in which he will be expected to use the language he is being taught. Such adequate command may be taken as evidence for the existence of what the Prague group terms 'linguistic consciousness' (and what is roughly comparable to N. Chomsky's 'intuition'). However vague this term may appear, the existence of its factual correlate can hardly be doubted (it is attested, among other things, by the interference of the pupil's mother tongue into the patterns of the foreign language which he is expected to master). As a matter of fact, the existence of this linguistic consciousness or awareness appears to be the only safe ground on which the teaching of a foreign language can build, despite the fact that the said consciousness functions here more as a set of instincts than as an established system of strictly delimited concepts.

A few words remain to be said on the teaching of the mother tongue. This process, as conceived by B. Havránek and his colleagues, and as exemplified in their above-mentioned textbook of Czech, has as its professed aim the derivation from the above-mentioned instinctive use of the patterns of the mother tongue a fully conscious system, underlying a conscious, functionally orientated use. It is only in this way, not in establishing and handing over a highly abstract edifice of dehumanized schemes and paradigms, that the teaching of the mother tongue can result in a truly adequate knowledge of the system of that tongue, and only in this manner will this teaching arrive at results useful not only practically but also socially. It may indeed be said that this regard for the social and human underlies the linguistic theory of the Prague group, and that it is for this reason that its application to language teaching turns out to be so profitable.

Bibliography*

O. Akhmanova & G. Mikael'an, *Theory of Syntax in Modern Linguistics.* (The Hague, 1969), especially pages 64 ff.

* Complemented by the editor V.F.

E. BENEŠ & J. VACHEK (eds.), *Stilistik und Soziolinguistik. Beiträge der Prager Schule zur strukturellen Sprachbetrachtung u. Spracherziehung* (Berlin 1971).

K. BÜHLER, *Sprachtheorie* (Jena 1934).

T. V. BULYGINA, 'Pražskaja lingvističeskaja škola'. In M. M. Guchman & V. N. Jarceva (eds.), *Osnovyje napravlenija strukturalizma* (Moscow 1964).

F. DANEŠ & J. VACHEK, 'Prague Studies in Structural Grammar Today'. *TLP* 1 (1964), 21–32.

J. P. FAYE & L. ROBEL (eds.), *Le cercle de Prague. Change No. 3* (Paris 1969).

J. FIRBAS, 'Comparative Word-Order Studies'. *BSE 4* (1964), 111-28.

V. FRIED (1965), 'The Prague School and Foreign Language Teaching', *AUC—PSE* 11, 15–30.

V. FRIED, 'Comparative Linguistic Analysis in Language Teaching'. In *Modern Language Teaching* (ed. Jalling), (London 1968), 38–46.

C. C. FRIES & K. L. PIKE, 'Coexistent Phonemic Systems', *Lg.* 25 (1949), 29–50.

E. GARRONI (ed.), *Il Circolo Linguistico di Praga. Le tesi del' 29.* (Milano 1966).

P. L. GARVIN (1963), Czechoslovakia in *Current Trends in Linguistics*, ed. by Th. A. Sebeok, Vol. 1: Soviet and Eastern European Linguistics (1963), 499–522.

P. L. GARVIN (ed.) (1964), *A Prague School Reader on Esthetics, Literary Structure, and Style* (Washington, 1955—3rd printing 1964).

P. L. GARVIN (1969), The Prague School of Linguistics. In *Linguistics Today*, ed. by A. A. Hill (New York 1969), 229–38.

P. L. GARVIN (1969), *Aspectos sociolinguísticos de la lengua nacional: La experiencia checa y el trabajo de la escuela de Praga* (Sympósio de Sâo Paulo 1969).

P. L. GARVIN & M. MATHIOT, 'The Urbanization of the Guarani Language', A Problem in Language and Culture; in *Selected Papers of the Fifth International Congress of Anthropological and Ethnological Sciences* (Philadelphia 1956), 783–90.

B. HAVRÁNEK (1932), 'Úkoly spisovného jazyka a jeho kultura'; (The Tasks and Cultivation of the Standard Language), in *SČJK*, 32-84. In part translated by P. L. Garvin under the title The Functional Differentiation of the Standard Language, *PSRE*, 3–16.

B. HAVRÁNEK (1936), 'Zum Problem der Norm in der heutigen Sprachwissenschaft und Sprachkultur'. *Actes du Quatrième Congrès international de Linguistes* (Copenhagen 1936) 151–6. Reprinted in *PSRL*, 413–20.

B. HAVRÁNEK (1962), *Studie o spisovném jazyce* (Studies in the Standard Language) (Prague 1962).

B. Havránek, L. Kopeckij, E. Starý & A. Získal, *Cvičebnice jazyka českého pro 1-4 třídu středních škol* (Prague 1933–1936).

K. Horálek, 'Les fonctions de la langue et de la parole'. *TLP* 1 (1964), 41–6.

R. Jakobson (1929), 'Remarques sur l'évolution phonologique du russe comparée à celle des autres langues slaves'. *TCLP* 2 (1929). Reprinted in *SW*, 7–116.

R. Jakobson (1963), 'Efforts towards a Means-Ends Model in European Linguistics in the Inter-War Period'. In *Trends in European and American Linguistics* (1930–1960) II (Utrecht 1963). Reprinted in *PSRL*, 480–85.

A. Jedlička, 'Česká jazykověda a otázky jazykového vyučování' (Czech linguistics and problems of language teaching). *Naše řeč* 40 (1957), 15–28.

N. A. Kondrašov (ed.), Pražskij lingvističeskij kružok (Moscow 1967).

H. Kučera, 'The Czech Contribution to Modern Linguistics'. In *The Czechoslovak Contribution to World Culture* (ed. M. Rechcigl, Jr.) (The Hague 1964), 93–104.

V. Mathesius (1911), O potenciálnosti jevů jazykových (On the Potentiality of the Phenomena of Language), *Věstník Král. české společnosti nauk, třída filos.-histor.* (Prague 1911). For the English translation see *PSRL*, 1–32, for the Russian translation Kondrašov, 42–69.

V. Mathesius (1928), 'On the Linguistic Characterology of Modern English'. *Actes du Premier Congrès International de Linguistes à la Haye* (1928) 58-63. Reprinted in *PSRL*, 59-67.

V. Mathesius (1929), 'La structure phonologique du lexique du tchèque moderne'. *TCLP* 1 (1929) 67–84. Reprinted in *PSRL*, 156–76.

V. Mathesius (1932), 'O potřebě stability ve spisovném jazyce' (On the Need for Stability in the Standard Language). *SČJK*, 14–31.

V. Mathesius (1934), 'Zur synchronischen Analyse fremden Sprachguts'. *Englische Studien* 70 (1934) pp. 21–35. Reprinted in *PSRL*, 398–412.

V. Mathesius (1936), *Nebojte se angličtiny*! (Do not be afraid of English) (Prague 1936).

V. Mathesius (1961), *Obsahový rozbor současné angličtiny na základě obecně lingvistickém* (A Functional Analysis of Present Day English on a General Linguistic Basis) (Prague 1961). With a detailed summary in English (edited by J. Vachek).

R. S. Meyerstein, *Functional Load* (The Hague 1970).

J. Mukařovský (1931), 'La phonologie et la poétique'. *TCLP* 4 (1931), 278–88.

J. MUKAŘOVSKÝ (1932), 'Jazyk spisovný a jazyk básnický' (The Standard Language and the Poetic Language). *SČJK*, 123–56. In part translated by P. L. Garvin in *PSRE*, 17–30.

J. MUKAŘOVSKÝ, (1948) *Kapitoly z ceské poetiky* (Chapters from Czech Poetics) (Prague 1948). German translation by W. Schamschula *Kapitel aus der Poetik*. (Frankfurt a.M. 1967).

J. NOSIL, *Poznejte němčinu* (Get acquainted with German) (Prague 1942).

P. NOVÁK and P. SGALL, 'On the Prague Functional Approach'. *TLP* 3 (1968), 291–9.

H. PAUL, *Prinzipien der Sprachgeschichte*, 2nd ed. (Halle 1886).

S. POTTER, 'Limits of Functional Shift'. *Studies in Language and Literature in Honour of Margaret Schlauch* (Warsaw 1966), 307–12.

S. POTTER and B. TRNKA, *Učebnice jazyka anglického* pro střední školy I–III (Prague 1926–1928).

P. S. RAY, *Language Standardization* (The Hague 1963).

P. SGALL, E. HAJÍČOVÁ, V. NEBESKÝ, *A Functional Approach to Syntax in Generative Language Description* (New York, London 1969).

J. ŠIMKO, *Word-order in the Winchester Manuscript and in William Caxton's Edition of Thomas Malory's Morte d'Arthur* (1485) (Halle, Saale 1957).

N. S. TRUBETZKOY, 'Grundzüge der Phonologie'. *TCLP* 7 (1939). French transl. Paris 1949; Russian, Moscow 1960; English, The Hague 1969.

J. VACHEK (1961), 'Some Less Familiar Aspects of the Analytical Trend of English.' *BSE* 3 (1961), 9–78.

J. VACHEK (1964a), Notes on Gender in Modern English. *SPFFBU* A 12 (1964), 189–94.

J. VACHEK (1964b), 'On Peripheral Phonemes of Modern English'. *BSE* 4 (1964), 7–109.

J. VACHEK (1964c), 'Prague Phonological Studies Today'. *TLP* 1 (1964), 7–20.

J. VACHEK (ed.), *A Prague School Reader in Linguistics* (Bloomington 1964).

J. VACHEK (1966a), *The Linguistic School of Prague: An Introduction to Its Theory and Practice* (Bloomington and London 1966).

J. VACHEK (in collaboration with J. DUBSKÝ) (1966b), *Dictionnaire de Linguistique de l'École de Prague* (Utrecht 1966).

J. VACHEK, *Dutch Linguists and the Prague Linguistic School*. (Leyden 1969).

Z. VANČURA, 'The Study of the Language of Commerce'. *TCLP* 6 (1936), 159–64.

R. WELLEK, 'The Literary Theory and Aesthetics of the Prague School'. In *Discriminations: Further Concepts of Criticism* (Yale 1970), 275–303.

V. A. ZVEGINCEV, *Istorija jazykoznanija XIX i XX vekov v očerkach i izvlečenijach* (Moscow 1964–65, 3rd edition).

2 Learning the Spoken Language*

Vladimír Barnet

Both the rapid development of human enterprise in all fields and growing international co-operation demand rapid exchanges of information about new developments and knowledge. Under these conditions the learning of foreign languages not only serves as communication between nations, it also furthers economic effort. Society makes great demands on the teaching of foreign languages. This fact must stimulate pedagogy and linguistics to consider methods which can reach greater efficacy than those usually employed hitherto. A further reason for developing new methods lies in the rapid progess registered in recent times in the field of educational technology.

Up to now the textbook has been the prime instrument in the learning of a foreign language. Frequently even the spoken language was practised by means of writing. The rapid rise of technology in the realm of communication (tape-recorder, language laboratory) has led to a higher regard for audio-oral methods in foreign language teaching. The textbook and electro-acoustic apparatus have become aids of equal value in language teaching. The methodology of language teaching cannot escape this fact. The significance of the new technical teaching media for foreign languages is so great that it raises questions about the very nature of this teaching and requires the reappraisal of language teaching, its linguistic, methodological, educational, and psychological bases and their interrelation.

THE SPOKEN LANGUAGE AND THE WRITTEN LANGUAGE IN FOREIGN LANGUAGE TEACHING

Two areas are clearly defined on the linguistic side of language teaching: the spoken and the written word. Each area has its specific object and its specific learning-procedure, and now its specific aids as well.

In a number of countries work has been proceeding for some time on the new methods which integrate the technical media with teaching.

* Translated by H. Gross from the German original first published in 'Praxis des neusprachlichen Unterrichts Vol. 1/67, Dortmund, with bibliographical additions.

The individual research centres differ from each other in that either audio-oral or audio-visual components are placed in the foreground and in that different functions of the teacher are emphasized in the teaching process. The Prague centre, in the Department of East Slavonic Languages in the Philosophical Faculty of the Caroline University, is concerned with the theoretical analysis of spoken expressions in Russian and with the development of methods which can best record this field of study.

I should like to indicate here how this centre examines the spoken language, specifically, from the point of view of teaching-goals, and how it exploits its findings in the further development of audio-oral methods.

Let us ask the first question: what data on the spoken language and its relationship with written forms must audio-oral teaching take into account? We can best distinguish the essentials of the spoken language by means of a comparison with the written form.[1]

1. Hitherto language teaching has started from an insufficiently clearly defined relationship between the written and the spoken languages. In the mother-tongue the spoken language is very much in the foreground. This is where foreign language methodology started out in seeing, above all, a symbolization of the phonic content in the graphic system. It regarded the graphic system as a collection of symbols and signs with whose help, having regard to the rules of orthography and transcription, one could transpose the spoken language into its written counterpart, just as one transmutes written texts into their spoken form on the basis of orthophonic and orthoepic rules. The graphic system, however, is not just a vehicle for the phonic system, any more than the phonic system is solely a vehicle for the graphic system. It is a matter of two autonomous, and from the functional point of view, independent systems which however, correspond to each other in every language. We know, however, that this correspondence is not always exact in all languages.[2] This is exemplified in cases where one phoneme corresponds to several graphemes. For

[1] For greater detail see V. Barnet: 'Audioorální metody vyučování jazykům a lingvistická teorie' (Audio-oral methods of language teaching and linguistic theory), *SaS* 26, 1965, pp. 186–91.

[2] В. Мотш, 'К вопросу об отношении между устным и письменным языком' Вопросы языкознания 1, 1963, p. 93 (W. Motsch: 'The Question of Relationships between the Spoken and the Written Language' *Koprosy yazykoznanya* 1, 1963 p. 93); Г. Гак,' Орфография ь свете структурного анализа', Проблемы структурной лингвистики, Москва 1962, стр. 210. (G. Gak: 'Orthography in the light of structural analysis', *Problems of Structural Linguistics*, Moscow 1962, p. 210.)

example, in *die Liebe* the one phoneme /iː/ corresponds with the two graphemes *ie*. Conversely several phonemes can correspond with one grapheme, for example in the Russian word поворот a strong phoneme /o/ and a weak phoneme /ɑ/ or /ə/ corresponds to the one grapheme *o*—orthoepically [þəvɑrót].

Among other things, the fact that the graphic system can fulfil its distinctive function independently of the phonic system points to the autonomy of the graphic and phonic systems.[1] We know that it is possible to learn to understand a written text whose phonic form remains unknown. The graphic differentiation of homophones gives the clearest indication of this autonomously distinctive function of the written form. The following frequently quoted English words may serve as example: *rite*, *wright*, *write*, *right*; phonetically they all have the form /rait/.

It is important to underline the functional independence of the graphic and phonic systems because in language teaching this justifies the separation of the two systems in the teaching process and the selection of the appropriate order of acquisition at any stage on methodological grounds. Whereas in the mother-tongue the path leads from the spoken to the written form, development in foreign language teaching usually goes in the opposite direction. If audio-oral methods are applied in the initial stages of language-learning to the exclusion of the written form of the language, it becomes possible to bring the acquisition of the foreign language closer to the learning of the mother-tongue. The introduction of audio-oral methods thus radically alters the function of the graphic system in the teaching of foreign languages. In a teaching course leading from the written language to the spoken language, from grapheme to phoneme, the graphic system acts as a trigger. In the reverse order, leading from phoneme to grapheme, it takes on the role of an intermediary. It is a means of transposing the language into its written form.

2. The relationship between the graphic system and the phonic system is naturally not the only thing to which attention must be paid in language-teaching. The differences between the written language and the spoken language also derive from the idiosyncrasies of the graphic and phonic materials.

Already in 1912 Baudouin de Courtenay in his work Об отношении русского письма к русскому языку (*Concerning the Relationship between*

[1] A. McIntosh: 'Graphology and Meaning' *Archivum linguisticum*, 13, 1961, pp. 107–20 (reprinted in A. McIntosh and M. A. K. Halliday, *Patterns of Language*, Longmans 1966, pp. 89–110).

Russian Writing and the Russian Language) pointed out that the difference between the two forms of language consists in the written form being fixed, having the characteristics of a document, whereas the spoken expression is more or less an affair of the moment without any stability. The Prague School has concerned itself with the problem since the 'thirties, and in the work of the Czech anglicist, J. Vachek, it has produced a self-contained theory of written and spoken linguistic expressions.[1] In recent years Vachek has arrived at the concepts of the *written language norm* and the *spoken language norm* and their functional definition. He explains: 'The spoken language norm is a system of phonologically realizable language elements whose function it is to react to a given impulse (which is as a rule urgent) in a dynamic manner, that is, in a rapid and immediate manner, which brings into play the rational-conceptual aspects as well as those of emotion and volition. The written language norm is a system of graphically realizable language elements whose function it is to react in response to a given impulse (which is as a rule not urgent) in a static manner, that is, in an easily surveyable and to a certain extent a rationally conceptual manner.'[2] In various situations *one* of the norms is usually regarded as appropriate. According to Vachek there exists a mutually complementary relation between the two existing language norms with regard to various situations in which they are used. The concepts of written language norm and spoken language norm are thus broader than the concepts of 'orthography' or 'orthoepy' and distinguish the specific autonomy of both forms of language better.

The teaching of foreign languages can benefit from these new attitudes in many respects. The documentary character of the written language makes it easier to obtain an overall view of it. The reader has the written text lying in front of him. He can return at any moment to any place he chooses. This means that dealing with a written or printed text does not make such great demands on the memory as dealing with spoken utterances. It is well known that auditory impressions only fix themselves upon the memory in limited measure and therefore the auditory memory does not provide as much help in the learning of linguistic expressions as does the documentary character of the written text.

These facts suggest that it is more profitable in practising spoken expression to start out from relatively short texts and that, alongside

[1] See, especially, 'Two chapters on written English', *BSE* 1, Prague 1959, pp. 7–38.
[2] See 'K obecným otázkám pravopisu a psané normy' (General problems of orthography and the written norm), SaS 25, 1964, p. 121.

the essential material to be treated, such exercises must be practised as will develop the auditive memory.

The documentary quality of the written form and the transitory quality of the spoken language carry with them further consequences for foreign language teaching. They revolve round the rate of assimilation in encounters with both forms of language. The rate of assimilation of the written form is basically individual; the reader determines it for himself. The rate of assimilation of spoken utterances, on the other hand, is determined by the speaker. Accordingly, in audio-oral teaching both listening and linguistic responsiveness must be practised. We can observe that in practising the written and spoken language forms each has its specific problems.

3. As well as the differences in character between the written and the spoken forms resulting from the difference in the substance involved, there are significant differences in the very structures of the two linguistic forms.[1]

Fundamentally every written expression can be transposed into spoken language and conversely every spoken expression can be captured graphically. Reading aloud, however, does not in every case necessarily denote speech in the sense of the spoken language norm. Language teaching has not yet drawn its conclusions from the general realization that we speak differently than we write. The situations in which the spoken word or the written word are used differ as well as the manner in which both language forms realize communicational content.

The specific structural characteristics of spoken expressions depend on many factors. The situational reference of the spoken word clearly emerges in the frequent incompleteness of its sentence-construction; the speaker's turning to a bystander shows itself in expressions which establish contact; deficient sentence-perspective precipitates pleonastic utterances, inadequate preparation and improvization creates numerous strings of utterances, and requires the use of linking phrases, etc. The objective content of communication is accompanied in spoken utterances by expressive and effective elements expressed by means which have no equivalent in written expression. It is a matter of *phonological means* (for example, intonation, melody and pitch, pause, rhythmic articulation), of *visual means* (facial expression) and finally of

[1] For thirty years the Prague School has been concerning itself with problems of functional and stylistic differentiation of the literary language. See, especially, B. Havránek: 'Úkoly spisovného jazyka a jeho kultura' (Tasks of the literary language and its culture), *SČJK*, Prague 1932, pp. 41 ff. and now 'Studie o spisovném jazyce' (Studies in literary language), Prague 1963.

motor means (gesture). These means heighten in significant measure the effectiveness of communication by spoken expression. The difference between written and spoken expressions is also manifest in the choice of denomination.[1]

The Brno linguistician, M. Grepl, formulates the difference between the language-forms very aptly. He says: 'In written expressions the communicational content is conveyed by *one* semiological system (language system), whereas in spoken expression it is conveyed by the fusion of three semiological systems, that is by linguistic, phonemic and motor means.'[2]

That is why in many situations spoken utterances can be more economical than written ones and they differ from each other in their overall lexical and semantic construction. Let us cite an example from Russian. The above-mentioned difference emerges clearly when we attempt to transpose a sentence from the special style of the written language into the everyday form of speech. In specialized style the sentence goes as follows: Итак, зависимость восприятия от особенностей личности, от всей нашей психической жизни влечет за собой значительные различия в восприятии—Psichologiya 1948, p. 131 (And thus the dependence of perception on personal qualities, on our entire psychological lives, entails significant differences in perception.) In everyday form the sentence may run as follows: Значит, так как люди разные по себе и в том как переживают, каждый человек по—разному смотрит на вещи. (And so, as people are different in themselves and in the way they experience things, each person looks at things differently.)[3] The communicational content of both sentences is, as comparison reveals, basically the same, but the manner and means of rendering it are different.

We make this point because the idea that the difference between the written and spoken forms of the language consists primarily in the communicational content being transmitted graphically in the first

[1] A. M. Peshkovskij ('Obyektivnaya i normativnaya tochka zrenya na yazyk', Sbornik statei, Leningrad/Moskva 1925, p. 117) speaks of a type of economy of the spoken language created by the common situation and the common previous experience of the participants involved in communication. For factors leading to differentiation of spoken expressions see 'Otázky slovanské syntaxe' (Questions of Slavic syntax), Opera Universitatis Purkynianae Brunensis, 85, Prague 1962, pp. 313–406, especially essays by K. Hausenblas '*O studiu syntaxe běžně mluvených projevů*' (About the study of the syntax of current spoken utterances) pp. 313–23, and J. Chloupek 'O specifičnosti nářeční skladby' (About the specificity of dialect-composition) pp. 325–36.

[2] M. Grepl: '*K podstatě a povaze rozdílů mezi projevy mluvenými a psanými*' (The substance and nature of differences between spoken and written utterances) (op. cit., ibid, p. 343).

[3] See V. Barnet, op. cit., p. 189.

instance and acoustically in the second has not been completely overcome in the practical application of methodology. Acoustic perception and the reading of what were originally written expressions in no way teach the spoken language and they are bound to fail in this purpose.

From the foregoing discussion it will be clear that audio-oral teaching must start out from a thorough and reliable knowledge of what must be learnt, that is, from knowledge of the specific properties of the spoken language. We have drawn attention to a few points. To summarize: it is a matter above all of the correspondence between the graphemic and phonemic systems, of the differences which spring from the graphic and acoustic substance or from the respective lexical and grammatical construction of the language-form in question. The audio-oral teaching-methods must naturally profit from those qualities which make up the essence of the spoken language-form.

We have thus answered the first question which we put to ourselves. As we have explained what the essence of the spoken utterance consists of, we can turn to the second question: what procedure is suitable for the learning of the spoken language?

LEARNING THE SPOKEN LANGUAGE AND PROGRAMMED INSTRUCTION

The process of practice to achieve fluency must be as close as possible to natural speech communication. This demand is obviously met by a type of exercise in which natural linguistic responses form the methodological basis of the exercise unit. Let us represent this unit schematically in three phases:

$$A \qquad B \qquad A_k$$

Hence:

A is the utterance containing the stimulus.

B is the response which expresses the linguistic behaviour of the pupil in reaction to the stimulus. This behaviour may be an imitation, a variation, or an independent answer. Technically phase B appears as a pause for the pupil's response.

A_k represents the correct solution to the set task whose point of origin was the stimulus.

From the point of view of foreign language methodology this type of exercise can be the means of practice (for example, in training pronunciation, stress, intonation) or also in itself the point of practice.

For example, in practising those Russian verbs whose various forms have different stresses, this type of exercise is only the methodological vehicle for the teaching material. The word-stresses are practised with the help of everyday language constructions.

A вы ку́рите? (Do you smoke?)
B нет, не курю́. (No, I don't smoke.)
Similarly:
A вы лю́бите ходить в кино? (Do you like going to the cinema?)
B нет, не люблю́. (No, I don't.)

In practising the colloquial phrase да что вы! (You don't say!), expressing rejection and amazement, the item to be exercised is itself the object of the learning process.

A вам эта книга нравится? (Do you like this book?)
B да что вы! (Of *course* not!)

The type of exercise in which natural linguistic response is the focal point brings audio-oral teaching nearer to genuine speech-communication. It has, however, other merits as well. It makes it possible to apply the principles of programmed instruction very advantageously.

Programming for language teaching can be related to various areas:

1 to the teaching of knowledge about the language
2 to the teaching of practical spoken language skills
3 to the testing of what has been learnt.

Work in the Prague research centre has hitherto been concerned with the second area, that is to say, with taking into account the principles of programmed instruction in practising skills in the spoken language.

On what principles of programming can this practice be based? It is a matter of the following principles:

(a) splitting the subject matter into small, methodologically optimal doses (teaching items)
(b) active and constant participation by the learner
(c) systematic feedback to the learner
(d) controlling the pace of the learner's linguistic behaviour.

Let us briefly characterize these principles.

THE PRINCIPLE OF SMALL DOSES

In programmes for exercising spoken language skills the dose (teaching item) consists of instructions for the learner, the example (model) of the phenomenon to be practised and a series of sentences of the same type with the help of which actual practice follows. We shall quote an example from the gramophone record course 'Speak Russian With Us', which attempts to apply the principles of programming to the acquisition of speech skills in Russian. We shall also use this example to clarify the other principles.

Instructions: You will hear a sentence to which you are to respond with an objection. Use the Russian construction

да ведь не такой уж . . . (But it isn't so very . . .)

Example

Programme: Какой холодный ветер! (What a cold wind!)

Pupil: да ведь не такой уж холодный! (But it isn't so very cold!)

Programme: да ведь не такой уж холодный!

After the instructions and the example there follows on the tape a corresponding series of sentences with pauses for the pupil's responses with corrections following immediately.

A Какой крепкий мороз! (What a hard frost!)

B . . .

A_k да ведь не такой уж крепкий! (But it isn't so very hard!)

A Какой жаркий день! (What a hot day!)

B . . .

A_k да ведь не такой уж жаркий! (But it isn't so very hot!)

A Какой сильный дождь! (What heavy rain!)

B . . .

A_k да ведь не такой уж сильный! (But it isn't so very heavy!)

A Какой густой туман! (What a thick fog!)

B . . .

A_k да ведь не такой уж густой! (But it isn't so very thick!)

The theme of the exercise quoted is the weather. With its vocabulary, however, it only offers material for practising the syntactic colloquial utterances (with special regard to intonation) which express the subjective attitude of the speaker towards the statement in the stimulus. The above-quoted responses represent a structure expressing some kind of objection. The practising of the spoken language is thus not only a vocabulary exercise as in traditional 'conversations' but it has reference to a genuinely spoken utterance as a linguistic unit.

THE PRINCIPLE OF ACTIVE PARTICIPATION

Active participation is a particularly important principle for the practising of spoken language skills. The ordering of teaching-items in scheme

A B A_k

[1] *Mluvte s námi rusky* (Speak Russian With Us) (A Handbook for the Gramaphone Record Russian Course with Programmed Exercises), Prague 1964, p. 127. Authors: V. Barnet, D. Brčáková, K. Koževniková, and J. Kryuková *et al.*

which provides a pause for the student's response, makes this participation possible to a particular extent. It is not, however, a matter of a mechanical drill which naturally reduces the pupil's attention and thereby also his activity. It can clearly be seen from the examples quoted that one and the same Russian structure да ведь не такой уж . . . (But it isn't so very . . .) is lexically varied in each example да ведь не такой уж крепкий! (But it isn't so very hard); да ведь не такой уж жаркий! (But it isn't so very hot), etc.
Thus the response demands activity on the pupil's part, the lexical completion of the structure corresponding to the stimulus.

THE PRINCIPLE OF FEEDBACK

In the scheme A–B–A_k the last phase contains the correct solution of the set task. It fulfills the function of feedback on the psychological level.

The correct version given by the programme itself, that is A_k, reinforces the student's self-assessment which does not, however, develop in any way mechanically. Experience with programmed instruction up to now has revealed that the efficacy of self-correction depends upon the measure of success in bringing the pupil to an accurate assessment of his own response. This demand is best met by contrast exercises in which the student learns to distinguish the essential differences.

CONTROLLING THE PACE IN LINGUISTIC BEHAVIOUR

It has already been stated that in spoken utterances the pace of reception by the listener is determined by the speaker. In programmes containing information and explanations, e.g. in mathematics, the pace of the programme is subordinate to the individual pace of the pupil. In the exercising of practical spoken language skills, on the other hand, it is expedient for the pace to be determined by the programmer on methodological grounds. Readiness to respond and speed of response in linguistic behaviour should, as has already been stated, also be practised in language teaching.

CONTROL OF STUDENT'S LINGUISTIC BEHAVIOUR

We now come to the most important point among the principles of programmed learning quoted earlier. Control may be exercised in different ways. Let us return to our example. The student's linguistic behaviour is firstly controlled through the instructions which direct what is to be practised and how, and secondly through the model structure, through the pattern provided. The most important means of control, however, is the first phase, the stimulus itself. In agreement with the methodological aim it contains the key-word, the necessary additional information for the exercise; for in practising spoken language skills the information contained in the stimulus is the direct point of departure for the pupil's response. In the example Какой холодный ветер! (What a cold wind!) this additional information is contained in the adjective холодный (cold). The structure to be practised is completed by this very adjective; Да ведь не такой уж холодный! (But it is not so very cold!).

Finally the correctness of the student's terminal linguistic behaviour is controlled through the third phase of the programme, i.e. through A_k, with the correct solution.

The measure of control also determines the degree of independence in linguistic behaviour on the part of the pupil. Control and independence in behaviour are in inverse ratio to each other. The more the pupil's behaviour is controlled, the less room is left for his initiative, and vice versa. On the basis of reciprocal diminution of control and increasing independence, various types of exercise are being designed at the Prague centre. We classify these as being *reproductive* and *productive* exercises according to the activity which they demand. Imitation which limits independent activity on the part of the pupil belongs essentially to the reproductive type of exercise.

Reproductive exercises—Examples:

1 Pure repetition

Instructions: Notice what expressions Russians use in introducing people. Repeat these expressions in the pauses.

Teacher: Разрешите познакомиться (Allow me to introduce myself.)

Pupil: (*repeats in the pause*) Разрешите познакомиться! (Allow me to introduce myself.)

Correction: Разрешите познакомиться etc.

2 Repetition with lexical substitution

Instructions: You will hear a sentence. On that model make another sentence using the words which the teacher tells you.

Teacher: Благодарю вас за любезность (Thank you for your kindness) за помощь (for your help) etc.

The pupil repeats the pattern of the initial structure and uses the suggested structure

Благодарю вас за помощь (Thank you for your help.)

Correction: Благодарю вас за помощь, etc.

3 Repetition with extension

Instructions: Repeat the expression given and add the expression of politeness пожалуйста (please).

Teacher: Проходите! (Come in.)

The pupil repeats the expression and forms a new construction by adding the required word.

Pupil: Проходите, пожалуйста! (Come in, please.)

Correction: Проходите, пожалуйста, etc.

4 Repetition with selective extension

Instructions: Repeat the sentences which you will hear. Use one of the expressions which the teacher will give you.

Teacher: Он здоров. (He is well.) совершенно (completely), совсем (quite), абсолютно (absolutely)

The pupil freely chooses one of the expressions given and thereby extends the construction.

Pupil: Он совсем здоров (He is quite well), etc.

With this type of exercise the correction disappears.

PRODUCTIVE EXERCISES

The essence of these exercises consists in the pupil's being led on the basis of a given stimulus to practise certain elements of self-contained utterances, and above all to practise speech responses. These exercises are intended to put the pupil into the environment of a natural conversation.

1 Practising linguistic responses following a given model

Instructions: Express your regret that you cannot accept the offer. Use the expression Мне очень жаль, но я не смогу. (I am sorry, I shall not be able to.)

Teacher: Вы придете сегодня в 7 часов? (Are you coming at 7 o'clock today?)

Pupil: мне очень жаль, но я не смогу. (I am sorry, I shall not be able to.)

Correction: Мне очень жаль, но я не смогу, etc.

2 Practising speech responses with alterations

Instructions: Following the teacher's direction, form a construction in the imperative.

Teacher: Скажите Тане, пусть она оденется потеплее. (Tell Tanya to dress a bit more warmly.)

The pupil reacts according to the model in the instructions with an altered response.

Pupil: Таня, оденься потеплее! (Tanya, dress more warmly.)
Correction: Таня, оденься потеплее! etc.

3 Practising speech responses with lexical variation.[1]

The principle of control plays an important part in the audio-oral teaching process as it has been adopted by the Prague research group since 1959. That is why we call it the *audio-oral method of controlled responses*, or *programmed response methodology*.

The audio-oral method of controlled responses is, as we have been able to see, founded on the theoretical analysis of spoken utterances as well as on the principles of programmed instruction. Attention was equally paid to the principles of contrastive analysis which are exploited in the exercises, particularly in the choice of phenomena of the foreign language which are difficult from the point of view of the student's mother-tongue, and in the methodological emphasis placed upon them.

Experience with courses in phonetics, intonation, morphology, syntax and conversation which have already appeared for the Russian language[2] has shown that the types of exercises exploiting the method of guided responses have the following advantages:

1 they permit the natural sequence, at least in partial elements, of the most frequent forms of speech-communication

2 they make it possible to apply the most important principles of programming, which without any doubt represents a step forward in the teaching of foreign languages

3 they allow both the role of listener and that of the speaker to be effectively brought to bear upon the methods of practising, something that has hitherto been scarcely possible to achieve.

At the beginning of our observations we described how two autonomous but reciprocally corresponding areas are emerging in the methodology of foreign language teaching: the area of practising the written language and the area of practising the spoken language. Audio-oral methods naturally make effective work possible in only one part of foreign language teaching, namely in the realm of spoken

[1] Cf. *Mluvte s námi rusky*, pp. 4 and 9.

[2] *Rusky se správným přízvukem* (Russian with the correct accent), Prague 1966 (with tapes), by K. Koževniková, D. Brčáková, V. Nekolová; *Rusky se správnou výslovností* (Russian with the correct pronunciation), Prague 1966 (with tapes), by P. Adamec and I. Camutaliová; *Audioorální cvičení z ruské morfologie* (Audio-oral exercises in Russian morphology), Prague 1966, by V. Nekolová, M. Holoubková *et al.*; *Audioorální cvičení z ruské syntaxe* (Audio-oral exercises on Russian syntax), Prague 1966, by P. Adamec, O. Kafková and S. Beková.

utterance.[1] We are often asked whether we are experiencing a revolution in foreign language teaching. We shall, perhaps, be able to speak about a revolution if, starting from the present state of linguistic science and educational theory, we succeed in reconciling the mastering of the written form of the language and the process of acquisition of the spoken form of the language. This task in foreign language methodology is, however, but a programme for the future.

[1] V. Barnet: *Místo audioorálních metod v cizojazyčném vyučování* (The place of audio-oral methods in foreign language teaching) in *Koncepce cizojazyčného vyučování a audioorální a audiovizuální komunikativní zařízení* (The approach to foreign language teaching and audio-oral and audio-visual communicational media), Prague 1967, pp. 21–31, V. Barnet et al.: *Základy audioorální metody řízených odpovědí ve vyučování jazykům* (The Audio-oral Method of Controlled Responses in Language Teaching), Prague 1969.

3 Sentence Patterns in the Theory and Practice of Teaching the Grammar of French as a Foreign Language

Antonie Menšíková

I. THE IMPORTANCE OF THE PRINCIPLES OF THE PRAGUE SCHOOL IN THE TEACHING OF FOREIGN LANGUAGES

The methodics of language teaching is based on the results of linguistic studies, on a certain description of the given foreign language. Language, however, is a very complex and many-sided reality. It changes and develops, is a means of thought and communication, has various levels and forms. Different linguistic trends approach the investigation of language from different viewpoints, investigate different aspects. This results in differing concepts of language which are then reflected in the teaching of foreign languages. The Prague School of Functional Linguistics formulated its conception of linguistics in contrast to the principles of the Neogrammarian philology. If we want to demonstrate the importance of the Prague School for the specific problem of sentence patterns, it is necessary first to draw attention to the difference existing between the two linguistic conceptions and to the consequences arising from them for the teaching of foreign languages.

The Neogrammarians attempted by the comparison of related languages to discover their older common stage. Despite its undoubted contributions to the development of linguistics, the Neogrammarian philology also had certain drawbacks which the founder and first chairman of the Prague Linguistic Circle, V. Mathesius, summed up under three basic points. 1. By observing the development of isolated linguistic phenomena sight was lost of the language system as a whole. 2. The Neogrammarians had at their disposal only written records of the language that obviously could not show the language in all its aspects (e.g. the acoustic aspect is completely ignored) and that would be further determined by the style of the literary record in question. 3. The adherents of the Neogrammarian school approached language exclusively from the viewpoint of the reader, completely ignoring that of the speaker or writer.[1]

These shortcomings are reflected in the shortcomings of what is called the traditional method of teaching foreign languages. 1. Pupils learn isolated words and their paradigms and form sentences from them on the basis of individual grammatical rules. The formative value of the grammar of a foreign language is considered to be in this atomizing process which requires continuous performance of a number of logical operations. The grammatical categories valid for one language are mechanically transferred to all other languages. 2. The bases of teaching are printed texts and exercises that are also used as the starting point for oral practice. Here the pupils learn to 'talk' according to rules the formulation of which is based on the norm of the written language. 3. In the teaching procedure the reader's viewpoint prevails; through the analysis of the text one arrives at an understanding of its contents.

The basic theses of the Prague School were directed against the shortcomings of Neogrammarian philology. 1. In the synchronistic investigation of a language its systemic character comes to the fore. The language is a system of linguistic values and not a sum total of minute unconnected phenomena. The systemic character of the language permits communication. Language is an instrument of communication and thought. In communication linguistic devices fulfil a certain function, have a certain task. No language element can be fully understood and evaluated unless its relations to the other elements are analysed and unless its functions, especially its communicative function, are taken into consideration. Every language has its specific system of devices to express identical communicative needs. By a synchronistic comparison of languages, in particular differing languages, we arrive at a more profound comprehension of the importance and function of linguistic facts. 2. The study and analysis of various functional styles also arises from the conception of language as a system of devices serving the various communicative needs. The Prague School, inter alia, devoted great attention to the study of the relations between spoken and written utterances and to the determination of their functional specificity. 3. The functional principle put into practice by proceeding from function to form corresponds in real life

[1] *V. Mathesius, Obsahový rozbor současné angličtiny na základě obecně lingvisticském* (A Functional Analysis of Present-Day English on a General Linguistic Basis), edited by J. Vachek (Prague 1961), pp. 5–6.

to the speaker's (writer's) viewpoint 'who has to find linguistic forms for what he wishes to express.'[1]

Let us now consider the changes introduced into the linguistic conception of the teaching of foreign languages by the linguistic principles of the Prague School. 1. The pupils do not learn the grammar of a foreign language to be able to carry out complicated mental gymnastics but to be able to communicate in the foreign language. They must learn the grammatical system on the basis of its encoding function and in the way it actually functions in communication, for example in spoken utterances in organic interaction of phonological, lexical and grammatical means. 'Thinking in a foreign language' is arrived at by penetrating more and more profoundly into the system of functional oppositions of the foreign language differing from the mother tongue. '. . . The fully formative value of foreign languages is given—apart from their stylistic make-up—by a certain degree of their basic grammatical difference from the mother tongue.'[2] 2. Taking into consideration the functional specificity and structural differences of the written and spoken utterances, it is also necessary to differentiate the processes of how we learn to write and to understand a written text from the processes on the basis of which we learn to speak and to understand the spoken word. When the aim is combined, i.e. when we aim at mastering all types of communication, the best method for combining both processes must be looked for.[3] 3. The differences must be simultaneously borne in mind between the proceedings of the speaker (writer) and those of the listener (reader). Whereas the speaker (writer) knows what he wants to say and is looking for means to say it, the listener (reader) hears or sees how it is said and must discover what is being said. The speaker must be therefore able to produce formal means of expression corresponding to his communicative purpose, the reader must know how to identify them.

Sentence patterns are means of learning the grammatical structure of a foreign language in the way in which it functions in its spoken form. We are therefore interested above all in the problem of the form of spoken utterances. The specificity of the spoken form, however, cannot be assessed without comparing it with that of the written language.

[1] V. Mathesius, 'New Currents and Tendencies in Linguistic Research, *MNHMA* (Zubatý Volume), Prague 1927, pp. 188–203.

[2] B. Trnka, 'Význam funkčního jazykozpytu pro vyučování moderním jazykům (La linguistique fonctionnelle au service de l'enseignement des langues modernes), *SaS* 3 (1937) p. 238.

[3] Cf. V. Barnet, 'Audioorální metody vyučování cizím jazykům a lingvistická teorie', (Aural-oral Methods in Teaching Foreign Languages and Linguistic Theory), *SaS* 26 (1965) pp. 186–91. See also his contribution to this volume.

2. WRITTEN AND SPOKEN GRAMMAR

The great pioneer of the modern aural-oral method, Harold E. Palmer, characterizes the traditional approach to grammar as follows: 'Grammar only exists in written language.' And answers appropriately: 'If the grammar of the written language only exists in the written language, the grammar of the spoken language only exists in the spoken language.'[1]

What, however, represents the specificity of the written and spoken norm? The analysis of the function of the literary language and its comparison with the vernacular speech, the study of the influence of this function on the phonological and grammatical structure of Czech in the works of B. Havránek[2] and the functional justification of written and spoken norms in the works of J. Vachek,[3] answer this question and point to a number of aspects to be taken into account in the teaching of foreign languages. The written norm sometimes speaks more clearly to the eye than the spoken norm to the ear (cf. *il parle—ils parlent*). From the graphical viewpoint a French verb of the type *parler* has five endings: -e, -es, -ons, -ez, -ent; from the viewpoint of acoustic realization only three: (-ə), (-õ), (-e). Both systems can fulfil their distinctive function independently of each other. But if our aim is to master all types of communicative activity, then their mutual relations must be investigated in a very concrete way.

The differences in written and spoken utterances that arise from their different graphical and phonetical realization, however, are far from accounting for their specific features. Reading aloud is not yet speaking. Further and more profound differences are revealed by the investigation and recognition of the functions performed by them.[4]

The functional specificity and the differing situations in which spoken and written utterances are used therefore influence the manner in which the two norms transmit the content to be communicated, their stylistic and structural make-up. We speak differently and write differently. These differences are particularly evident if we compare the two norms in their most typical manifestations, for example the written norm of literary works and scientific papers and the spoken norm of

[1] Harold E. Palmer, *The Principles of Language-Study* (London 1964), (2nd edition) p. 99.

[2] B. Havránek, 'Influence de la fonction de la langue littéraire sur la structure phonologique et grammaticale du tchèque littéraire, *TCLP* 1 (1929) pp. 106–20. Úkoly spisovného jazyka a jeho kultura', (Tasks of a Standard Language and its Cultivation, *in SČJK*), (Prague 1932), pp. 32–84. Reprinted in *PSRL*, 252–69.

[3] J. Vachek, Two Chapters on Written Language, *BSE* 1 (1959), pp. 7–39. 'Zum Problem der geschriebenen Sprache' *TCLP* 8 (1939), pp. 94–104, etc.

[4] See J. Vachek, op cit.; cf. a more detailed account in V. Barnet's contribution to this volume.

colloquial speech.[1] In the teaching of grammar of foreign languages these findings influence above all the selection and arrangement of teaching materials with regard to the given aim. For example, in colloquial speech with its typical form of dialogue, we shall begin practicing the verb in the contrast of first person singular and second person plural. This contrast simultaneously enables us to ask the pupils from the very beginning questions that concern themselves. If for example the aim is to learn to understand scientific papers in a foreign language in the shortest possible time, then, on the contrary, we shall begin with the contrast of the third person singular and third person plural. Linguistic facts, for example the fact that some forms are used exclusively in the written norm of language, will also influence the type of exercises. In modern French such a form is the *passé simple* which is replaced in the spoken norm by the *passé composé*. The bookish character of the *passé simple* determines the identifying way of mastering it. Exercises: *Put into the passé simple*! occurring in the traditional textbooks are therefore conceived incorrectly not only as far as the formal grammatical formulation of the task is concerned, but also in their demand for productive knowledge.

The unsuitability of the traditional exercises for oral practice arises also from the fact that in spoken utterances, apart from the intellectual aspect, the emotional aspect also plays a part, expressed not only by grammatical devices but also by stress, rhythm and melody. Traditional exercises: *Fill in the form omitted! Put the infinitive in brackets into the correct form! etc.* are to be done orally by the pupil. But when doing so the pupil must carry out a number of logical operations. The fluency of expressing himself in the foreign language is therefore constantly disturbed by his thinking about the language, and the important element of the spoken norm of the language, its phonological system, is completely ignored.

Very important consequences for the teaching and learning of written and spoken grammar arise from the understanding of the static nature of the written norm of the language and the dynamic character of its spoken norm. If we do not understand a foreign language text on the first reading, we attain understanding by an analysis of the text, by looking up unknown expressions in the dictionary and the recalling of grammar rules. The understanding of a spoken utterance, however, requires ready and immediate reaction. There is no time to look up words in the dictionary, nor to recall rules.

[1] See, for more detail, the contributions to this volume by J. Dubský, J. Camutaliová and K. Koževníková.

Similarly, if we want to speak in a foreign language and express a certain content, we have no time to think simultaneously of what we want to say and how we are to say it, what words, what word order and what endings are to be used. This is why for oral communication a mere knowledge of the grammar rules is insufficient, since their use must be automatic. This automation is a complicated process in which a well balanced relationship must be found between the awareness of the system of functional oppositions of the foreign language and its practical use. This problem brings us to the actual problem of sentence patterns.

3. SENTENCE PATTERNS—THE BASIS OF AURAL-ORAL GRAMMAR PRACTICE

The specific features of the spoken norm of the language lead to the demand of a specific procedure in the learning of 'spoken grammar'. This is the aural-oral approach. We teach and learn grammar by listening and speaking, not, however, by mechanical listening and unguided speaking about everything and nothing, but by organized and guided listening and speaking. The basis of this guided aural-oral grammar practice is sentence patterns.

Before attempting the explanation of our concept of sentence patterns, let us recall one of the great and stimulating thoughts of H. E. Palmer concerning the relation between 'memorized matter' and 'constructed matter'. Most of our utterances consist of constructed matter: their component parts have been memorized integrally, but the complete units are constructed. It is most important for the learner of foreign languages to learn how to form new sentences from concrete never repeated utterances. Different methods of achieving this follow different roads. The so-called grammar-translation method is not suitable for the aim of learning to speak a foreign language not because it uses translation—which is after all a valuable teaching device—but because it leads the pupil to form new sentences by unsuitable means.[1]

Palmer himself wanted to imitate as much as possible the procedure by which a child learns its mother tongue. It is impossible to repeat the procedure by which we learned our own mother tongue if we learn a foreign language under entirely different conditions: at a time when the systemic devices of the mother tongue are already firmly connected with our expressing of the extra-linguistic reality, in a limited number of normal teaching hours and in the surroundings of the

[1] Harold E. Palmer, op. cit., 116–26.

mother tongue which constantly strengthens in us the habitual means of expression. Whether we proceed directly or indirectly, whether we realize it or not, the concepts and categories of the mother tongue automatically pervade what we want to say and how we say it in the foreign language. The influence of the mother tongue cannot be excluded by ignoring it, we must consciously deal with it. This is why—as has been said by one of the outstanding Prague linguists, B. Trnka—the pupils must realize within the first teaching hours that they have entered the ground of differing functional phonological, morphological and syntactical contrasts where no interference on the part of the mother tongue is permitted.[1] The first precondition of success is the awareness of the system of the foreign language against the background of the learner's own mother tongue.[2]

Another statement referring to our problem has been made by one of the representatives of the second generation of the Prague School, M. Dokulil.[3] Dokulil speaks of the suitability of distinguishing the region of syntagmatized expressions from lexicalized units. In the case of lexicalized units we fully depend on the ready formulas alone. In the field of syntagmatized expressions we can make use of our constructive will in the foreign language as well if we know the laws by which words are joined into syntagmata. To be able to express in the foreign language our individual intellectual, emotional and volitional attitude in the endless number of real situations, we must know the laws by which we may connect words to form meaningful units. Naturally, mere knowledge is not enough—on this point we agree with Palmer. If we are to react promptly and readily, as required by the specificity of the spoken norm of the language, we must know how to use this knowledge automatically. What we shall therefore automize during practice are not ready-made, previously inflected and composed units, but the formation of such units. This is why we concentrate the pupil's attention on a particular relationship functioning in the foreign language so that he might become aware of its regularity, however, on the basis of concrete language materials by first hearing the given item in a certain connexion, then repeating it, then forming it himself and finally using it more and more freely. And this is the essence of our conception of sentence patterns.

Let us choose a simple example for the purposes of demonstration: the contraction of the definitive article in French with the preposition

[1] B. Trnka, op. cit., 240.
[2] Cf. I. Poldauf's contribution to this volume.
[3] M. Dokulil, 'Nová cesta k cizím jazykům' (New Way to Foreign Languages) *SaS* 8 (1942) 208–9.

à. This preposition is functionally very overloaded in French, since it expresses a number of relations rendered in Czech either by case endings or by different prepositions. The pupils will get to know these functions gradually. To be able, however, to use the given preposition for the expression of different relations, it is necessary to automatize the manner in which it is connected with nouns. Our sentence pattern will be as follows:

J'aime LA campagne.	*Je vais souvent À LA campagne.*
J'aime L'opéra.	*Je vais souvent À L'opéra.*
J'aime LE théâtre.	*Je vais souvent AU théâtre.*
J'aime LE cinéma.	*Je vais souvent AU cinéma.*
J'aime LES concerts.	*Je vais souvent AUX concerts.*
J'aime LES conférences.	*Je vais souvent AUX conférences.*
J'aime LES expositions.	*Je vais souvent AUX expositions.*

All the lexical meanings are known to the pupils, who also know the definite article and its sound image (for example the sound contrast *le* and *les* in the plural), as well as the fact that gender is not differentiated in the plural. In the previous lesson they were also introduced to and used the unit: *Je vais à la campagne*, *à la gare*, *à l'opéra*, *à l'aéroport*. Our sentence pattern thus links up with an already known phenomenon and contrasts it with a new phenomenon. At the same time it contrasts within the framework of two series of sentences placed opposite each other the form of the article and the manner of connecting the preposition *à* with this unit.

The series of sentence pairs of the given sentence pattern is first spoken by the teacher at normal speed, rhythm and intonation (he does not overstress the definite article and its connection with the preposition, this is stressed only in the written forms). The pupils must first learn to listen carefully, to cultivate their sense for perceiving the foreign language and its structure. We naturally perceive more easily an organized than a chaotic reality. This is why we present to the pupils in the sentence patterns a language reality organized in such a way as to simplify and speed up its comprehension. The aim of listening and then repeating the given sentence pairs after the teacher is to make the pupils realize the regularity of the given phenomenon.

During practice we change the original sentence pattern in such a way as to give it the form of a small dialogue between teacher and pupils. The practice sentence pattern will thus be made up of replication pairs as follows:

Teacher:	*J'aime le théâtre.*	*Pupil:*	*Et vous allez souvent au théâtre?*
	J'aime le cinéma.		*Et vous allez souvent au cinéma?*
	J'aime le restaurant de Bruxelles etc.		

In the teaching phase proper the teacher will first introduce separately the singular masculine noun beginning with a consonant, then the plural noun beginning with a consonant and finally the plural noun beginning with a vowel. In the testing phase all suitable lexical units will be used in turn, for example:

J'aime le restaurant de Bruxelles, la campagne, les jardins de Prague, les expositions, l'opéra, le cinéma, la Bibliothèque Universitaire etc.

Then we shall go on to the form of question and answer: *Vous allez souvent au théàtre? Ou est-ce que vous allez ce soir? Et demain vous restez à la maison? etc.* Here the pupils must answer, but they will also ask the teacher and one another questions. This exercise follows up on the previous practice on the basis of sentence patterns, but is already of a different nature: the conscious attention of the pupils is transferred from the way in which to say it to what they want to say. In the course of the lessons the pupils will successively be introduced to various functions of the preposition *à*. In this way even the form of its connexion with the definite article will continuously be strengthened.

The methodological importance of sentence patterns lies in the fact that they combine the practical explanation of the rule with its use. This procedure differs from the traditional method in a number of points.

1. Let us compare our procedure with the rule as it is formulated in traditional textbooks: 'The preposition *à* merges with the definite article of the masculine gender into *au* before an initial consonant. In the plural the preposition *à* merges with the definite article into the form *aux* in the masculine and feminine gender.' This formulation of the rule is based purely on the written norm of French. The fact that no French determiner signals the gender in the plural is interpreted as if referring only to the form *aux*. The verbalization of the rule requires a knowledge of grammatical terms. Our procedure is based on a different description of French. This description bears in mind the differences in sound and graphical realization. It sets out from the fact that the gender is signalled by the definite article only in the singular noun beginning with a consonant. The description is more accurate, the formulation of grammar rules, however, much simpler. The rule gives a directive for action; in its formulation the pupils rely on already known forms of the definite article and they can, but need not, use grammatical terms.

2. When using the traditional method the pupils memorize the rules, i.e. they learn by heart their verbalized formulations. On the basis of sentence patterns they can derive the rules themselves (whether we shall use induction or deduction depends on the character of the language phenomenon in question). In any case, however, the pupils get to know the rule actively and this contributes to its retention.

3. In the traditional teaching of grammar, after the rule has been explained, an exercise of the following type follows: *Fill in the preposition à and the definite article: Je travaille . . . usine. Téléphonez . . . docteur. Qui est . . . appareil? . . . murs de cette salle, il y a de beaux tableaux* etc. Throughout the exercise there is not one example of the plural noun beginning with a vowel, again only the written form is taken into consideration. A still greater shortcoming, however, is the procedure by which the pupil now forms sentences with the use of the above-mentioned formulation of the rule. First he must determine whether he is working with a noun in the singular or plural. If the noun is in the plural he always fills in *aux*. If the noun is in the singular he has to determine correctly its gender. If the noun is feminine, he fills in *à*. If the noun is masculine, he must note whether it begins with a vowel, or a consonant. If it begins with a vowel he fills in *à*. If it begins with a consonant, he fills in *au*. Thus the pupils learn to carry out a number of logical operations, but they do not learn to speak a foreign language.

In the aural-oral approach the pupil learns to use the correct form on the basis of analogy: *le cinéma—au cinéma*, therefore: *le restaurant—au restaurant* etc. The teacher's stimulus in the beginning supplies the necessary information, the prompting. For example, if the pupil is to learn how to form the *imparfait* the teacher's stimulus will in the teaching phase contain the form of the first person plural of the present: *Maintenant, nous n'allons pas souvent à la campagne.—Autrefois, nous allions souvent à la campagne* etc. In the testing phase the cue will be faded: Teacher: *Cette année, je ne fais pas beaucoup de promenades.*—Pupil: *Et l'année passée, vous faisiez beaucoup de promenades?* etc. Or: Teacher: *Aujourd'hui, le professeur a oublié quatre fois son parapluie.*—Pupil: *L'an dernier, il oubliait son parapluie à chaque cours*, etc. The pupil thus gradually learns to use the correct form automatically even without the teacher's prompting.

4. Substitutions and variations are used also in traditional teaching. In the aural-oral approach based on sentence patterns, they are used, however, in a specific manner. The problem is not how to form by means of substitution and transformation as many sentences as possible from

the given sentence. Neither do we use transformation in the sense of modern linguistics, where it is a form of the description of the relations between the elements of the language system. To investigate a language and to learn a language are two different things. We do not transfer to the teaching of foreign languages linguistic methods of investigation, we only make use of the results of such investigations. The transformations that we are carrying out in sentence patterns of the monologue and replication type place opposite each other an already known item and a new one derived from it or one with which it is in functional opposition. We are thus dealing here with a certain relationship in the system described by linguistics and recorded in the school rule. Substitutions, carried out within these changes then serve to further comprehension, retention and prompt use of the rule valid for a whole number of phenomena of the same type. In this sense, transformation connected with substitution then permits the formation of new sentences.

The transformation may involve a change in tenses (the example with the *imparfait*), but also pairs of different sentences whose common point is a certain syntagma and its change (contraction of article). Whether this or that type of change is concerned, we shall always attempt to produce a natural communicative connexion between the two sentence series so that the transformation should not remain merely formally grammatical but should possess a certain communicative content as well. We therefore do not let the pupils declaim: *Je travaille beaucoup, je ne travaille pas beaucoup. J'aime danser, je n'aime pas danser* etc. The formation of the negative in French is demonstrated by a sentence pattern in monologue: *Je travaille beaucoup, mais je ne travaille pas le soir. J'aime danser, mais je n'aime pas danser la valse* etc. And the practice of the negative is then carried out in replication pairs, for example: *Je travaille beaucoup* (J'aime danser etc.)—*Moi, je ne travaille pas beaucoup* (*Moi, je n'aime pas danser* etc.).

On the other hand, though we are trying to approach as closely as possible the natural connexion of two statements, we are aware that sentence patterns remain only a means of training, and what is more, an artificial means. We are using this means, since we cannot under current conditions of learning a foreign language repeat the process by which we have learned to speak our own mother tongue. Sentence patterns are an artificial link that we place between the habitual use of the devices of the system of the mother tongue and the unusual use of the devices of the system of the foreign language. Even though the sentence patterns have a certain communicative content, the pupil himself does not communicate anything, he is not forced to formulate his own thought, to choose independently adequate foreign language devices for what he wishes to say. We all agree that to know a grammatical rule does not necessarily mean to know how to use it. And similarly, to know how to use promptly foreign language devices in practice, guided by sentence patterns, does not mean that the pupil will know how to use them independently in real communicative situations. And therefore, apart from exercises on the basis of sentence patterns, which we shall call *structural* exercises, another type of exercise is essential, which we shall call *communicative* exercises. Here the pupil must use foreign language devices for communications independently.

The system of exercises for every item must thus contain both types of exercises; the overestimation of one type at the expense of the other is always harmful. On the other hand, in the case of communicative exercises we must also bear in mind their methodological gradation. A well-tried means to make the pupil really tell us something is to ask him a question. Let us compare, however, the following three questions: 1. Is your mother strict or indulgent? 2. Is your mother strict? 3. What is your mother like? The first question is an alternative question and presents the pupil with the lexical unit and form. The pupil in his answer only selects one of the solutions presented. The answer to the second question may be positive or negative, concise or longer, for example: 'My mother? My mother is very strict indeed' or 'She is not strict at all, on the contrary, she is too indulgent.' The second question thus presents more possibilities than question 1; it is more open and the answer will require greater independence in the selection of lexical and grammar means. The third question is completely open and the answer requires an independent selection of words and their independent arrangement. The differentiation of closed and open questions permits us to proceed from the simpler to the more difficult and simultaneously gives us a criterion for assessing the language level that has been achieved. If we were not to differentiate in this way we might mistakenly consider prompt answers to closed questions as the expression of the ready mastery of the foreign language.[1]

Sentence patterns are thus merely the basis of aural-oral grammar practice. Structural exercises (exercises based on sentence patterns) are only one type of aural-oral exercise. The second type is formed by communicative exercises. These exercises follow up structural exercises and must be alternated with them. The better the sentence patterns

[1] Cf. J. Guénot, *Clefs pour les langues vivantes* (Paris, 1964) 162–6.

are formulated, the more they respect the communicative function of the grammatical devices of the language, and the easier the transition to exercises in which the pupil thinks of what he wants to say and not of the way he must say it.

4. STRUCTURAL EXERCISES AND PATTERN PRACTICE IN THE USA

Our structural exercises have some common features with pattern practice as carried out in the USA, but differ basically in others.

Points of contact are given by common features of the structural approach to language. In fact, one of the representatives of American applied linguistics, Pierre Delattre, speaks of it as the direct successor of the Prague School of the thirties 'et du dieu phoneme qu'elle avait inventé . . .'[1] The Prague School naturally did not and does not limit its activities merely to the field of phonology and together with the viewpoint of system it has always applied that of function as well. The application of the viewpoint of function permitted—and still does so—a more profound linguistic analysis. For example, the investigation of the relationship between the spoken and the written norm of language from the viewpoint of their functional specificity and their functional equivalence leads to a more subtle analysis of their stylistic lexical and grammar structure. Mathesius's approach to the sentence from the viewpoint of the speaker's communicative needs gave rise to his theory of functional sentence perspective.[2] This theory has been further developed by a number of younger Czech linguists, for example J. Firbas.[3] For our needs it is sufficient to explain the basic concepts which we shall use in the comparison of our own and the American conception of pattern practice.

Mathesius divides the sentence into its starting point, the so-called theme (which does not supply new information and serves as a necessary link with the general context) and the 'rheme' or 'nucleus' which supplies the new information conveyed by the sentence. Under functional sentence perspective we understand with J. Firbas 'the arrangement of sentence elements as it is viewed in the light of the actual situation, i.e. in the light of the context, both verbal and situa-

[1] Pierre Delattre, 'Le français et les laboratoires de langue, *Esprit* 11 (1962), 599.

[2] V. Mathesius, 'Zur Satzperspektive im modernen Englisch', *Archiv für das Studium der neueren Sprachen*, Band 155, Jahrgang 84 (1929), 202–10. 'On Some Problems of the Systematic Analysis of Grammar, *TCLP* 6 (1936), 95–107. 'Ze srovnávacích studií slovoslednych' (From Comparative Word-Order Studies), *ČMF* 28 (1942), 118–20. Reprinted in *PSRL* 306–19.

[3] Cf. the contribution to this volume by J. Firbas.

tional.'[1] Functional sentence perspective has become an important means of synchronistic language comparison for the Prague School. The comparison of languages on the basis of the manner in which they express functional sentence perspective makes the linguistic analysis of their specificity more profound and the results of these investigations are in turn most fruitful also for the teaching of foreign languages.

The basic differences in the linguistic conception of American Descriptivism and the Functional Structuralism of the Prague School are reflected in the differences between the American pattern practice and our structural exercises in several ways. Both conceptions set out from a comparison of the native language and the target language. American Descriptivism, however, first of all compares form, position and distribution of language elements both in the system of the native language and that of the target language. The Prague School compares the ways in which these forms actually function in the languages in question. For example R. Lado[2] states that in the English and the corresponding Spanish pattern a different word order exists, in one case an uninflected form is used, in the other an inflected one, etc. The Prague School questions what function word order has in the languages under comparison, in what way for example English and French express what Czech expresses by means of flexion. The results of the difference in comparison are also seen in the difference in selection and arrangement of the teaching materials.

American Descriptivism isolates form from content, the language system from the extra-linguistic reality it conveys. It only takes note of the invariant systematic meanings of form and their formal signals. For example, it states by what formal means the question is signalled. For the Prague School the consideration of both form and content was always characteristic, which protects it from an antisemantic bias.[3] For example, the question not only has form, but expresses—as Mathesius says—an appeal to the listener to submit an explanation of the stated fact or a group of facts.[4] This different conception is again reflected in the differently conceived exercises. American exercises aim at training such formal means that signal the question. The exercises may then appear as follows: *He is a doctor* (*a teacher*, *an engineer*, etc.)—*Is he a doctor?* (*a teacher*, *an engineer*, etc.). Under our

[1] J. Firbas, 'Thoughts on the Communicative Function of the Verb in English, German and Czech', *BSE* 1 (1953), 39.

[2] R. Lado, *Linguistics across Cultures* (Ann Arbor 1957), 57.

[3] Cf. F. Daneš and J. Vachek, 'Prague Studies in Structural Grammar Today', *TLP* 1 (1966), 21–8.

[4] V. Mathesius, 'Několik slov o podstatě věty' (Some Words on the Essentials of the Sentence), *ČMF* 10 (1924), 1–6.

conception the difference in intonation between the Czech and French question will be practiced as follows:

Il travaille à l'usine. Il est ouvrier?
Il travaille à l'hôpital. Il est médecin?
Il travaille à l'école. Il est professeur? etc.

In the same way, if the pupil is to learn to form the question by means of the phrase *est-ce que*, we shall not present him with the exercise: *Il travaille. Est-ce qu'il travaille?—Il parle français. Est-ce qu'il parle français?* but with the exercise: *Il travaille beaucoup. Est-ce qu'il travaille bien?—Il parle français. Est-ce qu'il parle bien?* etc.

If we set out from the sentence merely as a syntactic system unit with invariant syntactical features, we can replace the noun in such a sentence by a pronoun, for example: *Il examine les résultats. Il les examine. Il cherche la serviette. Il la cherche.* If we set out, however, from the functional definition of a sentence as a communicative system unit, as an 'elementary expression of an attitude to some reality carried out by linguistic means'[1] we shall approach the practising of pronouns in another way. In conversation we use the pronouns if we hold a view-point differing from the statement, for example: *Je ne connais pas cette jeune fille—Moi, je la connais.* Or if by asking we require the supplementation of a previous communication, for example: *Il examine les résultats.—Pourquoi est-ce qu'il les examine?* Or if we answer a question: *Vous aimez le football?—Non, je ne l'aime pas.* And this functioning of the pronouns in real communication will be the basis of our sentence patterns serving the practising of pronouns.

The isolation of form from content, formal means of expression from the extra-linguistic reality that is being expressed, is the reason why American pattern practice in a number of cases remains equally formal as the traditional exercises. The difference is then to be found in the aural-oral practice and the use of modern language laboratory techniques. If we say that we teach grammar by speaking, we do not have in mind simply performing exercises aloud. If we speak, then we say something. When we teach grammar by speaking, we teach grammatical devices as they are used to convey something.

[1] V. Mathesius and J. Vachek in Mathesius' *Obsahový rozbor . . .*, 220, fn. p. 44. The distinction between the sentence as an individual utterance and the sentence as a unit of the grammatical system, expressed most fully in Mathesius's study 'On Some Problems of the Systematic Analysis of Grammar', *TCLP* 6 (1936), 95–107, reprinted in *PSRL* (1964), 301–19, has been further developed by M. Dokulil and F. Daneš in their paper 'K tzv. významové a mluvnické stavbě věty (On the so-called Semantic and Grammatical Organization of the Sentence) in *O vědeckěm poznání soudobých jazyků* (On Research in Contemporary Languages), (Prague 1958), 231–46. See also F. Daneš, 'A three-level approach to Syntax,' *TLP* 1 (1966), 225–40.

Concentration on form and disregard of content is also seen in exercises of the following kind: Substitute the words and make necessary changes in the Class 2 expressions: *Mary is watching the play.* (*John*, *we*, *studying*, *every day*, *he*, *now*, *last week*, *they* etc.)[1] As R. L. Politzer points out, pattern practice contains the danger that the students learn to react automatically only to a given stimulus, but that they will not be able to select independently suitable linguistic means in a real conversation.[2] This danger, in our opinion, becomes a concrete danger in exercises like those mentioned above, in which, for example, adverbs of time are no longer a prompting of function but become a mere stimulus of form. We consider this type of exercise particularly harmful where there is conflict between the formal grammatical agreement and the function of the given grammatical unit in real communication, as is the case in the exercise quoted by Geneviève Delattre: *Jean a une soeur* (*Paul et Henri*, *tu*, *vous*, *Paul et toi*, *je* etc.)[3] First of all, in the stimuli, the French system—whereby only the accented forms of the personal pronouns can be used when they occur alone—is violated. We would have to supply the stimuli for the changes in the forms of *moi*, *toi* and not *je*, *tu*. Simultaneously, however, there occurs a violation of the function of the grammatical category of the first and second person expressing the contrast of the speaker and the listener addressed. If the teacher carries out the aural-oral practice in class, he appears in the role of the speaker when expressing the stimuli and the pupils in the role of the listeners. If the pupils answer the teacher, they are the speakers and the teacher is the listener or addressee. If, however, in the above exercise the pupils react to the stimulating *moi* with the sentence: *J'ai une soeur* and to the stimulus *vous* with the sentence: *Vous avez une soeur*, they carry out a formal grammatical agreement in conflict with the function of the grammatical category of the person in the actual communication. And thus, when the teacher passes on to communicative exercises and turns to the pupils with the questions: *Vous avez une soeur? Est-ce que vous aimez votre soeur? Est-ce que je parle trop vite?* etc., a number of pupils will answer him: *Vous avez une soeur. Vous aimez votre soeur. Je parle trop vite*, etc. He has acquired the reflex of grammatical agreement in opposition to the function of the category of person. The exercise is again merely in formal grammar. This is why we do not practise the formal agreement of verb and subject like this but in the form of

[1] C. C. Fries and R. Lado, *English Sentence Patterns, Understanding and producing grammatical structures*. (Ann Arbor 1962), 34.
[2] R. L. Politzer, 'Some reflections on pattern practice', *Language Journal* 1 (1964), 26–8.
[3] Geneviève Delattre, 'Les différents types d'excercices structuraux', *Le Français dans le Monde* 41 (1966), 15.

communications and questions: *Moi, j'ai une soeur, et vous?—Moi aussi, j'ai une soeur—et votre ami?—Lui aussi, il a une soeur* etc.

If we consider the sentence merely a syntactic system unit of invariant syntactical features and if we disregard its function in communication, we cannot fully elucidate the problem of interference of the mother tongue either. As one of the representatives of the third generation of the Prague School, O. Leška,[1] has shown, the invariant system meaning is the basis of these functions, but such functions are realized only in a stylized view of reality. The real function is the 'connexion of the devices with the necessary result of communication.'[2] And only when we start to express our thought by foreign language devices interference of the mother tongue occurs. In the question of French word order, for example, there is very strong interference from Czech, arising from the difference in function of word order in French and Czech. In French—and similarly in English—word order has a grammatical function (the sentence position of an element is determined by the syntactic function of that element). The French sentence puts the noun that is to function as subject before the predicative verb which is made to precede the noun that is to function as object. In Czech the function of the subject and object is differentiated by case endings. Free word order becomes the main means of expressing functional sentence perspective and preserves the theme-rheme sequence. The Czech speaker has therefore a strong tendency to use word order in French as if it functioned similarly to that in Czech. Interference, however, does not always occur, but only in such cases where the theme of the statement is not in agreement with the grammatical subject and where therefore in Czech the thematic object will stand before the predicative verb. The Czech sentence with the object first, however, is no longer a syntactical unit but already a communicative unit and can therefore serve for the practising of French word order in the very act of communication. Thus, we shall draw up for this case a bilingual sentence pattern, in which the teacher will say a series of Czech sentences with the object in the first place and the pupil will react (naturally according to the pattern previously given by the teacher) with a series of adequate French sentences. This must not be regarded as a translation of sentences of different character

[1] O. Leška, 'K systémovému a funkčnímu pohledu na jazyk' (Some notes on System and Function of Language), in *Problémy marxistické jazykovědy* (Problems of Marxist Linguistics) (Prague, 1962), 129.

[2] I. Poldauf, 'Strukturalismus a americký deskriptivismus' (Structuralism and American Descriptivism), in *Problémy marxistické jazykovědy* (Problems of Marxist Linguistics) (Prague 1962), 82.

containing a number of individual difficulties, as used to be the case in the grammar translation method. The translation concentrates the pupils attention on one phenomenon only, the different functioning of Czech and French word order, and connects awareness of the different function of the French word order with its use. Let us compare this procedure with the so-called multiple substitution drill currently used in the USA, in which the pupils are to insert lexical units of various word classes in the correct place of the syntactical scheme, for example:

Elle cherche un quartier tranquille (cue: *trouve*)
Elle trouve un quartier tranquille (cue: *élégant*)
Elle trouve un quartier élégant (cue: *chapeau*)
Elle trouve un chapeau élégant etc.[1]

C. C. Fries in his work 'Teaching and Learning English as a Foreign Language' recommends that pattern practice should refer as far as possible to situations in the lives of the pupils. 'English Pattern Practices' (R. Lado, Director—C. C. Fries, Consultant) are accompanied by a clever scheme of picture charts each of which can be used for the practicing of different patterns. Approaching the situations in the lives of the pupils, however, concerns only the lexical contents of the patterns and the charts serve as stimuli for lexical substitution. Neither the one nor the other mean a really situational approach. On the other hand, it is impossible to realize in structural exercises, i.e. guided exercises requiring unambiguous answers, a situational approach in the same manner as it is possible in communicative exercises. The attempt to approach communicative situations in structural exercises leads us to choose the replication type of exercise, in which the connexion of the replication always expresses a certain attitude adopted by the person that is addressed to the speaker's statement. The situational approach is realized on the basis of general intellectual, emotional and volitional attitudes which are called forth by the request to carry out the exercises: 'Express agreement, doubt, joy, wishes, ask for supplementary information, take up the opposite point of view etc.', always, naturally, according to the given pattern. Therefore we want to stress once more that we are aware of the differences between the repetition of the attitude given by the sentence pattern and the expression of the speaker's own attitude to the situation or the statement about it. This is also the reason why it is essential to alternate systematically structural and communicative exercises.

[1] Geneviève Delattre op. cit. fn. p. 58.

The replication exercises naturally also occur in the American pattern practice; they are, however, not principally used, but kept separate and merged with a number of formal drills. The difference is also evident in the proportion of pattern practice to communicative exercises.

We do not want to deny the merits of American applied linguistics in the development of aural-oral grammar practice. We are of the opinion, however, that the functional structuralism of the Prague School offers reliable support in overcoming the one-sidedness, formality and lack of liveliness which have so often been the mark of grammar exercises, and will enable us to seek for the solution of one of the basic problems of learning grammar by speaking: the conflict between the requirement of automation and methodological gradation on the one hand and the wide variety of real communicative situations on the other.

4 Language Awareness

Ivan Poldauf

Experienced teachers suggest that it is between eight and ten years of age, in the course of normal elementary education that a child becomes aware of his mother tongue as a language. He is then not only capable of acceptable word-formation and acceptable patterning of new sentences relative to the style actually used by him, but he is also capable of indicating certain word formations and certain patternings of sentences as acceptable and others as unacceptable, and also begins to produce first imitations, however amateurish, of other people's words and sentences of individual or social import. Reference to the content of a communication ('what she said was true') may henceforth be complemented by metalinguistic pronouncements in the form of a communication ('what she said was rather high-flown, slangy, bad grammar'). Awareness is the ability, no matter how conscious, to view a language objectively, that is, as a phenomenon. Earlier nursery rhymes and nursery talk, seemingly also created out of objectively present language material, are partly due to older children's influence or are actually created by adults; partly they are mere 'words without a song', a play on words, on sentence fragments or fragments of narration, as the most syntactically advanced pieces of language available. They show language prevalently in its 'poetic' function (to use Roman Jakobson's term).

When teaching a foreign language to a child before such an awareness of the mother tongue has been formed, the school may attempt a distant simulation of the rise of bilingualism. After it has been formed, such a procedure is not only a waste of time but runs more and more against the grain of the learner. The simulation of bilingualism is made possible through the psychic factors which make a child ready to play on words etc. and the generally prevalent readiness (though not with child learners of all types) to imitate.

The approach through trial and error in learning one's mother tongue is for a long time devoid of comprehensive generalization. The corrections concern individual errors (*don't say . . ., but say . . ., don't say* '*she*' *of Uncle Joe . . .*). What the child generalizes is forms and procedures, not their comprehensive evaluations. Retorts like *why can't I say* or *why must I say . . .* do not aim at universal systemic solutions. It makes no difference if reference to language is worded by adults in universal formulas. *One doesn't say* means *you shouldn't say, because it is not proper*, that is, 'because I don't want you to say so'. This is not the case after awareness has been formed, when interest in language has become systemic. No doubt when beginning to learn the written form of one's mother tongue reading and writing and learning about one's own language strengthen the objective attitude towards it, but these do not seem to be the only factors contributing to the rise of mother-tongue awareness. Psychic factors, through which man becomes capable of observing less material data around him and which at a certain stage of the general development of the human mind evidently come to the fore, are of indubitable importance here.

From this stage on, foreign language learning becomes prevalently conscious. Not that every unit and every principle of construction (rule) has to be learnt separately, but they are grasped as units and as single principles to which parallels in the language of which one is already aware are sought and at least provisionally found. A curious situation arises. In one's mother tongue one is aware of a certain incompleteness (*that's a new word to me, this is a new turn, why ever does he put it in that way?*), but what one knows of it allows one to wield it within the limits of one's needs to both the speaker's and the hearer's satisfaction. In the foreign language, one is forced to speak as if the knowledge were complete (the learner is expected to 'communicate') though both the learner and whoever listens to him evidently do not fully accept the learner's knowledge as satisfactory and quite up to the situation. Most satisfaction is brought about when the learner is able to 'say as much as he wants to say with that little he knows of the language', when he is able to say it in a fluent and phonetically acceptable way. For then he will find himself accepted as a foreigner 'with whom you can converse'.

In any case, this means breaking away from a language in which the learner can achieve all this without much effort, but which is at the same time the projection chart of his whole communicable world and hence cannot really be broken away from. The dilemma leads to the well-known experience that the mother tongue is at the same time the learner's greatest friend and his greatest enemy. It helps him to connect new units with something, not merely to place them in a vacuum. The assumption that there is a new direct connexion between the language being acquired and the reality to be communicated is demonstrably wrong. The direct method has shown that a rational approach to the printed word is not the way to highly automatized spoken use, but it has not convinced anybody that through it the learner's mother tongue can be wiped out from the background of foreign language learning. A kind of *horror vacui* always introduces it. The translation method unduly stresses a mirror-image relation of the two languages, and where relations are automatically present it forces the learner to express them consciously in a crude and one-to-one manner.

The best way of dealing with a powerful enemy is to make him one's ally. We would suggest that this be done in the field of language awareness.

There is another reason for reckoning with language awareness in the fundamentals of foreign language teaching. We consider the pupil who will go on living in his own language community to be the characteristic type of a foreign language learner. In countries where the knowledge of the foreign language is a necessary condition of general education (e.g. English or French in most developing countries in Africa) the situation is different: the language of general education re-conceptualizes the learner's view of the world and the higher the education the more it pushes the mother tongue concepts into the background or creates a new spiritually creolized view of the world. What we have in mind is a situation in which the knowledge of a foreign language is one of the accomplishments of a person possessing a general education, parallel and more or less equivalent to the others. As the school subject, a foreign language comes closest to art and physical training with its gradual elaboration of abilities, but it is just the fact that it is foreign, that is foreign to the learner's situation, that makes it different from them. For art on various levels does exist round the learner (we do not teach music in a society without song or musical instruments). The foreign language, however, does not exist in a monolingual society, at least not in all the possible shapes and uses a language normally has in its own society underlying it. But it has its functional counterpart all round it: in the mother tongue as language of instruction, as language of out-of-school life, as language of home life, etc. The pupil's attitude to a foreign language is that there is nothing expressible in his mother-tongue that should not be expressible in the foreign language. It is the characteristic attitude of the encoder and the decoder: what he wants to encode and what he thinks he is expected to decode are *a priori* codable for him. However objective the teaching may be, no matter how ingeniously the learner may be induced to produce linguistic solutions of life-like situations, the awareness of his own mother-tongue cannot disappear and, owing to the natural coding approach, it as it were calls for the gradual development of a parallel awareness of the language that is being acquired.

It is universally accepted that a language may have several forms, in particular the spoken form and the written form. (With certain losses, the spoken form may be taken down in writing, as in the records of a hearing in court, which again may be read out, and the written form read aloud and by way of dictation again taken down.) There are also various functional styles (now frequently denoted as *registers* with perhaps an undue stress laid on differences of contact between social levels). The question arises: is a learner's awareness of his mother tongue different according to which forms of the language he uses, actively or passively, and according to the width of the span between the highest and the lowest styles used by him?—No doubt a learner is only aware of those forms and those types of a language which he actually wields. One who is a regular reader of a popular daily paper cannot be expected to be able to view quite objectively the language of, let us say, the *Financial Times*. Since, however, the forms and the styles are not self-enclosed, using between them much common linguistic material and many common linguistic procedures, common to all or to some forms or styles, the user of a language as his mother tongue may inflate the sphere of his awareness and assume an objective view of the residual material and procedures as well. Thus, for instance, the user of an inflected language need not leave the field of language awareness when an uninflected loanword is introduced with other grammatical qualifications adhered to, though he cannot fully or correctly, or at all, attach a lexical meaning to the unknown word. In this way the field of language awareness has a kind of blurred outer circle, where guessing, an important factor in language 'perception', is at home. And it is through transfer from this outer circle into the field of awareness proper that one's awareness of language grows, comprising more and more forms and styles, more and more professional and other special vocabulary etc.

Now, if a learner of a foreign language only knows the spoken form of his mother tongue, he can gradually build up the awareness of the language he is learning on that of his own as far as the spoken form is concerned, but the awareness of the written form of the foreign language will have to be elaborated separately with perhaps only the field of guesswork to give him any help. If he only knows the colloquial style, the same will happen if we teach him, in the foreign language, the style of belles lettres.

It is a well-known precept in foreign language teaching that a learner should not be asked to perform more than he can do in his mother tongue. This may sound right pedagogically, but it is not quite to the point. For a learner with no habit of writing in his mother tongue or perhaps a speaker of a language with an oral tradition only would then be barred from getting instruction in the written form of the foreign language. Rather, it should be said that if language awareness is to be quickly developed in the foreign language it is advisable to develop it in that form and style of the language that have been best mastered in the mother tongue, as it is for that form and that style (those styles) that awareness already exists, so that now only a parallel, not a brand-new, kind of awareness is to be developed.

How does language awareness compare with linguistic competence and linguistic performance (or with active presence of *la langue* and *la parole*)? Linguistic *competence* is the presence and readiness for prompt use in a language user's mind of linguistic material and rules for application in encoding and decoding a communication. The material and the rules are linguistic since they connect sound (or graphic representation) with communicable facts, thus making the sound (or the representation) a sign. Linguistic competence, like any ability, is a potentiality. Linguistic *performance* is time- and space-bound materialization of this ability (acoustic or visual) with part of the material and part of the rules applied in such a way as is made possible by the natural classification and stratification of the material and the rules. It is necessitated by the character of language communication that the materialization is sequential (in time or on a two-dimensional plane), that is, that the performance results in or interprets strings of units, superimposed upon one another, but with the units partially or wholly co-occurring only due to the fact of belonging to different strings. Whatever occurs in language over and above this is but a constitutive part of a unit (a distinctive feature). Whereas linguistic competence is practically always present in a speaker's mind as a whole, though the elements of the material and the single rules may be sunk in the mind to different depths, so that the readiness to use them may differ, linguistic performance is limited in time to those occasions when the need to encode or to decode a communication has arisen and been met by the language user. Language *awareness*, on the other hand, implies an ability to regard linguistic performance as the materialization of linguistic competence in all or most of its components, to combine and evaluate, socially and otherwise, combinations of units as signals as well as units as mentally present linguistic material and rules. It is very much like perceiving a work of art with the eye or ear of one who knows about the technique of the art, no matter how ably he himself can apply it or how expertly he can express himself about it. Language awareness is not expert knowledge in the sense that it should make use of scientific description and terminology. It is not the ability of a linguistic scholar, but an everyday ability of any mature and hence competent language user. Any statement or thought such as *why does he use that particular word*, *why doesn't he prefer to say . . .?*, *how had I best put it?*, *I have not expressed myself well*, etc., is expressive of the presence of such an ability. The ability itself becomes evident in such statements as: *you* (or *I*) *should have said . . .*, *because . . .*; or in nominal definitions as: *a glass is . . .*, *whereas a tumbler is . . . .* Nor is language awareness based on elements always comparable to the units and procedures discovered by linguistic scholarship. When questioning informants who share his mother tongue, the scholar is often surprised to hear on what they base their notions about words, meanings and constructions. Relatively correct notions (that is, to be more exact, acceptable to a modern linguistic scholar), are found, on examination, to be prevalent. It is also well known that such an unsophisticated informant may provide the linguist with an unexpected clue to a scholarly solution.

How can a similar awareness be gradually developed in a pupil? By the tactics used in teaching, which should proceed from what is common to the two languages—the foreign language and the mother tongue—to what is less similar and further to what is contrarily opposed.

Let us take for instance the procedure derived from generative grammar, opening with 'kernel sentences' of the very simplest type, such as *I read*, *John returns*, *She comes*, representing the noun-phrase plus verb-phrase combination. This should be modified if the pupil's mother tongue is fully inflectional. 'When saying what a single person or a single thing does (now) add *-s* to the verb or add *-s* and put *he* or *she* or *it* before the verb, if you do not expressly say who the person is or what the thing is.' 'If the person is the speaker put *I* before the verb, if it is a group including the speaker put *we* before the verb, if it is the person addressed or a group comprising this person put *you* before the verb.' 'When saying what more than one person or thing does (now), put *they* before the verb, if you do not expressly say who the persons are or what the things are.'—There is of course a natural short cut to say, e.g. in the case of Czech: 'For *-u* or *-m* place *I* before; for *-š* and *-te* place *you* before; for *-me* place *we* before; for *-ou* and *-í* (*-i* for more) place *they* before, if you do not say who or what does; otherwise choose between *he, she* and *it*, placed before on the same condition, and add *-s*.' This procedure can be visualized as follows:

. . . *-u*, *-m*	I . . .	. . . *-me*	we . . .
. . . *-š*, *-te*	you . . .		
. . .	he, she, it . . . -s	. . . *-ou*, *-í* (more)	they . . .
	x . . . -s		x . . .

Outside the third person the awareness of parallel facts in a language like English is quickly elaborated for an inflected-language speaker, for learning the required procedure is very near to learning vocables and the fact that *I, you, we* can be represented in Czech by independent words, pronouns, though rarely used merely to refer to the grammatical person of the verb, is a further help. (Too much of a help, for later on, *like I, better than I, nobody but I, it is I* seem to a Czech learner to be the natural way of saying the thing.)

In the third person things become complicated not merely because in the singular something has to be so frequently put before and something after (*he reads* for Czech *čte*), but also because of the insistence of the new language on *saying* 'they' or 'he' or 'she' or 'it' and, what is worse, on *choosing* between them on the basis of criteria which have to be learnt separately, and—to top all this—to apply this procedure only when denoting the person or persons or the thing or things that perform the action and on applying it but partially (termination *-s*) if it is one person or one thing. For the Czech learner it is sometimes difficult to find out quickly whether there is (are) such. There are a great number of feminines and neuters in Czech not distinguishing the singular from the plural, a certain number of verbs not distinguishing in the present indicative the singular from the plural form, and this number is even greater with some speakers. Apparently, this is parallel to the English situation with *sheep*, *can* or *may* and (also further extended by some speakers) *he don't*, but the relevance of these phenomena is greater in Czech if for no other reason than because of the numerical weight of the respective nouns and verbs. The Czech learner is not used to grammaticalized word order, so that *ovce slyší*, though more likely to stand for *the sheep hears* or *the sheep hear*, can also stand for *he hears the sheep*, *she hears the sheep*, *it hears the sheep*, *they hear the sheep* (or *it is sheep he hears*, etc.). A Czech pupil will tend to say (instead of *he reads*): *reads*, *read*, *he read* and *father he reads*, *father he read*, *father read.* It will also take him some time not to say 'he' or 'she' in reference to things, but here awareness of the state of things in English can be elaborated relatively quickly because of its fundamental simplicity. From all this it follows that the Czech teacher will have to concentrate on the third person and elaborate a new bit of awareness: 'In English, you always must have a word saying what or who does the action preceding the verb. Choose between *I*, *you*, *we*, as you choose between terminations in Czech. Elsewhere add *-s* to the verb or use *they* and add *-s* to the noun.' The last bit is of course a half-truth (consider *says*, *has*, *does*, *is*, the modal auxiliaries and the nouns not taking—or not merely taking—an *-s* to form their plural). But all language awareness, even that of one's mother tongue, is elaborated gradually, with corrections successively made to the preceding stages. Teachers are usually well aware of this, knowing they cannot impart language through all-comprising definitions. Somebody said once: 'You always learn a foreign language through a rising pyramid of white lies getting nearer and nearer to the crystal truth, which is so clear that you no longer think of its possible impurity'. Foreign language awareness also grows through gradually crystallizing bits, and so does the knowledge of a foreign language.

Even from our simple example it should be clear that language awareness can be elaborated without any truly linguistic apparatus. No doubt it would be more exact to say that it is the subject which precedes the verb or that it is a noun (or a representative of such a noun) of such a type as the lexical nature of the verb requires, that is the noun-phrase (of generative grammar). But that would introduce more unknowns than a practical approach. Moreover, the awareness already present in the learner, that of his mother tongue, is likewise based on non-scientific concepts.

Those in favour of a direct, intuitive approach would prefer to make the pupil combine proper names, common nouns and pronouns with verbs, teaching him when to provide the verbal form with an *-s* (*he*, *she*, *it*, singular noun). But they are suprised to see that when in the give-and-take of conversation the scheme of prescribed models is given up, the same mistakes (due to the extreme awareness of the mother tongue) appear again. Especially *he go* and *father go* are frequent, which shows that the representative schema (*speaker-hearer-neither* in any language) is more quickly acquired than the signal of a grammatical category (person and number). But even incorrect pronouns are not uncommon (*we go* for *you go*). All that has happened is merely that the concentrated endeavour to build up the foreign language awareness has been replaced by haphazard, unchannelled attempts on the part of the learner to achieve the same. He eventually learns that *we* is said of an action predicated of a group including himself, the speaker, and *you* of the hearer alone or included in a group, but he has done it by combining at the back of his mind the English pronoun with the respective Czech pronoun and sharpening his attention to the appurtenance of a Czech termination to a Czech pronoun and finding out which termination and hence which of the possible pronouns it is. Neither the procedure aiming at elaboration of awareness nor the intuitive approach are translation from the mother tongue, since translation is a consistent activity, evenly distributed throughout the whole context. Here we have only discontinued and, as the language experience grows, only sporadic reflexes of the mother tongue. Awareness of the second language develops with an ever-diminishing lag behind the development of that of the mother tongue, but develop it does and the teacher's mastery may speed up the process and help in the fixation of its components.

Sometimes it may appear desirable to reach out for a minority phenomenon in the mother tongue. Here is another example from a Czech's learning English. The use of the expanded form can be elaborated on two facts of the Czech language: 1. the majority of verbal meanings are each expressed by a pair of verbs, differentiated as to the *vid* (they are such verbs as answer the question *What has happened?*); statal and relational verbs have only one form. In English these are not pairs of verbs, but neatly opposed forms (*I write—I am writing*), some statal and relational verbs also having only one form (*I know, I belong*);—2. a group of some eight verbs (the most common verbs of motion) distinguish activity as a mere fact and activity as a process bound to a definite space at a definite time (*he goes to school* = he is a scholar—*he is going to school*). It is important to make the Czech pupil aware that all non-statal and non-relational verbs make this very distinction: *he smokes* = is a smoker, frequently smokes, though perhaps not now—*he is smoking*. We will therefore make our pupil aware of the approximate nature of the relation of the two verb forms on the basis of parallels to the Czech verbs of motion. It is true that the form corresponding to *he goes* in Czech occasionally serves the meaning 'is just now repeatedly -ing' (e.g. 'he is just now walking and walking round the table, circling the table'), but the existence of markedly deviant use should not prevent us from gradually elaborating the necessary awareness. There is similarly the good old tradition in teaching English of saying that *I am -ing* denotes what is going on just now in spite of the marked deviant use as in *I am always forgetting things* or *you are continually leaving the door open.* Hence the teacher's work with the Czech pupil should proceed on a line from *he is going to school, his sister also goes to school, but she is not going there now* (two different verbs in Czech) . . ., via *he is just bringing us our paper, he brings us a paper every morning* (two different verbs in Czech) . . ., to *he is smoking a cigarette, mother also smokes, but she is not a heavy smoker* (one verb in Czech). It is of little use trying to elaborate the same distinction by once showing a film of a person smoking and once presenting a photograph of a smoker. The awareness elaborated in this respect for the mother tongue is not based on differences in actual sensual observation. And trying to 'perform' before a class by saying '*Now I am taking a book in my hand. Now I am putting it back on the desk. Now I am writing on the blackboard*' is a well-known mistake, for in English denoting single activities by their names implies a fact rather than a process, so that, just as Czech *kouřím* ('I smoke' or 'I am smoking') is not a good starting point for the elaboration of awareness, merely denoting actual processes is likewise inconsistent. No visualization, and certainly not the additional acting out of activities denoted by the verb, can build up the awareness of a linguistic distinction, which is accomplished by using an already existing awareness of an at least partly similar phenomenon as a springboard. Abstract categories in a foreign language (of which there are always more than the simpler, situation-based ones) can without exception be better grapsed on the basis of similar abstract categories than on concrete signals and situational realizations. Automation through drills is an important fixation, but it is not the best way of elaborating a conscious approach to a foreign language.

We will leave it to the pedagogues to answer the question of how the foreign language teaching methodology is to be modified if foreign language awareness is to be brought about quickly and so that it proves to be an effective and lasting asset. The linguist's role is to tell the pedagogue how it would be best to have the material (units of lexicon and grammar) selected, marshalled—in order to obtain a well-founded, gradually extended sequence—and presented with a well-thought-out strategy.

As to the *selection* of the linguistic material, this seems to be outside the sphere of consideration of language awareness. It proceeds according to the aim or the complex of aims stated for the particular course. It considers the form and the style (forms and styles) of the particular language that have to be taught and the factors making a selection necessary: age of pupil, time at the teacher's disposal, the pupil's likely psychic attitude, the teacher's mastery of the language, the pupil's future place in the society he is being educated for, requirements arising from the interlinking stages of an educational system, etc. If the acquisition of a form or a style of the language in a selected and fairly representative portion is thus given, no consideration of awareness can change it. For instance, no item can be left out merely because it is more difficult to build up language awareness in the field of that particular phenomenon than any other.

Not so in the case of *marshalling* the language material. Here the elaboration of a new language awareness will play an important role. Unless the general strategy reverses the order or the requirements of the teaching methodology, making adjustments necessary, the linguistic material, which consists of both lexical units and grammatical rules, should be arranged so as to form a concatenation of facts from those for which awareness is most easily elaborated on the basis of the mother tongue to those where this is difficult. Thus, for instance, words will first be introduced whose senses have counterparts in the mother tongue. If Czech distinguishes strictly between types of locomotion (go = walk, be carried on road or rail, be carried on water, be flown, etc.), it will be useful to introduce the verbs *walk*, *drive*, *fly*, *travel* first and only afterwards teach the comprehensive *go*, to which there is no counterpart. Otherwise the well-known misuse appears: *I did not go there, I took a tram.* Or the verb *enjoy* will have to be introduced so as not to evoke the impression of its being equivalent to *like* = find satisfactory, *gefallen/schmecken einem.* We start from *I enjoyed my stay here, I enjoyed your company* and then pass to *I enjoyed the film, I enjoyed the soup*, while elaborating a prohibition of *enjoy a picture on the wall* or connecting *enjoy* with *your girl* (for *like*).

In the field of grammar, for instance, the eternal problem of whether to start in English with the simple or the expanded verbal forms will be solved, from the point of view of elaboration of language awareness, according to whether there is a springboard in the mother tongue and hence whether it is easy to elaborate awareness of the respective difference. Where this is not so, the two forms should be introduced at a greater distance from each other and the simple form, if more in conformity with the mother tongue pattern, should be the first. The distance need not be so great in the former case. It is no burden for a Czech pupil to find *he goes to school* and *he is going to school* in close sequence. A German learner would find it burdensome (*er geht schon in die Schule* for both).

Since learning a foreign language is learning how to work something out in one's mind and then how to use a system, consideration of the actual frequency of a language phenomenon in the form and the style of the foreign language should not be of primary importance. Thus, for instance, the frequency counts of the simple present and the expanded present in the particular form and the particular style (or styles) of English should not be decisive. They should be dealt with in sequence from the more accessible to language awareness to the less accessible, no matter which of them is more frequent. A parallel case is that of the English perfect tense forms as opposed to the simple forms. If in the learner's mother tongue the *habeo scriptum* type exists not merely as a periphrastic form but as one endowed with resultative force, it may be introduced relatively earlier than if this is not so. The sequence of the English preterite and the present perfect tense form is likewise to be based on the consideration of which is the more suitable procedure for the elaboration of the awareness of this particular distinction. In Czech, for instance, the *habeo scriptum* type does exist and hence it is not difficult to elaborate awareness of the function of the form. But application of the type is limited to a few verbs of everyday use, and it can always be replaced by the preterite of the perfective verb, which is the norm with all the other verbs. Hence the relation has to be carefully weighed and the Czech learner must be prevented from connecting the three forms *he wrote—he was writing—he has written* with his distinction of the binary opposition imperfective preterite and perfective preterite.

This brings us to the linguist's third contribution to the teaching of a particular language: he should suggest the *strategy* of the approach to the linguistic phenomena. When considering the two languages and an action verb (*write*) and two status verbs (*sit* and *know*) he will be faced with the following configuration in the case of a Czech learner of English:

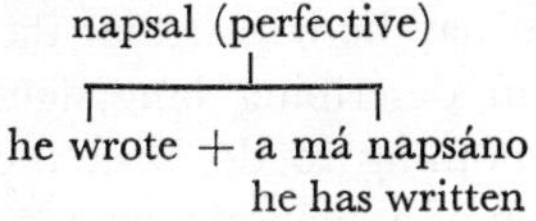

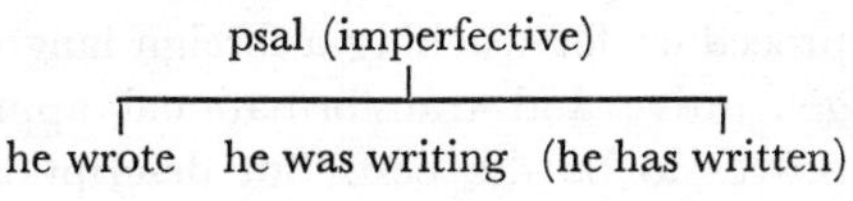

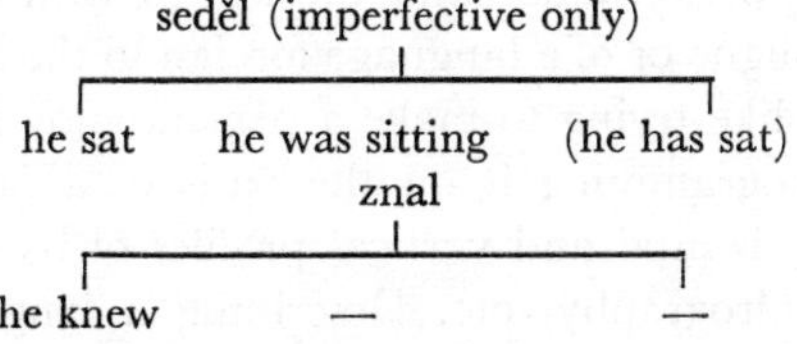

In order to simplify matters, we omit the expanded perfect—*he has been writing*, *he has been sitting*—and, with verbs having no expanded forms at all, its non-expanded counterpart—*he has known*, *he has been.*

There is a one-way correspondence: the English *he was -ing* always corresponds to an imperfective form. There is no other correspondence. There is only a *partial* one-way correspondence in that the Czech *napsal* if paraphrasable through *má napsáno* (*scriptum habet*) always corresponds to *he has written*. But it is limited to a few action verbs in Czech, being unknown for the status verbs (i.e. there is no similar paraphrase for *I have been*, *I have lived here*, etc.). The status verb perfect, as in *he has sat*, has negligible frequency in English (*sit* actually differs from *know* only in being expandable for special reasons). The Czech *psal* for *napsal*, *he has written*, is a mere stylistic variant of *napsal* (it seems to denote an act as part of one's daily routine, as one among many acts, sometimes as a professional act as opposed to an individual exploit). The strategy recommended by the linguist would be as follows. 1. Start from the present perfect of action verbs, connecting this with the *habeo scriptum* periphrasis in Czech. This will mean starting from those verbs which possess this periphrasis in colloquial Czech. But it is also possible to create further, hitherto non-existent periphrases of the type, which, thanks to their systemicity, will be comprehended by the learner. 2. Pass on to the simple preterite, contrasting it with the *habeo scriptum* type (*yesterday*, *at that time*, *two days ago* . . .). 3. Conclude with the expanded preterite as a parallel to the imperfective verb of other than purely status content, because here the conditions of the use of this form will have to be explained (for instance 'film-like background to an event or to a series of events'), that is the learner must be made aware of something which is not fully parallel to anything in his awareness of his mother-tongue.

It has become the fashion recently to declare the descriptive procedure of generative grammar to be at the same time an adequate procedure for teaching a foreign language. It may be hoped that the generative and transformational approach in describing languages proves to be the best. But description has nothing to do with the procedures in the background of the acquisition of human competence or performance and the less so with awareness either of the mother tongue or of a language foreign to the learner. Failing to recognize this is like trying to make a person enjoy his stay in a foreign country by programming it on the basis of a projection chart and all sorts of horizontal and vertical profiles of its surface, its geology, orography, hydrography, etc. Describing a language with scientific exactitude has nothing to do with imparting the knowledge of it. It is true, the more exact the linguist's knowledge of the language target and also of the learner's mother tongue, and the better his contrastive analysis of the two languages, the more valuable can be his advice to the methodologist as to the selection, marshalling and the strategy to be used in the process of teaching—which should itself be devised by the methodologist, that is, a specialist in didactics as a branch of pedagogy. Contrastive analysis will provide considerable help, though the recommendations of the methodologist will not be based only on the findings derived from it. Before we have a fully reliable description and a contrastive analysis of the two languages, the help the linguist can give to language teaching can only be provisional or tentative, but this does not exclude the possibility of change after new discoveries have been made. Impermanence is, however, the lot of all science and there can be no exception in the case of linguistics, no matter how great the pedagogues' impatience with the linguists may be.

Bibliography of works chiefly consulted by the author

BRAINE, M. D. S., 'On learning the grammatical order of words', *Psychol. Rev.*, 70, 1963, 323–48.

BROWN, R. W., 'Language and categories'. In Bruner, J. S., J. J. Goodnow, and G. A. Austin, A study of thinking. Appendix 1956, 247–312.

BROWN, R. W., and BELLUGI, U., 'Three processes in the child's acquisition of syntax', *Harv. educ. Rev.* 34, 1964, 133–51.

CARROLL, J. B., Language and thought. Englewood Cliffs, N.J., 1964.

CHOMSKY, N., 'Review of Skinner, B. F., Verbal behavior, 1957'. In: *Language* 35, 1959, 26–58.

COFER, CH.N. (Ed.), Verbal learning and verbal behavior. New York—Toronto—London 1961.

COFER, CH.N., and MUSGRAVE, B. S. (Eds.), Verbal behavior and learning: Problems and processes. New York—San Francisco—Toronto—London, 196.

HÖRMANN, H., Psychologie der Sprache. Berlin—Heidelberg—New York 1967.

JENKINS, J. J., 'Mediation theory and grammatical behavior'. In: Rosenberg, Sh. (Ed.), Directions in pyscholinguistics 1965, 66–96.

JOHNSON, N. F., 'Linguistic models and functional units of language behavior'. In: Rosenberg, Sh. (Ed.), Directions in psycholinguistics 1965, 29–65.

JUHÁSZ, J., 'Einige Bemerkungen zum Verhältnis zwischen Bewußtmachung und Automatisierung im Sprachunterricht.' In: Deutsch als Fremdsprache 2, 1963/5, 21–7.

LENNEBERG, E. H. (Ed.), New directions in the study of language Cambridge, Mass., 1964.

MILLER, G. A., GALANTER, E., and PRIBRAM, K. H., Plans and the structure of behavior. New York, 1960.

MILLER, G. A., and ISARD, S., 'Some perceptual consequences of linguistic rules'. *J. of Verbal Learning and Verbal Behavior* 2, 1963, 217–28.

OSGOOD, CH. E., 'A behavioristic analysis of perception and language as cognitive phenomena'. In: Bruner, J. S. *et al.*, Contemporary approaches to cognition, 1957, 75–118.

5 On the Interplay of Prosodic and Non-Prosodic Means of Functional Sentence Perspective (A Theoretical Note on the Teaching of English Intonation)

Jan Firbas

In a recent article in *English Language Teaching* (21, 210–17, 1966–67), John Halverson voiced the opinion that the 'neglected rhetorical notion of emphasis' should form the basis of teaching English intonation.

By emphasis he means 'a combination of heavy stress and high pitch that the speaker places on the words . . . that he takes to be most significant in his utterance' (215). In his opinion the rhetorical principle simplifies the whole procedure of intonation exercise, for once emphasis is placed where it belongs, the rest of the contour tends to fall, with minimal guidance, into a reasonable approximation of native speech.

Moreover, it is an illuminating and valuable experience for a student if he is obliged to decide which words are important and deserving of emphasis; if he has to decide what the sentence and the whole passage means, what the point of it all is (217).

I find J. Halverson's view very sound, and propose to give in the present article a brief outline of the theory of functional sentence perspective (=FSP) which in my opinion fully substantiates his conclusions. In the first part of the paper, I shall explain the basic concepts of the theory as they have been established by inquiries into the written language; in the second part, I shall attempt to apply the theory to the spoken language concentrating my attention on the prosodic features of the finite verb.

The paper is based on my previous researches into FSP[1] to which I

[1] See, e.g. my 'Non-Thematic Subjects in Contemporary English (= Non-Thematic Subjects)', *TLP* 2, Prague 1966, 239–56, and 'From Comparative Word-Order Studies', *BSE*4, Prague 1964, 111–26, where references to my previous papers on FSP and to other scholars' works (especially to those of E. Beneš, D. L. Bolinger, K. Boost, M. Dokulil, K. J. Dover, E. Dvořáková (= E. Golková), A. G. Hatcher,

have been brought chiefly by the works of V. Mathesius, F. Daneš, J. Vachek and D. L. Bolinger. Besides serving a practical purpose, it is an attempt at a theoretical contribution towards the solution of problems of structure and function, which have always been the object of intense interest at the Linguistic School of Prague.

1. One of the basic concepts I have attempted to develop in my researches into FSP is that of communicative dynamism (=CD). It is based on the fact that linguistic communication is not a static, but a dynamic phenomenon. By CD I understand a property of communication, displayed in the course of the development of the information to be conveyed and consisting in advancing this development. By the degree of CD carried by a linguistic element, I understand the extent to which the element contributes to the development of the communication, to which, as it were, it 'pushes the communication forward'. Thus if examined in its non-marked use, the sentence *He was cross* could be interpreted in regard to the degrees of CD as follows. The lowest degree of CD is carried by *He*, the highest by *cross*, the degree carried by *was* ranking between them.

I believe that much valuable light can be thrown on the function of language in the very act of communication by a *consistent* inquiry into the laws determining the DISTRIBUTION of degrees of CD over linguistic elements capable of carrying them.

The following note will be relevant here. I agree with D. S. Worth that a linguistic element—sentence, noun phrase, word, morpheme, submorphemic segment, etc.—may be singled out in order to establish a sharp ad hoc opposition (contrast):[1] *John WAS reading the local paper*, *Jenda ČETL místní noviny*. The fact that *ČETL* may appear in sharp ad hoc contrast, e.g. to *čte* ('is reading'), shows that the morpheme *-l* may become the actual bearer of the contrast. Under the circumstances it would be the only element conveying new information (and be

---

B. A. Ilyish, S. Ivančev, K. G. Krushelnitskaya, J. Mistrík, P. Novák, I. P. Raspopov, M. Schubiger, and others) pertaining to FSP can be found. All the conclusions presented in the present paper are based on the results of my previous researches. Part one of the present paper is an expanded version of my report 'On the Interplay of Means of Functional Sentence Perspective', read at the Tenth International Congress of Linguists in Bucharest, 1967. Section two is based on my study 'On the Prosodic Features of the Modern English Finite Verb as a Means of Functional Sentence Perspective (More Thoughts on Transition Proper) (= Prosodic Features),' *BSE* 7, Brno 1967, 11–48.

[1] See D. S. Worth, 'Suprasyntactics', *Proceedings of the Ninth International Congress of Linguists, Cambridge, Mass., 1962*, The Hague 1964, 698–704. Cf. also, my 'Prosodic Features', in which I treat of these phenomena in greater detail terming them—after D. L. Bolinger—cases of second instance.

therefore contextually independent), whereas all the other elements would convey known information (and therefore be contextually dependent). Normally, the morpheme *-l* would not carry the highest degree of CD as it does in the highly marked example under discussion; but even then, on account of its semantic content, it would have to be regarded as a carrier of CD. All linguistic elements, including morphemes and submorphemic exponents, are capable of carrying degrees of CD, as long as they convey some meaning.

It may have been gathered from the above note that elements become contextually dependent and in consequence carriers of the lowest degrees of CD owing to the operation of the context. They assume this function irrespective of the positions they occupy within the linear arrangement. (I avoid the term 'word order' here, because words are not the only elements concerned.) Strictly speaking, contextual dependence or independence is determined by what I have called the narrow scene, i.e. in fact the very purpose of the communication. Thus in the sentence *John has gone up to the window*, *the window* may be well known from the preceding context, but the purpose of the communication being the expression of the direction of the movement, *the window* necessarily appears contextually independent.

As to the determination of degrees of CD carried by the contextually independent elements, two further factors are in play: (i) the semantic structure, i.e. the semantic contents of the elements and the semantic relations into which they enter, and/or (ii) the positions of the elements within the linear arrangement.

Let me first illustrate the operation of the semantic structure on the level of FSP. If contextually independent, an object will carry a higher degree of CD than the finite verb. This is because the former expresses an essential amplification of the latter, and consequently becomes communicatively more important. (*I have read a fine book*, *Ich habe ein schönes Buch gelesen*, *Četl jsem pěknou knihu.*) Similarly, a contextually independent adverbial element of place will exceed in CD a verb expressing motion. Indicating the direction of the motion, the adverbial element is communicatively more important than the verb. ([*I did not know*] *you were hurrying to the railway station*, [*Ich wußte nicht,*] *daß du zum Bahnhof eilst*, [*Nevěděl jsem,*] *že spěcháš na nádraží.*) As to the subjects of the two discussed grammatical structures, each will carry a lower degree of CD than the verb and/or object/adverbial element of place provided, either the verb or the object/adverbial element of place, or both are contextually independent. This is understandable, for a known or unknown agent expressed by the subject appears to be communicatively less important than an unknown action expressed by the finite verb and/or an unknown goal (expressed by the object or the adverbial element of place) at or towards which the action is directed. (Under the circumstances described, the ultimate *purpose* of the communication is to state the action and/or its goal, not the agent.)[1] The situation is different if the subject is accompanied by a verb expressing 'existence or appearance on the scene' and possibly also by an adverbial element of place or time. Under these circumstances, provided the subject is contextually independent, it will carry the highest degree of CD. This is understandable, for an unknown person or thing appearing on the scene is communicatively more important than the act of appearing and the scene itself, i.e. the local and temporal settings. *An old man appeared in the waiting room at five o'clock. Ein alter Mann erschien im Wartesaal um fünf Uhr. Um fünf Uhr erschien im Wartesaal ein alter Mann. V pět hodin se v čekárně objevil starý muž.* (The ultimate purpose of the communication is to state who appeared on the scene.)[2] If, however, the subject of the discussed semantic and grammatical structure is contextually dependent, a contextually independent adverbial element of time or place becomes an important local or temporal specification, exceeding in CD both the subject and the finite verb. *The old man was sitting in the waiting room. Der alte Mann saß im Wartesaal. Der alte Mann ist im Wartesaal gesessen. Starý muž seděl v čekárně.* It is of utmost importance to emphasize in this connexion that under the described conditions the discussed semantic contents and relations signal the degrees of CD *irrespective of the positions* the elements occupy within the linear arrangement.

Not all semantic contents and relations, however, are capable of signalling degrees of CD in the way indicated above. The following are illustrations of how the linear arrangement itself operates on the level of FSP when unhampered either by context or semantic structure. Thus a contextually independent infinitive of purpose carries a lower degree of CD when occurring finally: *In order to see him, he went to Prague, He went to Prague in order to see him.*[3] Similarly with the direct and indirect object, provided they are contextually independent, the one coming later within the linear arrangement carries a higher degree of CD. *He gave a boy an apple, He gave an apple to a boy.* Or, a contextually independent adverb of manner ending in *-ly* evidently carries

[1] For a detailed discussion of these problems, see my 'Thoughts on the Communicative Function of the Verb in English, German, and Czech,' *BSE* 1, Prague 1959, 39–68.
[2] For a detailed discussion, see 'Non-Thematic Subjects' (footnote 1, p. 77).
[3] See E. Golková, 'On the English Infinitive of Purpose in Functional Sentence Perspective', *BSE* 7, Brno 1967, 119–28.

a higher degree of CD when following a finite verb than when preceding it. *He ate it up hastily*, *He hastily ate it up*. (I venture to suggest that under the indicated contextual conditions the adverb always carries a higher degree of CD than the finite verb, but does so conspicuously only when following it.)

In determing the degrees of CD, three levels are consistently to be kept separate: that of semantic sentence structure, that of grammatical sentence structure, and that of FSP.[1] The question may be raised as to the extent of coincidence existing between them. Somewhat modifying J. P. Raspopov's view, I have attempted to show[2] that a remarkably high degree of coincidence,[3] perhaps the highest within the system of language, is displayed by the temporal and modal exponents of the finite verb.[4] In their non-marked use in FSP, they mediate between the thematic and non-thematic sections of a sentence or clause, i.e. between the section carrying the lowest and the section carrying the highest degrees of CD. They carry the lowest degree within the non-thematic section and constitute what may be called *transition proper* (in correspondence to *theme proper*, i.e. the element(s) carrying the very lowest, and *rheme proper*, i.e. the element(s) carrying the very highest degree of CD within a sentence or clause). This conclusion is fully borne out by an inquiry into the prosodic features of the finite verb undertaken in the 'Prosodic Features' (see fn. 1, p. 77). The results of this inquiry have been incorporated in part two of the present paper.

I have attempted to show that the distribution of degrees of CD is the outcome of an interplay (co-operation) of means. This distribution takes place within distributional fields provided by grammatical structures arising through explicit (open) or (as has been shown by A. Svoboda)[5] implicit (hidden) predication. A distributional field of

1 The three-level approach has been suggested to me chiefly by F. Daneš's works. See, e.g. his 'A Three-Level Approach to Syntax', *TLP* 1, Prague 1964, 225–40. See also E. Beneš 'On Two Aspects of FSP', *TLP* 3, 1968, 267–74, and M. A. K. Halliday 'Options and Functions in the English Clause', *BSE* 8, Brno 1969, 81–8.

2 In 'A Note on Transition Proper in Functional Sentence Analysis (= Transition Proper)', *PP* 8, Prague 1965, 170–6.

3 The problem of coincidence between grammatical structure and FSP has also been touched upon by B. Trnka, 'On the Linguistic Sign and the Multi-level Organization of Language', *TLP* 1, Prague 1964, esp. p. 38.

4 (= TMEs). We understand by them all the formal expedients (such as the alternation of the stem vowels in *sing*, *sang*, *sung*, the verbal suffix *-ed*, the auxiliaries, etc.) used by the verb to convey its temporal and modal indications. We follow here B. Trnka (cf. his 'Some Thoughts on Structural Morphology' (1932) republished in *PSRL*, 329–34, in which see especially p. 330).

5 See his study 'The Hierarchy of Communicative Units and Fields as Illustrated by English Attributive Constructions', *BSE* 7, Brno 1967, 49–101, and also footnotes 38 and 40 in my 'Prosodic Features' and my 'It was Yesterday that . . .', *SPFFBU* A 15, Brno 1967, esp. pp. 142–3.

the former type would be a sentence, one of the latter type an attributive construction (headword plus its attribute). This points to a hierarchy of fields, also aptly dealt with by A. Svoboda. A distributional field of higher order, e.g. one provided by a sentence, may contain elements, e.g. clauses, which in their turn provide distributional fields, or rather sub-fields, of their own. I define FSP as the distribution of various degrees of CD over the elements within a sentence, the distribution being effected by an interplay (co-operation) of the semantic and grammatical structures of the sentence under conditions created by a certain kind of contextual dependence. Strictly speaking, it would be possible to speak of other kinds of functional perspective, e.g., that of a clause or that of an attributive construction. It should be added that the hierarchy of distributional fields implies a hierarchy of elements within these fields. This will become evident in the course of the discussion to be taken up in part two of the present paper.

In effecting the distribution of CD, the means of FSP either operate in the same direction as, or show deviations from, what I have termed the basic distribution of CD, i.e. a sequence implemented by elements starting with the one carrying the very lowest, and gradually passing on to the one carrying the very highest, degree of CD within a distributional field. The described interplay of means of FSP rules out the possibility of permanently linking up certain degrees of CD with certain positions within the linear arrangement, for example, theme proper with the beginning, transition with the middle, rheme proper with the end, of the sentence. Further, as a distributional field may be entirely contextually independent (*A girl broke a vase*), the theme need not always be contextually dependent. Contextually dependent elements, however, are always thematic. On the other hand, non-thematic elements are always contextually independent, but not every contextually independent element is non-thematic.

At this point two notes may be inserted. The first concerns the distribution of CD. The phenomenon may be viewed from two angles. Sometimes, it is necessary to concentrate on its linear implementation, i.e. the actual order of the carriers of the degrees of CD. On other occasions, it is necessary to concentrate on its implementation in regard to the *relations* between the carriers of CD.

Thus in *Pětku* (theme) *dostal* (transition) *i ze čtení* (rheme) (*Five he-got even from reading, i.e. He was marked five even in reading) and *I ze čtení* (rh) *pětku* (th) dostal (tr) (*Even from reading he-got five), the relations between the carriers of CD are practically the same, but their orders are different. In accordance with the structure of Czech, the second order is marked.

The second note is a terminological one. What is called here 'distributional field' and 'carrier' of CD (or simply 'element') is respectively referred to by A. Svoboda as 'communicative field' and 'communicative unit'. Svoboda's terms appropriately underline the common denominator of all the phenomena concerned—their function in the very act of communication.

It should be emphasized that the degrees (amounts) of CD do not constitute multiples of some basic unit or quantity of information. They are to be understood in terms of the mutual relations of the elements in regard to CD within a distributional field.

The fact that word order is only one of the means through which the distribution of CD takes place has far-reaching consequences. Susceptibility to FSP is by no means dependent merely on word order. In other words, the relations in regard to CD between the elements of a distributional field may remain the same in spite of differences or changes in word order. Synchronically speaking, the laws of the interplay of means of FSP are flexible enough to make room for differences between separate languages (English, German and Czech[1] for instance), or for differences between different standards or sub-standards of one language, or for stylistic differences within one of such standards or sub-standards. Diachronically speaking, the laws of the interplay are flexible enough to make room for changes in word order in the course of historical development. Thanks to the adaptability of means of FSP, demands on the system of word order raised by other systems of language in the course of historical development may be complied with without impairing the purpose of the communication. This is quite in keeping with J. Vachek's conception of language as a system of systems.[2] I should add here that although I hold that the means of FSP form a system, I do not hold that this system is a closed and rigid one. Even in this I concur with J. Vachek.

In the light of what has been very sketchily outlined here and in the light of researches offered in my earlier papers, I venture to draw the conclusion that the laws of the interplay of means of FSP are to be regarded as at least an Indo-European universal.

[1] And also Russian, as can be gathered from P. Adamec's book *Poryadok slov v sovremennom russkom jazyke*, Prague 1966.

[2] See, e.g. J. Vachek, 'Some Notes on the Development of Language Seen as a System of Systems', *Proceedings of the Eighth International Congress of Linguists, Oslo 1957*, Oslo University Press, 1958, 418–19.

2. Let us now see if an inquiry into the prosodic features of the finite verb corroborates the view that in their non-marked use in FSP the TMEs (= the temporal and modal exponents of the finite verb, see fn. 4, p. 81) mediate between the thematic and non-thematic section of the distributional field, carrying the lowest degree of CD within the non-thematic section and in consequence constituting what may be called transition proper. If this view, which points to a remarkably high degree of coincidence between FSP on the one hand and the semantic and grammatical levels on the other, is corroborated by the inquiry, the TMEs will prove to be a suitable starting point for further research into the relation of intonation not only to FSP, but to the other two levels as well. It is believed that the results of such research could be turned to good purpose in language teaching.

It should be pointed out in this connexion that valuable contributions to the study of interrelations between grammatical structure and intonation have recently been offered, e.g. by M. A. K. Halliday,[1] R. Quirk,[2] H. Wode.[3] Much useful pioneer research into the interrelations between FSP and intonation has been done by M. Schubiger.[4] The main justification of the present chapter, based on my 'Prosodic Features' (see fn. 1, p. 77), appears to be its attempt at a consistent, though limited, inquiry into the interrelations between intonation and the three above-mentioned levels.

By way of starting the proposed inquiry, a word must be said on the correspondence between the gamut of CD and the gamut of prosodic weight. As can be gathered from what has been said before, the gamut of CD is constituted by theme proper, rest of theme, transition proper, rest of transition, rheme excluding rheme proper, rheme proper. As to the gamut of prosodic weight, it is constituted by A. C. Gimson's four degrees of accentuation. The weakest degree is shown by unaccented syllables, which 'do not normally have pitch or other prominence'. Prosodically heavier are syllables bearing secondary accent without pitch prominence. Still heavier are syllables bearing secondary (pitch prominent) accent, pitch prominence being achieved 'by means of a change of pitch level (higher or lower)'.

Prosodically heaviest are syllables bearing primary (nuclear)

[1] *Intonation and Grammar in British English,* The Hague 1967.
[2] R. Quirk and others, 'Studies in the Correspondence of Prosodic to Grammatical Features in English,' *Proceedings of the Ninth International Congress of Linguists, Cambridge, Mass., 1962,* The Hague 1964.
[3] Englische Satzintonation', *Phonetica* 15, 1966, 129–18.
[4] *The Role of Intonation in Spoken English,* Cambridge 1935; *English Intonation, Its Form and Function,* Tübingen 1958.

accent.[1] In the present inquiry, the four types of syllable are for short referred to as unstressed (and left unmarked), partially stressed (marked ˙ or ˌ), stressed (marked ˈ and ˈˈ) and bearing a nucleus (marked ˊ, ˏ, ˋ, ˎ, ˇ, ˬ, ˆ, etc.). For the purposes of the present inquiry, I follow A. C. Gimson also in applying the term 'nucleus' to the prosodic features of a fully stressed syllable which stands out from among its neighbours (stressed, partially stressed and unstressed) in that it displays (at least through initiating it) a change of pitch direction, i.e. a fall, a rise or a combination of the two. The complex sentence *By the ˋtime we got to the ˏhouse, we were ˈall wet ˎthrough* therefore contains two nuclei; its animated variant *By the ˋtime we got to the ˇhouse, we were ˋall ˏwet ˋthrough,* five nuclei.

The correspondence between the two gamuts is to be sought within distributional fields. As has already been indicated, the carriers of CD within their fields are not all of one and the same order (or, to use A. Svoboda's term, rank). Thus the Subject, the TMEs, the Finite Verb to the exclusion of the TMEs, the Object(s), and the Verbal Modifiers, of a sentence are of one, basic order. Except for the finite verb with its TMEs, each of these items may provide a distributional field of lower order (a subfield). Within it, in accordance with grammatical dependence, a subfield or subfields of still lower order(s) may occur. The elements (carriers of CD) making up a subfield naturally share its order (rank). Examples will illustrate.

In *ˇSome people say ˈfrosts kill ˋoff all the ˏgerms* (43.10) and *They ˈsaid on the ˇradio last ˙night that a ˋthaw was exˌpected* (43.24),[2] the objects, in their entirety, function as extensive rhemes. They in fact provide subfields, i.e. display a kind of perspective of their own. In this way, the nuclei of *kill ˋoff* and *a ˋthaw* perform a double function: within the subfields, they respectively signal as rhematic the predicative verb and the subject (i.e. their very bearers: *kill ˋoff* and *a ˋthaw*); within the basic fields, the *entire* object clauses (*ˈfrosts kill ˋoff all the ˌgerms, that a ˋthaw was exˌpected*). It follows that if an element bears more prosodic features than one, its degree of CD is signalled by the weightiest of them. Needless to say, possible distributional subfields become eliminated if one element within a complex sentence passes into second instance, i.e. is singled out for the sake of sharp ad hoc

[1] See A. C. Gimson, *An Introduction to the Pronunciation of English,* London 1962, 244.

[2] All the examples in this paper are adduced from P. A. D. MacCarthy's *English Conversation Reader,* London 1956. They are referred to by page and line, with the exception of examples quoted from pp. 24–9, which are referred to by the number of the page and the number they are given in the book.

contrast (ˈ*This is the* ˈ*book I* ˎ*told you about* > *This* ˵*is the book I told you about*).[1]

One further note is necessitated by the fact that the gamut of CD is constituted by a greater number of degrees than the gamut of prosodic weight. It may be asked whether this does not lessen the correspondence between the two gamuts. The prosodic features, however, which within a distributional field are phonically equivalent in terms of the four degrees of 'accentuation' given above do not appear equivalent functionally. An important trait indicating the difference in functional importance is once again supplied by the linear character of the distributional field. The following general statement can be tentatively made in this connexion. Of two prosodic features phonically equal in the above terms, the one occurring further on within a distributional field will be functionally weightier (signalling a higher degree of CD). This implies that, if two or more nuclei occur within a distributional field, the one occurring last will be functionally weightiest (cf. the examples given on p. 85). Further research will have to modify this statement, but the extent to which it is valid is undoubtedly very great. Perhaps the most important of the necessary modifications is the following: if within one and the same distributional field a low rise occurs after a fall, it will be functionally less important than the preceding fall. (*I'll* ˋ*show them* ˌ*to you if you* ˏ*like* (39.12), *It's hardly* ˈ*ever* ˋ*used* ˏ*now, except* ˌ*possibly by the* ˌ*shop people who* ˏ*sell them* (36.26). Another modification is suggested by the occurrence of a low fall occurring within a group of low pitched syllables coming after a high fall (. . . *and I was* ˵*horrified to* ˌ*find how* ˎ*late it was when I got* ˎ*back* (34.08)). The modifications evidently cover special cases of interplay of non-prosodic and prosodic means of FSP.

In this connexion, an important question must be raised. Is it at all desirable that there should be a perfect correspondence between the gamut of CD and the gamut of prosodic weight? On the one hand, it seems that such a perfect correspondence would but impede language in fully coping with all its tasks. On the other, in order to make language capable of coping with all its tasks, a comparatively high degree of correspondence appears to be essential. The following observations are to throw some light on the matter.

It is evident that deviations from perfect correspondence can occur as long as the distribution of CD is signalled clearly enough by the

[1] By not speaking of 'pre-heads', 'heads', 'bodies', and 'tails', I do not dispute the usefulness of these concepts. But on the level on which the present inquiry is conducted I find it sufficient and profitable to work only with the concept of nucleus and use it in the sense defined above.

interplay of means of FSP, in which the non-prosodic means in no way play a negligible role.[1] A case in point is the well-known deviation which may be described as the *prosodic intensification* of the theme. It may take place for various reasons.

In *The pro'prietor/was/''most ˏfriendly* ('th/tr/''ˏrh—33.05) and *the 'first place I 'went and inˇquired at/had 'just had/a 'new 'coat of ˏpaint* (''ˇth/'tr/''ˏrh—32.24), the themes are expressed by elements (nominal subjects, one of which is expanded by a clause) which are *rhythmically* heavier than the transitional finites (forms of the verbs *to be* and *to have*).

In other cases, prosodic intensification may put the theme or one of its components into evident, though not heavy, contrast with some element mentioned in, or easily understood from, previous context (*ˇMine's from the ˋlibrary* . . . —30.17); or impart to the theme the additional meaning of 'as to/as for/concerning/in regard to/ . . .' (*The ˇfirst few looked 'rather ˏshabby* . . .—32.23) or simply make it carry some prominence of its own; or add to it some more or less emotive colouring dependent on the character of the prosodic features used and the contextual meaning of the thematic elements; cf. the animated variant of the example on p. 87). Needless to say, prosodic intensification may be due to more than one of these reasons at once.

Viewed in the direction from transition to theme, none of these cases shows straightforward coincidence between the two gamuts. This is evidently compensated by the high share the non-prosodic means of FSP have in signalling the theme. Nevertheless, the prosodic means are not entirely excluded from co-operation. It has to be borne in mind that the intensified elements would cease to be thematic were they not followed by bearers of functionally weightier prosodic features: prosodic intensification must remain within certain limits set by the requirements of FSP.

The same applies to the prosodic intensification of transition. To remain transitional, the respective elements must be followed by bearers of functionally weightier prosodic features. (*Well, I'd ˋˇlove a ˋdrink.*—34.22). No such limitations can naturally be imposed on rheme proper, which in any case carries the highest degree of CD. [*'Oh I ˋsee. Then perˌhaps there'll 'just be 'time for a cigaˏrette.*] *I'm ˋˋlonging for a ˏsmoke.*—34.29).

It follows that the possible lack of coincidence described between

[1] On the co-operation of language levels cf. J. Vachek's observations in 'On Functional Complementation as an All-Level Analytical Procedure in Language Research', *Symbolae Linguisticae in Honorem Georgii Kuryłowicz*, Warsaw 1965, 340–50.

the two gamuts does not forbid the interpretation of an unstressed finite verb accompanying a prosodically weighter theme as transitional. This may be further substantiated by the following observation.

A. Svoboda has convincingly shown that a thematic subject may be expanded and thereby raise its CD without becoming communicatively more important than the non-thematic rest of the sentence, the latter only correspondingly raising its CD. Thus in *A girl had broken a precious vase brightly painted with a fanciful hunting scene; A pretty girl with red lips, dark blue eyes, and curly black hair had broken a vase brightly painted with a fanciful hunting scene; A pretty girl with red lips, dark blue eyes, and curly black hair had broken a vase*, the subject merely provides the foundation (theme) upon which the information offered by the rest of the sentence is built. It follows that in all the three sentences the subject carries the lowest amount of CD, whereas the highest amount is carried by the object, the finite verb mediating between them. It also follows that in spite of its mediatory role, the verb is not included within the foundation. Even its TMEs (*had* plus *-en*) remain outside it. Supplying temporal and modal indications, they carry the lowest amount of CD within the non-thematic section and start building up the main information on the foundation provided by the theme. In this way, as has been discussed in greater detail elsewhere (see my 'Transition Proper', especially pp. 174–5), they are transitional *par excellence*, performing the function of transition proper. As I see it, they would perform it both in the written (printed) and in the spoken form of the discussed sentences, provided they do not appear in sharp ad hoc contrast. (According to context, they would then become either bearers of rheme proper or co-bearers of extensive theme proper.)

As to the phenomena causing prosodic intensification, they, too, raise the CD of the theme, for they also contribute to the communication. The respective thematic elements, however, will retain their status owing to the co-operation of non-prosodic means of FSP.

It has been shown that transition may be prosodically lighter than theme, the co-operation of non-prosodic and prosodic means of FSP efficiently coping with possible deviations from perfect correspondence between the gamut of CD and that of prosodic weight. On the other hand, it has been indicated that an element (elements) cannot be transitional if bearing the prosodically weightiest feature(s) within the distributional field. This means that in the transition-rheme direction the correspondence between the two gamuts may be expected to be well-nigh perfect. This conclusion is substantiated by an inquiry into the prosodic features of the finite verb the main results of which I am now going to offer. (The inquiry has been presented in full in 'Prosodic Features'). The material has been drawn from P. A. D. MacCarthy's *English Conversation Reader* pp. 24–5, and yields 419 *affirmative* finite verb forms.

The inquiry has revealed that there are at least six types of communicative functions the English finite verb can perform. They are illustrated by the following examples: 1. *ˊWhat did you ·say?* (25.16), 2. *ˇThey were ·booked ·up ·too, ˏreally . . .* (32.28), 3. *The proˈprietor was ˈˈmost ˎfriendly . . .* (33.05), 4. *Then I reˈtired to a ˈseat in the ˏpark and spent ˈhalf an ˏhour or so . . .* (32.06). 5. *We ˋmissed the ˌnews last ˏnight . . .* (43.26), 6. *ˈWell that ˎˎdoes sound nice* (33.08). Before giving the frequencies and characteristics of the types, let me first comment on the examples.

Type 1. As has been discussed elsewhere,[1] considered in the light of FSP, a question performs the following two functions: (a) to indicate the want of knowledge on the part of the questioner, (b) to impart knowledge to the informant as to the particular angle from which the question is to be approached (i.e. in what respect the indicated lack of knowledge is to be satisfied). Applying this observation to the structure *What did you say?*, we find that the first function is performed by the interrogative *what*, the second by the other elements, which for this purpose can appear in different kinds of perspective (cf. *ˈWhat ˈdid you ˎsay? ˈWhat did ˎyou say? ˈWhat ˎdid you say?*). If a *repetition* of a reply is required, the second function is no longer important, for not only is it obvious that something was *said*, but also that it *was* said and by *whom*. In fact, it would be possible, though less polite, simply to ask *ˊWhat?* It follows that the example under discussion shows an unusually high degree of contextual dependence, which has its share in signalling the request for repetition. This is why all the elements, including the TMEs, after the interrogative *ˊWhat* have been interpreted as thematic.

Type 2. The preceding context of the example under discussion (*ˇInside it was ·nice ˋtoo, but ˈunˇfortunately they were ˈbooked right ˋup. So I ˈwent to the ˈplace next ˋdoor,*) makes it clear that with the exception of its TMEs, the finite verb of the example has to be interpreted as conveying known information: it carries the lowest degree of CD and is thematic.

Though due to a different kind of interplay of means of FSP, the notional component of the finite verb also carries the lowest degree of CD and is thematic in (*They ˈsaid on the ˇradio last ·night*) *that a ˋthaw was*

[1] See my 'Some Thoughts on the Function of Word Order in Old English and Modern English', *SPFFBU* A 5, Brno 1957, 90–3.

ex,pected (43.24). Expressing 'appearance on the scene', it is communicatively less important than the subject, which expressed the phenomenon supposed to appear. (The entire that-clause is contextually independent.)

Type 3. Like all the other cases listed under this type, the quoted example contains a finite form of the verb *to be*. In their semantic weakness, the lexical components and the TMEs of *was* differ very little from each other. The same applies to the amount of CD they carry. This makes it necessary to regard not only the TMEs, but the entire finite verb form as bearer of transition proper. For the time being, it is only the finite forms of *to be* that have been interpreted in this way. This is because, semantically speaking, the verb *to be*, especially as a copula, is considered the weakest of English verbs. There are, of course, other verbs that because of semantic weakness come very close to it. (Cf. G. O. Curme, *Syntax*, Boston, 1931, 26.) On the other hand, on account of some of its lexical uses, *to be* may be shifted out of the sphere of the pure copula. An inquiry into these questions may eventually raise the number of verbs functioning as *Type* 3 cases, but would not affect the basic observation that these TMEs carry the lowest degrees of CD within the non-thematic section,

Type 4. In contrast with *Type* 3 cases, instances coming under the heading of *Type* 4 display a difference in the amounts of CD carried by the TMEs and the rest of the finite verb form. (The difference is naturally less distinct with verbs that because of their semantic weakness come close to the copulative *to be*.) In contrast with *Type* 5 cases, on the other hand, they do not contain verbs bearing the functionally weightiest prosodic feature within their respective distributional fields. In the adduced example, the verbs cannot perform this function, for they are respectively accompanied by a contextually independent object (cf. p. 88).

Type 5. In the adduced example, the finite verb bears the functionally weightiest prosodic feature. It does so on account of its notional component, which expresses rheme proper, the TMEs remaining transitional. The object and the adverbial element have been thematized by the preceding context (*They* ˈ*said on the* ˇ*radio last* ·*night that a* ˋ*thaw was ex,pected*).

Now, if—as in the adduced example—a finite verb bears a nucleus on account of its notional component and is at the same time *sole* nucleus bearer within the distributional field, it undoubtedly performs a *Type* 5 function. The situation, however, may not be so unequivocal and straightforward if the finite verb is not the only nucleus bearer.

In my material, there were 23 such cases out of the total of 71 verbs bearing a nucleus. Determining the functionally weightiest prosodic feature according to the criteria briefly outlined above (pp. 89-90), I interpreted 1 finite verb as performing function 3, 13 finite verbs as performing function 4, and 9 as performing function 5. All the 23 cases are adduced and discussed in 'Prosodic Features'.

As a detailed inquiry into the modifications of the basic observation on the functionally weightiest prosodic feature lies outside the scope of the present paper,[1] these interpretations must be looked upon as tentative, though in regard to the examined cases, the degree of tentativeness of the offered interpretations is comparatively very low. An obvious *Type* 3 case is . . . *but the* ˈ*fact* ˏ*is my* ˋ*watch had* ˏ*stopped while I was* ˈ*out* ˋ*shopping* (34.07). Obvious *Type* 4 cases are ˇ*Mealtimes and* ˇ*bedtimes and* ·*so on* are ˋbound *to be rather dis*ˇ*organised* (45.10); . . . *but it* ˈturned ˏout *that they'd* ˈ*just had* ˈ*several cancel*ˇ*lations for the* ˈ*second* ˈ*fortnight in* ˎ*August* (32.29); ˋ*Well, I*'d ˇˇlove *a* ˋ*drink,* (34.22). Obvious *Type* 5 cases are . . . *and I* ˈ*had the* ˏ*feeling we* should be ˈ*well* looked ˎafter *there* (33.06), *I*'ll ˋshow *them* ˌ*to you if you* ˏ*like* (39.12). The following two sentences were tentatively interpreted as *Type* 4 cases: *I* ˋlost *my* ˏ*old one at* ˋ*school,* . . . (39.24), *I* ˈ*generally* settle ˋdown *straight a*ˋ*way* (30.27).

Type 6. Like *Type* 5 example, the one illustrating *Type* 4 contains a finite verb which bears the functionally weightiest prosodic feature. The finite verb of 6, however, does not do so on account of its notional component but on account of its TMEs. *Does* becomes rheme proper on account of the semantic item of affirmation. Together with the rest of the sentence, the notional component of the finite verb constitutes an extensive theme proper. Neither in example 1 nor in 6 do the TMEs serve as transition proper. (In the examples 2–5, they do!) Both in 1, in which they serve as theme proper, and in 6, in which they serve as rheme proper, the TMEs signal a highly marked kind of contextual dependence of the distributional field.

The following two tables and the appended notes will give the frequencies and summarize the characteristics of the six types under discussion.

Type 1 is represented by 1 case (0·2 per cent) in my material. The finite verb is *entirely* thematic. *Type* 2 = 13 cases (3·1 per cent). The finite verb is thematic with the exception of the TMEs, which constitute transition proper. Both *Type* 1 and *Type* 2 are excluded from the sphere

[1] Relevant to such an inquiry are M. Schubiger's observations in *The Role of Intonation in Spoken English*, Cambridge 1935, 38–40. It follows from them that in determining the functionally weightiest prosodic feature in multinuclear distributional fields, the role played by the pause will have to be taken into consideration as well.

TABLE I

Type	The Finite Verb of the Sentence or Clause										The Non-Thematic Section of the Sentence or Clause[2] (not including the finite verb)	Total number of cases
	The Sphere of function in FSP of[1]		Prosodic characteristics of								Number of non-verbal nucleus bearers occurring within the non-thematic section that are functionally weightier than the finite verb	
	The TMEs of the finite verb form	The finite verb form to the exclusion of its TMEs	The auxiliaries (if present) of the finite verb form				The finite verb form to the exclusion of possible auxiliaries					
			Number of cases									
			Unstressed	Partially stressed	Stressed	Bearing a nucleus	Unstressed	Partially stressed	Stressed	Bearing a nucleus		
1	Theme proper	Theme proper	1	—	—	—	—	1	—	—	One	1
2	Transition proper	Theme	2	—	—	—	8	5	—	—	At least one	13
3	Transition proper	Transition proper	8	—	—	—	117	2	2	1	At least one	122
4	Transition proper	Transition	78	1	8	1	77	22	100	13	At least one	212
5	Transition proper	Rheme proper	17	—	1	—	3	2	—	56	None	61
6	Rheme proper	Theme[3]	—	—	—	10	3	—	—	1	None	40

[1] Strictly speaking, this column records how the finite verb functions in FSP through its semantic content.
[2] The term 'non-thematic' is always to be understood here in regard to the distributional field in which the examined verb functions.

TABLE 2

Type	Characteristics of the Finite Verb (Cf. Table 1)		Total	Percentage		
1	Theme proper	Theme proper	1	0·2	0·2	0·2
2	Transition proper	Theme	13	3·1	3·1	97·4 (types 2–5)
3	Transition proper	Transition proper	122	29·1	79·7 (types 3–4)	
4	Transition proper	Transition	212	50·6		
5	Transition proper	Rheme proper	61	14·6	14·6	
6	Rheme proper	Theme	10	2·4	2·4	2·4
			419	100·0	100·0	100·0

of stress bearers and nucleus bearers. *Type* 3 = 122 cases (29·1 per cent). The finite verb is non-thematic, functioning entirely within transition proper. With the exception of 3, all cases are excluded from the sphere of stress bearers and nucleus bearers. *Type* 4 = 212 cases (50·6 per cent). The finite verb is non-thematic, functioning in transition proper only through its TMEs, but not expressing rheme proper. In 100 cases it functions as a stress bearer, in 13 cases as a nucleus bearer. *Type* 5 = 61 cases (14·6 per cent). The finite verb is non-thematic; it expresses rheme proper, though through its TMEs it simultaneously functions in transition proper. 56 cases out of the 61 (91·8 per cent) are nucleus bearers. (Though not nucleus bearers, the remaining cases appear as the prosodically weightiest elements within the respective sentence or clause structures.) *Type* 6 = 10 cases (2·4 per cent). The finite verb expresses theme proper, this time through its TMEs; otherwise it is thematic.

As has been shown in the comments, borderline cases could naturally be established. They do not, however, invalidate the following conclusions. The finite verb displays an unmistakable tendency to function as a transitional element. In regard to degrees of CD, it is frequently heterogeneous, because the degree carried by the TMEs is frequently lower than the amount of CD carried by the rest of the finite verb form. On the prosodic level this heterogeneity becomes especially evident when the TMEs are separate words.

Now there are 127 cases in which the TMEs are expressed by

separate words (auxiliaries). In 10 of these cases they function as rheme proper and are nucleus bearers, in 1 case as theme proper and are unstressed, in 117 cases as transition proper and outside the nucleus sphere. If to the last mentioned group the 114 cases are added in which the finite verb form has no auxiliary, but occurs within transition proper, the number of cases in which transition proper is expressed by at least one separate word is raised to 241, i.e. 58·7 per cent of the total number of all the examined cases. The total number of nucleus bearers among these 241 cases amounts to 4.

All this is not at variance with the assignment to transition proper of those TMEs that are expressed by bound morphemes. The weight of the prosodic feature of a polymorphemic word naturally depends on that of its morpheme which carries the highest degree of CD.

To sum up. It is hoped that this inquiry bears out the conclusion that the TMEs show a remarkably high degree of coincidence between FSP on the one hand and the semantic and grammatical structures on the other. The TMEs, and in fact the finite verb, therefore provide a suitable starting point for further inquiries into the function of intonation on the level of FSP. Such inquiries may be expected to throw additional light on the function of the sentence in the very act of spoken communication and prove useful also in language teaching. As FSP (which makes the semantic and grammatical structures of the sentence function in a definite kind of perspective) plays a decisive role in controlling the intensity of the prosodic features, and above all in determining the location of the nuclei, the relation of grammar to intonation cannot be determined without due regard to FSP. This gives substantial support to the view recently voiced in *English Language Teaching* (see above, p. 77) that the 'neglected rhetorical notion of emphasis' forms an appropriate basis of teaching English intonation.

6 Verbal Aspect and Manner of Action in French—a Slavonic/Czech view

Jan Šabršula

I. Introduction

I.1. This paper deals with the verb, particularly from the point of view of its aspect and the manner of verbal action. We shall also consider the problem of time and tense, as well as mood and the potential lexico-syntactical classes of the verb. (A bibliography of the author's previous works in this field, published between 1959 and 1966, appears on pp. 110-11).

I.2.1. Many authors have dealt with the French verb tenses and one should refer to the bibliography in P. Imb's monograph *L'emploi des temps verbaux en français moderne* for details.[1] Some of the authors included there have made contributions which have been helpful in the writing of this paper: in particular authors such as Brunot, Yvon, Tesnière, Sten, R. L. Wagner, Marcel Cohen and P. Imbs himself. However none of these gives a complete picture of the ways in which aspect and manner of action are expressed, and certain authors (Buffin, Togeby, Guillaume) put forward points of view which we contest.[2]

I.2.2. The idea of aspect was already known to the Ancient Greeks, as we are reminded by Jens Holt in his 'Studies in Aspect'.[3] In the seventeenth century evidence of research on verbal aspect appeared in the work of certain Czech grammarians (Benedictus of Nudožery and W. J. Rosa)[4] and in the nineteenth century we encounter notions of verbal aspect in comparative Indo-European grammars, as well as in the works of many Russian authors.

Among the important contributions to this field we should mention

[1] Paris 1960, 255–61.

[2] Cf., e.g. my 1959: 67–9 and 1962b: 1/I—§§ 2 and 25 and 1/II—§ 5.

[3] 'Etudes d'aspect', *Acta Jutlandica* 15/2 (1945) 4. He himself quotes Bekker's *Anecdota Graeca* II, p. 889.

[4] Benedictus of Nudožery, *Grammaticae bohemicae ad leges naturalis methodi conformatae et notis numerisque illustratae ac distinctae libri duo*, 1603; W. J. Rosa, *Thesaurus Linguae Bohemicae* and *Grammatica Linguae Bohemicae*, 1672.

the Czechoslovak linguists F. Trávníček; and more recently, B. Havránek, A. V. Isačenko, V. Mathesius, F. Kopečný, I. Němec; and anglicists B. Trnka, I. Poldauf, M. Jindra, J. Krámský. The most thorough monograph dealing with the problem of aspect from the point of view of Slavonic and general linguistics is the work of A. Dostál entitled *A Study of the aspect system in Old Slav.*[1] However the authors who have studied aspect do not use the same methods of approach nor do they adopt the same criterion for defining aspect. Romance linguistic works are weakest in this respect.

Scholarship during the period characterized by the comparative grammar of Brugmann and Delbrück was based on morphology, for example W. Streitberg,[2] G. Herbig who deals with Greek[3] or W. Porzig[4] who concentrates on the Indo-European morpheme *-sk-*. Slavists concentrate on the suffix or prefix and attempt primarily to isolate those suffixes and prefixes which have no lexical content (i.e. classificatory, entirely aspectual formemes).

Similarly, Jens Holt[5] studies all the verbal forms of Ancient Greek and asserts that they are formed from four roots, the present, the future, the perfect and the aorist. Since it is possible to build from certain roots forms which can express three tense distinctions, he deduces that the difference between these roots is not one of tense but rather of aspect. So, leaving aside the future root, he arrives at a system of three roots which, in his opinion, represent three distinctions of aspect. It is unclear how he arrives at the conclusion that these differences are aspectual in nature.

I.2.3. Among the Romance scholars, G. Guillaume divided the French verbal tenses into simple and compound forms and gave the name 'aspect' to these two groups.[6] When we use the term 'aspect' in such cases we gain nothing. This only increases the confusion in terminology. We might remind Guillaume here that French is a polysystemic language in which the differences between the Compound Past (*passé composé*, *passé indéfini*) and the Simple Past (*passé simple*, *passé défini*) are stylistic; these two tenses occur in *different* functional styles and the essence of the difference between them lies here.

A valuable discussion on aspect took place in 1958 (cf. *Revue belge de Philologie et d'Histoire*; L. Rocher, M. Leroy, A. Maniet and M. Maline

[1] *Studie o vidovém systému v staroslověnštině* (Prague 1954). For bibliographical details on the authors mentioned above, see my 1962b: 182.
[2] 'Perfektive und imperfektive Aktionsart im Germanischen', *PBB* 15 (1891), 70–177.
[3] 'Aktionsart und Zeitstufe', *Indogermanische Forschungen* 6 (1896) 157–269.
[4] Zur Aktionsart indogermanischer Präsensbildungen', *IF* 45 (1927) 152–67.
[5] Op. cit. Cf. my 1962b: 1/I—§§ 4 and 22.
[6] 'Temps et verbe', *Théorie des aspects, des modes et des temps* (Paris, 1929).

took part in this discussion, and Jacques Pohl made an important contribution on verbal aspect in French). However here once again each of the authors meant something different by 'aspect'.

I.2.4. This is linked with the general problem of choosing the contrastive comparison of systems or of function (and if we decide in favour of the latter, how are we to define function?).

If we accept the pragmatic point of view, which we must if we are to be of any use to the teacher and student of a foreign language, then we must consider language and thought as unified, see the function of language as a vehicle of thought and communication, and assume that all languages indirectly reflect objective reality. Despite the doubts expressed by the linguists of the Humboldtian school, in the works of Sapir, Whorf and Weisgerber, we maintain that different languages are capable of expressing the same objective reality—or our subjective thought concerning this reality—in different ways. With this premise as a basis we wish to attempt an onomasiological definition of verbal aspect and of manner of action, and afterwards to list the corresponding means of expression. This method has been used in our previous work, published between 1959 and 1966 (see bibliography, pp. 110-11).

I.3. We now propose to give an onomasiological definition of aspect and manner of action, from the point of view of the Slavic observer (we generalise from the Slavic aspect system with, of course, certain reservations).

I.3.1. We define the term 'aspect' as the concept of action by the subject who is speaking: the action can be conceived as perfective or imperfective (i.e. as global or non-global). The semantic definition of aspect was first made by the Czech E. Černý, and de Saussure, Hermann and Hjelmslev also came close to this definition,[1] A. Dostál above all successfully defended this definition of aspect in his study, mentioned above. He explains that 'perfective' is not the same as 'accomplished', as Curtius, Miklosich, Delbrück, Jagić, Fortunatov, Gebauer, Hartmann, Brugmann, Streitberg, Tesnière and others thought, and that imperfective aspect is not to be identified with the objective duration of the verbal action.

If we take as a basis a semantic definition of aspect, we can speak of the *aspect of the verbal action* without being obliged to identify aspect solely with a few traditional forms.

[1] Cf. A. V. Isačenko, 'Slovesný vid, Slovesné akce a obecný charakter slovesny' (Verbal aspect, verbal action and the general character of the verb), *SaS* 21 (1960), 9–10, and F. de Saussure, *Cours de linguistique générale* 2 (1922), 162.

Aspect of verbal action presents a binary opposition, i.e. the perfective and imperfective; apart from these two, there are no other aspects.

I.3.2. Naturally there are phenomena which are closely related to aspect. In Indo-European studies, Germanic studies, Classical philology, sometimes in Slavic linguistics and, at the moment, only occasionally in Romance linguistics the term 'manner of action' (*Aktionsart, azione, ordre de procès, subaspect*) is used alongside the term 'aspect'. We wish to reserve the term 'manner of action' to indicate the phase of action (inceptive, continuative, terminative), for the progressive character of action, semelfactive, distributive, iterative, frequentative, durative, and for a few other modifications of the character of verbal action. I am not thinking here of non-indicative modal modifications, since mood and manner of action are two different things, although the non-indicative mood is sometimes found in a special relationship with manner of action. For example, the conative mood implies, it appears, the imperfective aspect, e.g. Czech imperfective verbs can express simultaneously intention: 'Otec kupuje dům' = 'Otec *se snaži koupit* dům' 'my father *intends to buy* a house'. Similarly the French imperfect indicative tense may, in certain circumstances, express the conative mood of the action, e.g. 'Un enfant de deux ans se noyait dans la Sarre. Un passant l'a sauvé in extremis.' 'A two-year-old child *was drowning* in the River Sarre. A passer-by saved him just in time.' (Czech: 'Dvouleté dítě *se topilo* v S., chodec je v poslední chvíli zachránil.'—Opp. *topilo se*, Imperfective, Eng. *was drowning*: utopilo se, Perfective, Eng. *drowned*.)

I.3.3. The fact that aspect can concern a subjective conception may be shown by the following example. In this French context the same action which, from an objective point of view, happened only once is expressed twice: once in the global, perfective conception, and again in the non-global, imperfective conception:

J'allais à la fenêtre et j'ouvris. Au moment où j'ouvrais, midi sonnait partout. (Daudet) Eng.: 'I went to the window and *opened* it. As I *was opening* it, all the bells were chiming midday.' (Czech: 'Šel jsem k oknu a *otevřel* (Perfective conception) jsem je. V okamžiku, kdy jsem je *otvíral* (Imperfective conception), všude odzvánělo poledne.')

The global or non-global concept of action may express the relationships which exist in the world of objective reality, for example in the Incidence-Scheme:

*J'*écrivais *quand il* entra. 'I *was writing* when he *came* in'. (Czech: *Psal* jsem, když *vstoupil*. *Psal jsem* Imperf., *vstoupil* Perf.)

The sentence *J'écrivais quand il* est entré has an identical meaning.

At this juncture let us recall once again that the Compound and Simple Past tenses have the same meaning in contemporary French; their co-existence has become a feature of *functional style*: the Simple Past is not the tense of *normal spoken language*.

In a few cases only the Compound Past may have the meaning of the resultative present: *Il est mort* can correspond to a Preterite ('he died') and in this case the meaning is the same as, in *regional French*, the form *Il a moru îr*. In other cases, this form may have a resultative meaning ('he is dead') and in *popular language* which is not governed by codifying institutions, we find the equivalent '*Il est mwèrt dispoy lontins*'.[1]

The fact that the objective duration of the action must not be confused with aspect and that aspect represents rather a subjective conception may be shown by other examples. One such example may be found in Mr Bonnard's article in *Le Français Moderne* 2 (Avril, 1964) 96: 'Short as was Caesar's victory over the King of Pont, it lasted longer than it takes to say *Veni, vidi, vici.*'

II. Concerning Comparative Material and Documentation

II.1. The person whose mother tongue is Slavic notices immediately that the tense system of the French language is richer than that of Slavic. In French the number of past indicative tenses in particular is very large.

Quite often when comparing languages, one makes over-simplified parallels: for example, the opposition *imperfect* : *aorist* in different languages or the opposition *imperfect* : *perfect*, etc., is often compared with the Slavic *perfective* : *imperfective* verbal forms.[2] Nevertheless our view of the problems would be wrong if we claimed certain analogies without recognizing their limits.

Again, one may affirm that the French imperfect indicative and present indicative verbal forms represent a kind of 'infectum', i.e. the imperfective aspect. That is to say that these forms combine two functions: the temporal classification of the action, and an indication of the non-global conception of the verbal action. Generally the action formulated as present can be conceived only as a non-global concept. If we use the present, a perfective conception may be imagined in those cases where this form has a secondary meaning (future or past); the present indicative becomes a *stylistic variant* of a past narrative tense or of a future. The other tenses, indicative or non-indicative

[1] These examples are quoted by Jacques Pohl, *Témoignages sur la syntaxe du verbe dans quelques parlers français de Belgique* (Bruxelles, 1962) 71–2.
[2] H. Paul, and others. Cf. my 1962b: 35–7.

(i.e. subjunctive, conditional, infinitives) are unmarked in this respect.[1]

If we examine these tenses in relation to their Slavic equivalents in a parallel text, we realize that the perfective equivalents are more frequent although they are not the only ones to be found. So we must examine these tense forms on their own in connexion with the lexical meaning of verbs and with the meaning of certain conjunctions and adverbs. Thus, it is not enough to examine solely the morphological system of the verb and the grammar without heeding the lexicon.

II. 2. *Lexical meaning of verbs*

II.2.1.1. Conclusive and non-conclusive verbs. There are certain verbs: e.g. *chercher* (to seek'), *circuler* ('circulate'), *stationner*, *être en stationnement* ('to be parked'), *pourchasser* ('pursue'), *régner* ('reign'), *jalouser* ('to be jealous'), *compatir* ('commiserate with', 'sympathize with' *consister* ('consist'), *travailler* ('work' in the intransitive sense), *agir* ('to be active'), *converser* ('converse'), *haïr* ('hate'), *agoniser* ('to be in agony'). These verbs always correspond to imperfective forms of Slavic verbs, whereas verbs like *trouver* can only be translated by a Slavic perfective form as long as they are not in the present or imperfect indicative.

One could designate these two groups with the terms 'conclusive' (e.g. *trouver*) and 'non-conclusive' (e.g. *chercher*).[2] The large class of conclusive verbs represents a few sub-groups, among which appear the verbs called 'momentaneous', a few semelfactive, inceptive, terminative verbs etc. There is also a third group of amphibological verbs such as those which, in the Slavic languages, are translated by perfective or imperfective equivalents according to the context (conjunction, adverb, etc.) or situation (except when the verb is in the imperfect or the present indicative tense).[3]

The differences between conclusive and non-conclusive verbs are clearly seen in the passive. In Czech the passive of the imperfective verb expresses action conceived in a non-global light; the 'passive' of perfective verbs expresses the state implied by a completed action.

[1] Cf. my 1963a: 72–85.

[2] Cf. my 1960–61, 1962b, and 1963d. In the nineteenth century Diez (*Grammatik der rom. Sprachen* 3, p. 202) distinguished between these categories, followed by H. Lindroth (*PBB* 31, p. 238, and *Over adjectivering of participie*, Lund 1966) and others. The terms *conclusive* and *non-conclusive* are found in Jespersen (*A Modern English Grammar on historical principles*, Part IV: Syntax, Vol. 3: Time and Tense, London, 1932 p. 92). H. B. Garey ('Verbal aspect in French' *Lg*. 33, 1957, 106–9) distinguishes *telic* and *atelic* verbs, which are not the same as conclusive and non-conclusive verbs.

[3] Cf. my 1959: 73, 1961a, 1962b, 1963d: 166–79, etc.

In French (and in English) the passive of certain verbs (e.g. *il est cherché* 'he is sought', Czech 'je hledán', Imperfective) also describes a process conceived as imperfective. They may mean the state which is the consequence of a completed action. These verbs acquire this second meaning (state) primarily in the present indicative tense or in the imperfect, but only occasionally in the simple past.

This results from the fact that the past participle of non-conclusive verbs is always kept, in any function, even as an attribute or an epithet expressing an action, e.g. *je suis aimé* 'I am loved', *je suis haï* 'I am hated', *mon fils aimé* 'my beloved son' or, rather, 'my son who is loved'.

However, the past participle of a conclusive verb expresses the result of the the action, for example, *la porte est fermée* ('the door is closed'), and hence a state. Certain past participles of non-conclusive verbs are only found in compound verb forms (*appartenu*, *agonisé*, *consisté* . . .), unless they are the result of an ellipsis. The past participles of conclusive verbs in the function of attribute or epithet often become adjectives expressing a state, e.g. *ils voyaient sa mine renfrognée* 'they saw his scowling face', *un petit coin parfumé* 'a small perfumed place', *une petite pièce blanchie à la chaux* 'a little room whitened with chalk', *bergers drapés dans des manteaux* 'shepherds wrapped in their cloaks'.

This may also be the case with intransitive verbs, e.g. *une pomme* tombée 'a *fallen* apple', *un homme* mort 'a *dead* man'.

However, in an appropriate context even the past participles of conclusive or amphibological verbs may express a 'continuous' action: *cette expression* n'est plus employée. 'This expression is no longer used'. The past participle may even have, in a suitable context, an iterative meaning: *les passions,* allumées *ou entretenues par des ministres, ont eu dans tous les âges, les effets les plus funestes.* (Diderot) 'Passions, *kindled* or preserved by ministers, have had, throughout the ages, the most disastrous effects.'

The resultative manner of action in an 'absolute' construction can be expressed only by a conclusive verb: *le soir* venu, *la soupe* mangée, *le petit neveu* couché, *Adèle Amable s'assied sur un banc et file ou tricote.* (R. Vailland) 'When evening falls, the soup *has been eaten* and the little nephew *has been put to bed,* Adèle Amable sits on a bench and spins or knits.'

In Slavic languages certain prefixes may express the perfective aspect (e.g. *učit se*, Imperfective, *naučit se*, Perfective). In French two different verbs may express this distinction, a non-conclusive verb and a conclusive verb (*étudier* : *apprendre*). The tense remains the same.

In English the situation is different; but there is some similarity: *What have you learnt for today? Don't you know your irregular verbs? Then what have you learnt/did you learn? What have you learnt = Qu'est-ce que tu as appris, What did you learn = Qu'est-ce que tu as étudié. J'ai étudié longtemps, mais je n'ai rien appris. I have been studying (I have studied) for a long time and I have learnt nothing.* Czech: Studoval jsem *dlouho* (Imperfective), or Učil jsem se *dlouho* (Imperfective), *ale nic jsem se* nenaučil (Perfective).

Conclusive or non-conclusive verbs represent two categories (cryptotypes) clearly definable by certain distributional processes.

The conclusive or non-conclusive character of Romance verbs is not, however, the same as the perfective or imperfective aspect. A conclusive verb may correspond to the imperfective aspect in the Slavic languages (or to an imperfective verb which expresses an unlimited iteration) if the verb is in the imperfect indicative. E.g. the two verbs *porter* : *apporter* represent a non-conclusive : conclusive opposition. The clause *Il a porté* (Eng. 'he carried', 'he has carried', 'did carry') corresponds to the Czech imperfective form 'nesl'. *Il a apporté* ('he has brought', 'he did bring', 'he brought') corresponds to the Czech perfective form 'přinesl'.

But, *Quand il apportait . . .* corresponds to the imperfective Czech form 'Když přinášel . . .' ('While he *was bringing* a book to me, something *happened*'—Incidence-Scheme); in this case even a conclusive verb corresponds to an imperfective or iterative-frequentative Slavic verb.

On the other hand, conclusive verbs resemble Slavic perfective verbs in that they represent a more general category than the different sub-aspects. For example, *porter* is non-conclusive and durative, *apporter* is conclusive and terminative, *apprendre* is conclusive, and, in a certain sense, resultative, *étudier* is non-conclusive and durative, *être* is linear, cursive, durative and non-conclusive in contrast with *devenir* ('to become') which is conclusive and resultative, but has the ability to express an imperfective or iterative action when the verb is in the imperfect indicative: *M. Haviland . . . mangeait beaucoup*, devenait *très* rouge, restait mélancolique *et ne disait rien.* (A. France.) 'Mr Haviland . . . ate (used to eat) a lot, and *from time to time he would become* very *red*, and (*would*) *remain melancholy* and (would) say nothing.' *Toute la table se retourna: on crut qu'il* devenait fou. (Daudet.) 'The whole table turned round: they thought he *was going mad.*' *Hélène grandissait*, devenait belle . . . (A. France.) 'Helen was growing up and *was becoming* beautiful.'

This is an example of gnomic iteration: *Lorsqu'on le* blessait *à la vanité*, devenait *aussitôt* méchant. '*Whenever* people *injured* his pride, he immediately *became* awkward.'[1]

The infinitive of a conclusive verb has an imperfective meaning even when it follows a verb expressing the phase of the action, with the meaning of 'to begin', or 'to continue', or 'to stop', e.g. *Nous commençons à* devenir, *je crois*, *de fort bons amis*. 'I believe we are beginning to be very good friends'. The Slavic equivalent of this periphrasis could be represented by an imperfective verb: Czech: Stáváme se *velmi dobrými přáteli*.

II.2.1.2. The lexical meaning of verb and tenses. At this juncture we can establish a synoptic table of the Slavic aspectual equivalents of certain tenses in French. For the past tenses of the amphibological group, we find the following equivalents:

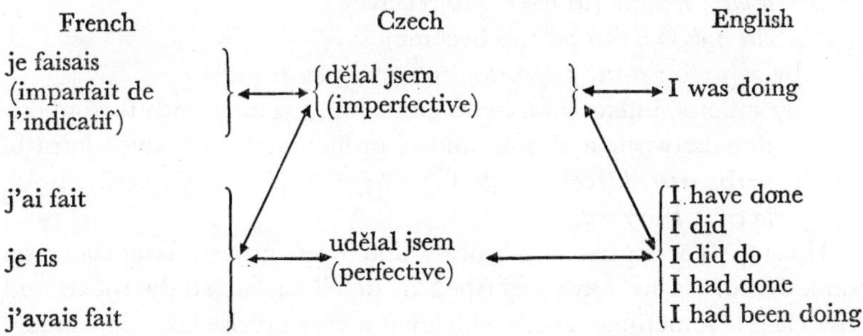

For genuinely conclusive verbs, we find the following equivalents:

French	Czech	English
quand j'arrivais	když jsem přicházel když jsem přijížděl (imperfective)	While I was arriving
je suis arrivé j'arrivai, etc.	přišel jsem přijel jsem (perfective)	I have arrived I did arrive I arrived, etc.

For non-conclusive verbs there is only one equivalent:

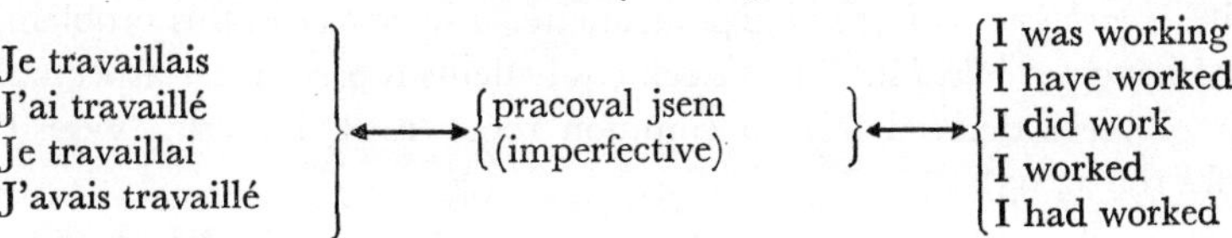

[1] The examples are taken from my 1962b: 115–19.

For the future simple, the table is less complicated:

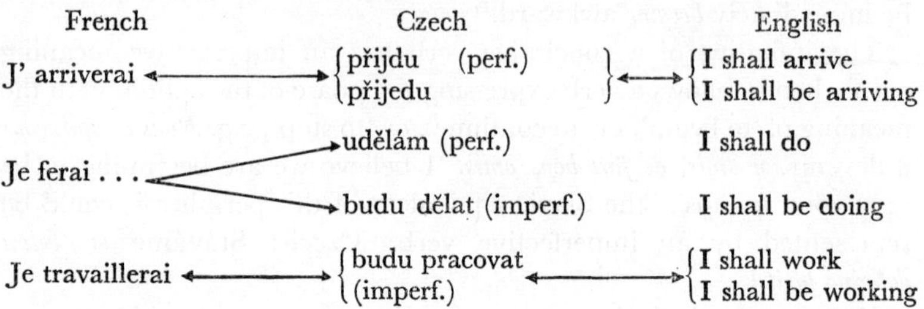

French
Czech
English
J' arriverai
přijdu (perf.)
přijedu
I shall arrive
I shall be arriving
Je ferai . . .
udělám (perf.)
I shall do
budu dělat (imperf.)
I shall be doing
Je travaillerai
budu pracovat (imperf.)
I shall work
I shall be working

The conclusive or non-conclusive character of the action can be indicated by

the root or the stem, e.g.

chercher : *trouver* (to seek : to find)

avoir : *recevoir* (to have : to receive)

être : *devenir* (to be : to become)

by a prefix: *porter* : *apporter* (to carry : to bring)[1]

by suffixes, infixes and, in certain cases, together with the opposition between a simple and a pronominal (reflexive) form of verb: *crier* 'křičet' (imperf.): *s'écrier* 'vykřiknout' (perf.), Engl. *to cry* : *to cry out*.

II.2.1.3. To express sub-aspects and even aspect, language uses supletivism. As we have described in detail in our study 1962b and elsewhere,[2] sometimes a verb which has a very precise lexical meaning, but which, from the point of view of conclusivity, is amphibological, is interchangeable with a verb having a poorer lexical content, but which, in respect to conclusivity, is clearer. E.g. *Il a lu ta lettre* (longtemps). 'He read your letter (for a long time)'. Cz. *Četl* tvůj dopis (dlouho) (imperf.). *Il a* parcouru *ta lettre*. 'He *glanced* at your letter.' *Pročetl* (perf.) (zběžně a rychle) *tvůj dopis* (1962b, 63–4).

For the verbs *résoudre*, *solutionner*, *chercher* (*trouver*) *la solution*. 'to solve', 'resolve', 'look for the solution' and 'find the solution', there are, in French, interesting 'equivalents' (i.e. verbs which, in certain contexts, are interchangeable with the expressions given above), one of which is conclusive, and the other non-conclusive: *traiter* : *trancher*. *J'ai* traité *ce problème, mais je ne l'ai pas* tranché. 'I have *tackled* this problem, but I have not *solved* it.' The Czech equivalents represent an aspectual pair of verbs derived from a common root: 'řešit' imperf., 'vyřešit' perf. (1963c, 95).

[1] In my 1962b: 55, fn. 2, and 1963c: 100, 4.1, we show, by means of certain examples, that prefixes in French can modify the manner of action but not verbal aspect.

[2] Cf. 1962b: 63–4 and 1963c: 93, etc.

II.2.2. Complex denominating units with a verbal character.

II.2.2.1. The conclusive or non-conclusive character of the action, and even 'aspect' itself are sometimes expressed by verbal periphrases—e.g. inceptive (1964, 83–6), terminative (1964, 87–91), pseudo-terminative (1964, 91–2), continuative, imperfective (1964, 96), and others. The progressive character of the verbal action is expressed, in certain cases, by periphrases such as *aller* (*être* plus participle in *-ant*). G. Gougenheim (*Étude sur les périphrases verbales de la langue française*, Paris 1938) deals with them. In our own comparative studies (1962b, 1964, 104–6) we give some recent examples: *L'agitation de Buteau* était allée en croissant, *il attelait et dételait du matin au soir, sans raison, et les gens se sauvaient.* (Zola.) 'Buteau's agitation *had been increasing*, he harnessed and unharnessed his horses from morning to evening, without any reason, and everyone fled.' and define certain homonymous periphrases, using distributional procedures. Note the use of the pluperfect tense in these examples.

II.2.2.2. Let us add an example where the repetition of the verb expresses an imperfective action, in some cases the durative, iterative or distributive sub-aspect: *J'ai couru, couru . . . mon pied a buté dans un casque.* 'I *ran and ran*, my foot stumbled against a helmet.'; *Il regarde, regarde . . .* 'He looks and looks.'; *Il* attelait et dételait *du matin au soir.* 'He *harnessed and unharnessed* his horses *from morning to evening.*'; *Elle se promena dans son jardinet,* passant et revenant *par les mêmes allées.* 'She walked around in her garden, *coming and going* along the same paths.'

II.2.2.3. The rôle of verbo-nominal constructions.

II.2.2.3.1. These constructions express the semelfactive sub-aspect: *Il* jeta un regard *rapide à travers la porte.* 'He *cast a* rapid *glance* through the door' ('He glanced rapidly . . .'); *Dingo* poussa un aboiement *lamentable.* 'Dingo *gave a* plaintive *bark*' (1962b, 80, 82, 87).

Together with the semelfactive sub-aspect these constructions also can express the smallness of the action: *Le père poussa un* léger *sifflement d'admiration.* (Maupassant.) 'The father *gave a small whistle* of admiration. *Ils on effectué une* légère *mise en train* (*L'Humanité* 31 March 1959). 'They carried out a *light* training-programme.' In Czech there are synthetic derivative equivalents ('zatrénovali si' perf.). *Faire un petit somme,* 'to have a short nap (sleep)'; *Fair la causette, fair causette,* 'to have a chat'; *Cette absence et le départ ont* jeté un froid *dans les rapports* franco-italiens. (*L'Humanité* 8 October 1958.) 'His absence and his departure *have cast a shadow* over Franco-Italian relations.' *Ébaucher un geste, ébaucher un sourire* ('He almost smiled', 'He gave the ghost of a smile', 'shadow of a smile', 'flicker of a smile'); *La jeune fille a marqué un temps d'hesitation.* (Laffitte) Czech: 'zaváhala', Eng: 'The girl showed a moment's hesitation.'

Sometimes the smallness of the action is expressed by the verbo-nominal locution containing the noun *coup: donner un coup de peigne* 'to run a comb through one's hair'. In other cases, these constructions express the abrupt nature of the action.

Special groups are represented by constructions containing the verbs *avoir* ('to have'): *il eut un geste* ('he made a sign'); *faire; jeter* and *pousser* (*-un cri* 'give a cry'); *donner* (*un coup de pied*, 'to kick'); *élever*, *porter*, *prendre*, *mettre* (e.g. *élever sa protestation* 'raise *an* objection' in contrast to 'object'); *porter secours* ('come to the aid of'); *prendre fin*, *mettre fin* ('come to a close', 'bring to a close').

II.2.2.3.2. Attributive constructions with the verbs *être*, *demeurer* ('remain'), *se tenir* ('stay'), *se voir* express the durative and linear sub-aspect, and constructions with the verb *rester*, *se voir*, *se trouver* sometimes the resultative sub-aspect: *Quand le docteur* se voit seul . . . 'When the doctor finds himself alone . . .'.

The verb *se trouver* forms, together with the participle of the verb in question, a true resultative compound past in the following example: Le rythme de la circulation . . . s'en est trouvé ralenti. (*L'Humanité* 16 August 1966, 'The rhythm of the traffic (was) slowed down.')

II.2.2.3.3. Constructions with the verbs *devenir* ('to become'), *se faire* ('to become'), *tomber* (*tomber malade* 'fall ill') and *rendre* ('to make', 'render') express the change of state. The opposition 'single verb: verbo-nominal attributive construction' represents, as far as content goes, the opposition 'non-resultative manner of action : resultative manner of action' (and sometimes the opposition 'intransitive : transitive'), e.g. *embellir: devenir beau* : *rendre beau* ('embellish', transitive only : 'become beautiful' : 'make beautiful' or 'beautify'). *Une petite fille très laide* embellit *en passant à l'adolescence, sans pour cela* devenir belle. (Lafay.) 'A very ugly little girl *improves* with adolescence, without *becoming beautiful* for all that.' In Czech the two equivalents are perfective ('stane se hezčí, aniž zkrásní). Similarly *On ne devient vieux qu'à force de vieillir* 'One only *becomes old* by *growing old*'. In the latter case, we find the perfective: imperfective opposition in Czech ('*Zestárneme* jen jako důsledek tobo, že stárneme'). In French it is a question rather of the conclusive : non-conclusive opposition: *Il a aiguisé* 'He has been sharpening the knife' corresponds to the Czech pair 'brousil' : 'nabrousil', 'He has been sharpening' = 'brousil', 'He has sharpened' = 'nabrousil' or 'brousil' *Il a rendu aigu* corresponds only to the perfective 'nabrousil'. Certain verbo-nominal constructions express the semelfactive sub-aspect and, at the same time, the conative modality, e.g. *Martha* fait un geste pour *parler*. ('Martha *makes a move* to speak'.)

II.2.2.3.4. The construction verb plus *un* plus noun in the imperfect expresses a habitual action which is characterized by a unique realization: *Quand . . . elle* faisait une grimace *de dégoût* '*Whenever* they gave her the bitter medicine, *she grimaced* in disgust.'

This is in opposition to the construction verb plus *des* plus noun: *Tandis qu'il se défendait, Tamango* poussait des cris *de rage*. 'While he defended himself, he *shouted* in rage'.

The verbo-nominal constructions with the complement in the plural (*pousser*, *faire des cris*, 'to cry out', *jeter des regards* 'cast glances', *faire entendre des aboiements* 'to bark', *faire des réflexions* 'to reflect', *faire des recherches*, 'to do research', *donner des coups de pied* 'to kick several times') often express the distributive or iterative sub-aspect.

Certain constructions with similar form do not, however, express the distributive or iterative sub-aspect, e.g. *présenter ses excuses* ('offer one's excuses', Czech 'omluvit se').[1]

II.2.2.3.5. The meaning of certain local modifications of action expressed by certain Czech aspectual prefixes may be rendered by lexically independent French verbs e.g. in Czech verbs *jíti* 'go', *přijíti* 'arrive' and 'come', *přicházeti* ('come', imperf.), *odejíti* 'go away', 'depart', 'leave' (*odcházeti* imperf.) correspond to the French verbs *aller* : *arriver*, *venir* : *s'en aller*, *partir*. Certain local modifications are expressed in French by periphrases, e.g. the Czech verb *běžeti* 'to be running', 'to run' corresponds to the French *courir*, and the Czech verb *vyběhnout* 'to run out', 'to be running out' corresponds to the French periphrase *sortir en courant*. Similarly, *přiběhnouti* 'come running' is equivalent to *parvenir en courant*. Let us add to this example a verbo-adverbial group *traverser au pas de course* (*la rue*), Czech *přeběhnout* (perf.) or *přebíhat* (imperf.) 'run across the street', 'to be running across the street'.

II.2.2.4. At this point we now turn to the problem of adverbs and verbo-adverbial constructions.

II.2.2.4.1. Verbo-adverbial constructions often express the phase of the action, for example, the inceptive manner of action. E.g. *entrer en fureur* 'to get into a rage', 'to get angry' (*se mettre en colère*), *éclater en sanglots* 'burst into tears'. Some verbo-adverbial constructions form pre-morphological paradigms (1966a, 183–92).

II.2.2.4.2. The adverb (or its equivalent) is an external element of

[1] Cf. my 1962b, 91.

the semantic constellation of the verb, from the point of view of distribution. Perfective verbs, or those which, in a given context, have a perfective sense, are incompatible with the indication of interval (*une heure* 'one hour', *quelques jours* 'a few days'). The adverbs show that K. Togeby (*Structure immanente de la langue française*, p. 173) is incorrect in thinking that the future simple in French is a form of the perfective aspect. Cf. *Il dormira longtemps* 'He will sleep for a long time', *A six heures du matin, nous dormirons encore* (H. Bonnard) 'We shall still be asleep at six o'clock in the morning.'

Certain adverbs indicate the perfective conception of the action: *Les habitants de la petite commune* furent réveillés *en sursaut par une terrible explosion*. 'The inhabitants of the small community were awakened (awoken) *abruptly* by a terrible explosion.'

A few adverbial expressions occasionally correspond to the Czech prefixes *u-*, *na-*, *vy-*, *do-* which in certain conditions express the perfective aspect, or the resultative or terminative sub-aspect. E.g. *Plusieurs* moururent à force de boire. 'Several people died through drinking' (Mérimée). Czech: *Mnozí se* up*ili*.

The rôle of the French adverb *net* is also important. E.g. *Le rire de Roselyne* se brisa net. *B.M.* stoppe net. (Vailland.) 'Roselyne's smile suddenly disappeared. Beau Masque stops dead (suddenly)'.

The resultative sub-aspect is indicated by the adverb *dès* or *une fois*, e.g. *Une fois la tâche terminée* . . . 'Once the task is completed . . .'

If we wish to express the meaning of the Czech verb derived from the prefix *po-* in the expression *pohleď*, which expresses an action of limited duration, we add to the French verb the adverbial phrase *un peu*: *Regarde un peu, Jean* (Zola) 'Take a look, John'. The Czech adverb *pořád* (*toujours* 'always') indicates the continuative manner of action and the imperfective aspect; the adverb *vždycky* (*toutes les fois que* 'whenever') indicates the frequentative sub-aspect.

II.3. *The role of conjunctions*

The conjunctions and conjunctive expressions *pendant que*, *tandis que*, *tant que*, *à mesure que* are marked from the point of view of aspect and indicate the imperfective aspect: *Pendant qu'il examinera* . . ., *Tandis qu'il regardera* . . . *Tant qu'il téléphonera* . . . *À mesure qu'il avancera* . . ., *Aussi longtemps qu'il parlera* . . . 'While he is examining', 'While he is looking at . . .', 'As long as he is telephoning . . .', 'As he advances', 'As long as he goes on speaking . . .'.

With momentaneous or semelfactive verbs, the conjunctive locutions above express the imperfective, distributive sub-aspect, e.g. *Tant qu'il sautera* 'As long as he goes on jumping (continues jumping) . . .'; *Tandis qu'il poussera des cris de rage* 'As long as he goes on shouting (keeps shouting) with rage . . .'; *Tandis qu'elle poussera des soupirs . . .* 'As long as she keeps sighing (goes on sighing)'; *Tant qu'elle fait des grimaces de dégout* . . . 'As long as she keeps grimacing (goes on grimacing) with disgust . . .'. It seems to us that the conjunctive locution *tandis que* is not compatible, in a similar case, with a verbo-nominal construction containing a complement in the singular (e.g. *pousser* un *cri* 'give a cry').

Tant que may be combined in this case with different tenses. Among the past tenses we find most often the imperfect indicative but we may also find the Compound past provided that the lexical meaning of the verb is not distinctly conclusive. This confirms that the Compound past or Simple past are not marked with regard to aspect. E.g. *Tant qu'il* a vécu *il a travaillé* 'He worked all his life (as long as he lived)'; *Tant qu'il* a crié *je me suis bouché les oreilles.* 'While he shouted (was shouting) I covered my ears.'; *Tout cela fut tel* tant que *Verlaine* vécut, *puis changea lentement.* (Jean Gallotti, *Le Paris des poètes et des romanciers*, 1946) 'Things were the same as long as Verlaine lived (was alive) but then they changed slowly.'

Tant que is compatible with resultative tenses and conclusive verbs in a *negative* clause in which the action expressed by the resultative tense and by the conclusive verb is at the same time negated: *Tant que je* ne *serai* pas *rentré, tu ne sortiras pas.* (Maupassant.) 'As long as I am away, you shall not go out.'; *Pas de sécurité en Europe, tant que* ne *sera* pas *déraciné l'impérialisme germain.* 'There will be no security in Europe until German imperialism is uprooted.'

À mesure que is a conjunctive expression which is doubly marked. Apart from the imperfective conception this expression also indicates the progressive manner of action.

III. Summary of findings

III.1. It follows that the asymetric character of the morphology of the French verbal system (revealed by the fact that for the future there is no opposition infectum: non-infectum) is compensated for by different suppletive means, verbal periphrases, adverbs, conjunctions. The lexical meaning of verbs also partly compensates for the lacunae in the morphological system.

III.2. We have also seen that the denominating units of the French language can be formed by several words, (e.g. verbal periphrases, or verbo-nominal or verbo-adverbial constructions), which are often interchangeable with single word units. The real unit of construction of the French clause is not the word, but the denominating unity, which can be either complex or 'simple' (i.e., consisting of a single word).

IV. Conclusion

If we examine the aspect of the verbal action from the onomasiological point of view, we observe that this is a complex phenomenon, expressed *both by grammatical* and *also by lexical* devices, and by certain *contextual* markers.

Our study has been based on a comparison of a Slavic language with the French language. This raises the question of the heuristic validity of such comparison, and its limits.

Comparative linguistics can be considered, on the one hand, as a theoretical approach (i.e. it is a part of descriptive linguistics which differs from general linguistics, and from general typology, in the concrete nature of its object), but one can also find practical applications for it. It can be applied in the teaching of modern languages, and its usefulness here cannot be contested.

But a comparison of two different language systems can also help to explain the way in which one of these systems works, and even a comparison based on practical application can influence theoretical conclusions. By means of a comparative study of aspect in Czech and French, from an onomasiological point of view, we have managed to find a few *complex units* of construction, and to define the *pre-morphological* character of certain of these units (1966a, 183–92). We have also confirmed Yvon's theory on the marked character (that is to say, marked with regard to aspect) of the French imperfect indicative, and defined the marked character of certain French *conjunctions*.

From the psycholinguistic point of view, we note that the linear character of the utterance, which is organized in a different way in each language, does not necessarily mean that the language is not capable of expressing the same content. The western European languages (e.g. French and English) express, in their own ways, the aspect of the verbal action, and all the associated nuances.

Bibliography of previous works by the author

1959. 'La notion d'aspect et la langue française', *AUC*, 3, *Romanistica Pragensia* I.

1960–61. 'K otázce slovesného vidu ve francouzštině' (On the problem of verbal aspect in French), *CJvŠ* 4, 97–105.

1961a. 'Les equivalents de l'aspect slave en italien' *PP* 4, 147–59.

1961b. 'Les locutions semelfactives et l'aspect perfectif en français', *AUC, Romanistica Pragensia* II, 99–111.

1962a. 'L'aspect et le caractère de l'action verbale en provençal', *Kwartalnik neofilologiczny* 9, 249–60.

1962b. 'Nominálně verbální konstrukce a povaha děje ve francouzštine' (Verbo-nominal constructions and the manner of verbal action in French), *AUC, Philologica, Monographia* II.

1962c. 'Contribution aux problèmes de méthode de la recherche dans le domaine de l'aspect verbal (langues romances)', *Actes du Xe Congrès international de linguistique et philologie romanes* I (Strasbourg; Paris 1965), 157–74.

1963a. 'Kapitoly z rozboru moderní francouzštiny I. Francouzské sloveso' (Chapters from an analysis of Modern French I: The French verb). Prague mimeographed.

1963b. 'Les systèmes d'expression du temps, du mode et de l'ordre du procès. A propos de leur agencement et de leurs relations syntaxiques, domaine français, domaine provençal', *PP* 4, 349–62.

1963c. 'À propos de quelques problèmes linguistiques de la lexicographie. L'aspect, l'ordre du procès et les dictionnaires', *AUC, Romanistica Pragensia* III, 87–103.

1963d. 'La signification des verbes françaises et les problèmes d'aspect (Étude comparative: langue française et langues slaves)', *Beiträge zur romanischen Philologie* 2, 166–79, Berlin.

1964. 'Kapitoly z rozboru moderní francouzštiny II. Nefinitní tvary slovesné' (Chapters from an analysis of Modern French II: Non-finite verbal forms). Prague, mimeographed.

1966a. 'Un problème de la périphérie du système morphologique: à propos des formations prémorphologiques', *TLP* 2, 183–92.

1966b. 'Les équivalents de l'aspect slave sur le territoire de la Romania Orientale (Le problème de l'influence slave sur le système roumain)', *Les Études balkaniques tchécoslovaques* I, 57–68, Prague.

1966c. 'Le plan prémorphologique de la langue française. Avec quelques aspects comparatifs'. *AUC, Romanistica Pragensia* IV, 65–80.

7 The Prague Conception of Functional Style

Josef Dubský

THE BASIS OF THE PRAGUE CONCEPTION OF FUNCTIONAL STYLES

I.1. The linguists of the Prague School formulated the principles of the stylistic differentiation of the standard language in the context of the conception of language as an open dynamic system of signs functionally utilized. The basis of the Prague conception of functional styles is a profound view about the correlation of language with its realization in concrete acts of speech, based at the same time upon the wider issue of the functions of language.[1] Another, no less important impulse leading to the formulation of this conception, arose out of purely practical views: in the 'thirties, the necessity of formulating a scientific conception of the linguistic norm arose when some conservative linguists were puristically evaluating and condemning certain language features in Czech technical, journalistic, and other specialized texts, assuming that these features contradicted or violated the norm of the language; in the course of years this practical aspect appeared in the application of functional stylistics to the teaching of the mother tongue and foreign language teaching, in the practice and theory of translation, and so on.

I.2. The main groups of questions that have occupied the Prague School in the field of functional stylistics are the following:

(a) the position of stylistics within linguistic science and the definition of basic concepts of functional stylistics;

(b) the definition of factors of style and the classification of the various styles of the standard language;

(c) the determination of the principal features and the tendencies of the basic functional styles of the standard language;

(d) the question of the linguistic norms and their codification;

[1] About the theory of the functions of language in the conception of the Prague School cf. the articles by K. Horálek, 'Staronová teorie jazykových funkcí (The Old-New Theory of Language Functions) *SaS* 28 1962, 126, and 'Les fonctions de la langue et de la parole' *TLP* I Prague 1964, 41. P. Novák, P. Sgall 'On the Prague Functional Approach' *TLP* 3, Prague 1968, 29i.

(e) the practical application of the principles of functional stylistics.

The Prague theory, apart from the problem of proper functional styles or dialects, thus deals with the problems of the norm and codification of (i) the linguistic means of expression and (ii) the standard language and the cultivation of language. An inseparable correlate of the Prague conception is concrete linguistic analysis and the establishment of general features, because a profound knowledge of style is possible only as the result of detailed stylistic analysis of concrete acts of speech, leading to the determination of the substance of the stylistic features within the linguistic system.

I.3. In this article we shall try to give a summary of the principal ideas of the Prague conception of functional styles, based on the studies by B. Havránek, V. Mathesius, J. Mukařovský and other members of the Prague Linguistic Circle[1] and the subsequent discussions on style in the forties[2] and in the years after 1950,[3] and finally in the light of contemporary research in the field of style by present-day Czechoslovak linguists.[4] This elaboration of some of the basic ideas of the Prague conception of style stresses their stimulating value and vitality.[5]

THE FUNCTIONAL ASPECT IN STYLISTICS

II.1. In the conception of the Prague School the theory of style is conceived of as the stylistic analysis of utterances; it is considered an integral component of linguistic analysis: any study of the language without stylistic analysis would be incomplete. While the lexical or

[1] Although we meet with the problems of functional stylistics in earlier works of B. Havránek, we refer here specially to his article 'Úkoly spisovného jazyka a jeho kultura' (The Tasks of the Standard Language and its Cultivation) *SČJK* (Prague 1932) 32; in the same volume cf. also: V. Mathesius, 'O požadavku stability ve spisovném jazyce' (The Requirement of Stability for a Standard Language), and J. Mukařovský, 'Jazyk spisovný a jazyk básnický' (Standard Language and Poetic Language).

[2] As to the discussion in the forties, see the journal *SaS* 7 (1941); cf. also V. Skalička, 'Problémy stylu' (The Problems of Style) *SaS* 7 (1941) 192.

[3] Cf. the report of L. Doležel in *SaS* 16 (1955) 56, and the following articles: L. Doležel, 'K obecné problematice jazykového stylu' (The General Problems of the Style of Language), in *SaS* 15 (1954) 97; K. Hausenblas, 'K základním pojmům jazykové stylistiky' (The Fundamental Concepts of Stylistics of Language) *SaS* 16 (1955) 1; M. Jelínek, 'O jazykovém stylu' (The Style of Language) *SaS* 15 (1954) 118; P. Trost. 'K obecným otázkám stylu' (General Problems of Style) *SaS* 16 (1955) 15.

[4] See specially: K. Hausenblas, 'Styly jazykových projevů' (Styles of Speech Utterances) *SaS* 23 (1962) 189; M. Jelínek, 'Definice pojmu jazykový styl' (The Definition of the Concept 'Style of Language'), in *SPFFBU*, A 15 (Brno 1965) 43.

[5] In this survey we differ from P. L. Garvin who, in his publication *PSRE* (Washington, D.C. 1964), takes note only of the principles published in the articles of B. Havránek and J. Mukařovský, in *SČJK* (cf. fn. 1, above).

grammatical analysis determines the different structural elements and processes, stylistics regards speech as a unit and tries to establish general stylistic features of each utterance; the subject of stylistic analysis is the structure of a concrete act of speech and the mode of selection and utilization of its particular elements. Hence linguistic stylistics determines the use of particular language devices in particular zones of the national language. Particular stress is laid, at the same time, on the functional view. One of the most important tasks of stylistics consists in the analysis of the adaptability of the linguistic devices of expression to the purpose and the function of the utterance.

II.2. When we consider the potential possibilities of expression of a given linguistic system and their concrete utilization in particular utterances according to their individual purpose or function, we must inevitably come to a differentiation of the standard language from the point of view of function. The functional and stylistic differentiation of the standard language is based on its lexical and syntactic aspects; phonological devices are used as well, though to a lesser extent. The functional aspect in the stylistics of the Prague School was elaborated mainly by B. Havránek, who distinguishes:[1]

(a) the communicative function in the area of everyday communication;

(b) the practical technical communication;

(c) the theoretical or scientific technical communication;

(d) the aesthetic function of the communication.

In this way he proposes the following functional and stylistic differentiation: (a) the conversational form; (b) the matter-of-fact (work-a-day) or technically communicative form; (c) the scientific form; (d) the poetic form.

In addition, Havránek distinguishes the following 'functional styles', determined by the concrete purpose of the response: (a) matter-of-fact communication, information; (b) exhortation, appeal; (c) general or popular explanation; (d) technical explanation, exposition, proof; (e) codifying formulation.

According to the manner of response, he distinguishes the private functional style and the public functional style, oral and written; their combination leads to the functional style of the private discourse, in dialogue or monologue, the functional style of public speech-making in the form of a discussion or speech, the functional style of the written

[1] Cf. fn. 1, p. 113.

private utterance in the form of a personal letter, the functional style of the written public utterance in the form of a notice, poster, journalistic or book writing.

B. Havránek distinguishes thus 'the functional style', determined by the specific purpose or function of the given act of speech ('parole'), and the 'functional language', determined by the over-all-purpose of the totality of means of expression, a function of the linguistic pattern ('langue').

II.3. These ideas represent the significant and permanent Czech contribution to the principles of stylistic theory, though some details have been re-evaluated in the course of time. Today the term 'functional language'[1] is not used to denote autonomous structures within the language: the functional differentiation of the standard language is based on the structural features which refer to the totality of the devices of expression and the differences between the different style strata do not concern only the provision of the devices of expression (e.g. lexical and grammatical doublets), but also the structural organization of the totality of the devices of expression. Nevertheless, all these differences are not so considerable as to create autonomous structures, which could be placed side by side, and the functional strata cannot be regarded as the autonomous components, or parts of the whole of the national language. The style of the language is a phenomenon 'sui generis', present in the act of speech, but not potentially involved in the structure of the language as are its other components.

The stylistic strata of a national language as the complex means of expression with their own stylistic specifications which serve to satisfy the communication needs of the given utterance, and the style of the language as the peculiar organization of the concrete act of speech as a whole, are the bases for further investigation within the field of functional stylistics.

When the act of speech is the result of individual use, we may speak about an individual subjective style, even about the style of a generation, a literary or scientific school, etc.; when its organization is interindividual, we may speak about a functional, objective style, determined by the function of the act of speech.

[1] B. Havránek, in his article 'K funkčnímu rozvrstvení spisovného jazyka' (The Functional Differentiation of Standard Language), *ČMF* 28 (1942) 410, reprinted in *Studie o spisovném jazyce* (Studies of Standard Language) (Prague 1963) 60, replaces the term 'functional language' with the term 'functional dialect' or 'functional stratum'; cf. also his article 'Funkční jazyk a styl' (Functional Language and Functional Style) *Studie o spisovném jazyce* 64.

Within a standard national language we therefore distinguish:
the style of individual utterances,
the style of utterances made by the same author,
the stylistic forms within particular objective styles (in the journalistic style, e.g., the leading articles, reports, etc.),
the objective, functional style (or style of language), e.g., the journalistic style, the scientific style, etc.

STYLISTIC FACTORS AND STYLISTIC DIFFERENTIATION

III.1. The specific means of expression used in different acts of speech or discourse are characterized by the selection (or the creation) of lexical or grammatical means of the language system. This selection depends on stylistic factors or on their various incomplete combinations.

The fundamental stylistic factor in functional stylistics is the concrete purpose of the utterance and this is determined by the conditions in which the act of speech takes place in a concrete area of human activity. We can distinguish four main aspects: the content of the discourse, the situation, the attitude of the speaker to reality, and his relation to the listener.

The different objective styles of standard language are determined by objective factors. The main objective factors can be summarized in three principal groups:

1. The factors connected with meaning:

(a) the function of communication, which can be communicative (colloquial style), practically professional (style of the official, technical and professional language), theoretically professional (the scientific language), function of mass communications (journalistic style), aesthetically communicative (works of art);

(b) the purpose of the act of speech, which can be an objective statement (the interpretative style) or an appeal (in the journalistic style);

(c) the speaker's attitude to the theme: it can be serious (official style), humorous (the comical nature of the utterance), depreciating (ironical or invective nature of the utterance);

(d) the mode of theme: dynamic (narration) or static (description);

(e) the degree of spontaneity (from the style of entirely spontaneous and that of prepared utterances).

2. The elements connected with the situation of the utterance:
   (a) private or official setting (the style of the private or official utterances);
   (b) bilateral (the style of dialogues) or unilateral speech (the style of monologues);
   (c) the contact between the author and the addressee (in the colloquial utterance), whether the addressee is present (style of situational utterances) or absent (broadcasting style).

3. The language substance used: phonic (the style of spoken utterances) or graphic (the style of written or printed utterances).[1]

Stylistic factors appear in complex groups; these groups, however, are not permanent, because their composition can change. Both the meaning and the degree of the impact of the different factors may differ. The impact of the objective factors is not constant in the history of language. The establishment of the stylistic factors meets with grave difficulties caused by the transitory fields or the overlapping of the different functional styles.

III.2. The analysis of the stylistic factors reflects the delimitation and classification of the functional styles of the standard language. The fundamental scheme of the stylistic differentiation of the standard language as presented by B. Havránek (cf. II.2. of this article) continues to be the basis for further classifications, though the number of the items is sometimes reduced (the practical technical style and the scientific technical style are often joined and the colloquial style is not classified as a functional style), or some new items are added (the technical style, the colloquial style, and the aesthetic style are combined with the journalistic, rhetorical and administrative styles).

III.3. On the other side, apart from the differentiation of the principal functional styles of the standard language, it seems to be necessary to work out their inner differentiation. The great sphere of the technical functional style appears subdivided into a series of styles: the unifying factor is the fundamental communicative function, but each of the different technical styles shows different tendencies. The inner differentiation of the technical functional style appears in the light of the functional standpoint and with regard to the setting, or according to the substance, of the discourse.[2]

[1] Cf. K. Hausenblas, *SaS* 16 (1955) 10–12, and E. Pauliny, 'O funkčním rozvrstvení spisovného jazyka' (The Functional Stratification of Standard Language) *SaS* 15 (1955) 17.

[2] J. Filipec, 'Rozbor odborného stylu a jeho vnitřní diferenciace' (Analysis of the Technical Style and its Inner Differentiation) *SaS* 16 (1955) 37.

The technical functional style can be subdivided as follows:

Technical functional style { proper
popular

Technical functional style proper { scientific
practical

Practical technical style { style of instruction
style of economics
style of law
style of administration

Technical functional style { written
spoken

Spoken technical style { read (lecture)
prepared (lecture)
unprepared (discussion)
in form of monologue
in form of dialogue (debates)

This subdivision of the technical style is only a rough one, the variety of concrete realization of each of the items indicated in our table leads to other subdivisions within each of them. The style of economics may be taken as typical in this way.

The scientific or economic discourse belongs to the technical style proper and presents features common to other scientific discourses, for example, a high degree of specialization of terms, the precision and exactness of utterances, the systematic classification and definition of concepts, mathematical symbols, etc., in so far as it corresponds to its theoretical function. The conception of the theme is static and the principal stylistic forms are (i) description ('Le capital n'est pas éternel. Généralement même, il ne dure pas très longtemps, parce qu'il se dvtruit par l'acte même, instantané ou indéfiniment répété . . .' C. Gide, *Cours d'économie politique* (Paris 1918[4]) 191. Capital is not eternal. Generally it does not continue long because it destroys itself by the act of production, instantaneously or indefinitely repeated . . .), (ii) the explanation or reflection ('Mais inversement, le capital peut-il se transformer en revenu? Non, s'il s'agit de capital instrument comme dans les exemples de tout à l'heure. Oui, s'il s'agit de capital sous forme d'approvisionnement ou d'argent'. *Ibid.* 181. But on the contrary, cannot capital be transformed into revenue? No, when we must use capital as in the above given example. Yes, when we use capital in the form of provisions or money); or, finally, in the enunciation of laws and definitions ('La valeur d'échange varie en raison directe de la demande et en raison inverse de l'offre'. *Ibid.* 349. The value of exchange varies in direct proportion to the demand and in indirect proportion to the supply), and so on.

On the other hand, the popular technical discourse in economics, published in a specialized review or in the newspapers, includes tendencies typical of the journalistic style (up-dating or archaization of the means of expression, individual or collective negligence, use of automatic introductory phrases as, for example, 'it should be recalled that', 'we suppose that', etc.). The popular technical style is one of transition and the tendencies which appear in it belong to different styles. In the same way, we could further differentiate the style of stock exchange reports and other economic articles published in the daily press, and the style of different kinds of commercial letters.

The number of the inner differences is increased by the so-called styles of transition, the classification is sometimes rather difficult (in the functional style in the field of economy we could mention here some types of commercial letters that are either commercial or official or legal.

MAIN FEATURES OF PRINCIPAL FUNCTIONAL STYLES

IV.1. The differentiation of the principal functional styles and their inner differentiation is connected with the determination of the principal features of the different styles of the standard language. In Czech linguistic writings we find at present many studies dealing with these problems, referring not only to the Czech and to Slovak languages, but also to other languages (such as Russian, English, German, French and Spanish). For the results of these investigations, see the respective papers included in this volume dealing with some special problems of the different functional styles. We, however, should like to point out some characteristic features of the principal functional styles which are discussed in the works of the linguistics of the Prague School.

IV.2. In his fundamental study, B. Havránek mentions intellectualization (or rationalization), automation and foregrounding as principal types of the specific use of the means of expression for different functions of the standard language.

The intellectualization (or rationalization) culminates in the scientific theoretical discourse, both in the lexical plan and in the grammatical structure. It is determined by an attempt to approximate the expression as much as possible to the rigor of objective (scientific) thinking, in which the terms approximate concepts and the sentences approximate logical judgements. From the lexical point of view, the characteristic features of the intellectualization consist in the introduction of new words, in technical terms, and in the change of the structure of the vocabulary, in which the number of unequivocal words, specialized words, abstract summarizing terms, means that express the existence, possibility, necessity, the relations of causality, finality, parallelism, etc., increases. Other features of the intellectualization of the style include a great number of nominal groups of adjectives with nouns, the use of the nominal predication with formal verbs, etc. As for the grammatical structure of the sentences, the intellectualization normalizes two-member sentences, uses more passive constructions, stresses the hierarchy of clauses and sentences standing on different levels, specifies conjunctions, etc.

Automation consists in a use of devices of the language, given in isolation or combination, which does not attract any attention, whereas by the foregrounding (*Fr. actualisation*) we mean the use of the devices of language in such a way that this use attracts attention and is perceived as uncommon, as non-automatic: the degree and the mutual proportion of both these means of language characterizes different functional styles (e.g. in conversation, both automation and foregrounding coexist, in the scientific discourse, automation prevails, while in the poetic style or in that of the essay, foregrounding predominates).

IV.3. The classification of the colloquial (conversational) style as one of the functional styles[1] is nowadays generally accepted. The colloquial style is classed with the practical and technically communicative styles in which the aesthetic purposes of the speaker are suppressed or eliminated. The function of the colloquial style is simply communicative and the language serves the direct communication of concrete contents and the emotional attitude of the speaker. The colloquial style is sometimes called 'conversational', 'social', or 'style of the dialogue' (the dialogues of fiction or drama are not usually classed within the sphere of the colloquial style, because the conversation

[1] Apart from the basic article by B. Havránek (see fn. 1, on p. 113), compare the following articles: K. Hausenblas, 'O studiu syntaxe běžně mluvenych projevů' (The Study of the Syntax of Common Spoken Utterances) in *Otázky slovanské jazykovědy* (Problems of Slavonic Syntax) (*OUPB*) (Prague 1962) 313; M. Ivanová-Šalginová, 'Hovorový štýl súčasnej spisovnej slovenčiny' (Colloquial Style of Present-day Standard Slovak) *Slovenská reč* 28 (1963) 17; M. Jelínek, 'Postavení hovorového stylu mezi styly funkčními' (The Position of the Colloquial Style among Functional Styles) *SaS* 27 (1966) 104.

itself constitutes a form of artistic style).[1] B. Havránek mentions, as the characteristic features of the colloquial style, the uniformity of the semantic plan, the free relation of the lexical units to the expressed content, the incompleteness of the utterance and its intelligibility provided by the situation, and the colloquial automatisms.

For the structure of conversation we may lay stress on the emotional attitude, expressed in the selection of expressive intonation, the choice of expressive patterns of syntax and the use of expressively coloured words and idiomatic means, and on the dependence of the communications upon the existence of the speaker and the addressee. It leads to the necessity of distinguishing the initial conversation acts of speech and the dependent conversational acts of speech replies. These features are reflected in the incompleteness of the acts of speech, in the great frequency of deictic means, in the use of monocentric sentence patterns, especially verbless sentences, etc.

As to incomplete acts of speech, we may distinguish[2] the fragmentary incompleteness, provoked by excitement ('where the deuce—'), by terminal position ('I don't—'), by sensation of shame or similar feelings ('Don't dance too much with—you know—'), by being interrupted, by loss of memory ('Eight years ago—that was in—'), etc., and the economical incompleteness, connected very often with the repetition by the speaker, taken by surprise, of a part of the communication ('Do you deny . . . ?'—'Deny? No, of course not'.), or when stressing ('It's a very serious thing to leave your husband. A very serious thing.'), or in answering ('Do you ever read the *Watch*?'—'Not necessarily read'), etc. The verbless sentences, the monocentric and the bicentric sentences, express a simple declaration, a question, an exhortation, an excited evaluation of the fact and so on. In this connexion it is necessary to stress the special position of the nominal constructions, adjectival constructions, infinitive forms, participal and gerund constructions in the replications, etc.[3]

Among the other features of the colloquial style we can also mention a lesser frequency of hypotactic conjunctions as a result of syntactic relaxation and the conversational implication of the relations, the

[1] Cf. M. Jelínek. 'Míšení funkčních stylů v soudobé umělecké próze slovanských národů' (Mixture of Functional Styles in Contemporary Fiction of Slavonic Nations) *Československé přednášky pro V. sjezd slavistů* (Czechoslovak Papers for the Fifth Congress of Slavists) (Prague) 1963. Cf. also the contributions by J. Camutaliová and K. Koževniková in this volume.

[2] Cf. the manuscript of I. Poldauf's thesis 'Outlines of a Functional Syntax of Present-day Colloquial English', (Prague 1937) 19–23.

[3] Cf. also J. Dubský. 'El infinitive en la réplica.' *Español actual* (Madrid) 8 (1966) i.

presence of the 'additional constructions and expressions'[1] as a result of the improvised character of the acts of speech made in colloquial style (the additional constructions or expressions are the sentence members which are added, because the speaker feels that his communication is not complete, e.g.: 'Not bad, your idea'), the deformation of the member schemes (e.g. contamination, zeugma) and many others. Whilst some authors do not consider the colloquial style to be very important for the development of the language, the Prague School emphasises the significance of this style, within which the language finds its most frequent realization, and gives it much attention.

IV.4. Less attention is paid to the technical style, but many interesting results have been obtained even here.[2]

B. Havránek characterizes the technical style as follows: the semantic plan of the practical technical style and that of the scientific style is uniform; the relation of the lexical units to what is expressed in the practical style is definite and determined by the convention of the word/term relation, in the scientific style it is exact, being determined by the word/concept relation; the practical style is definite and its definiteness is determined by the conventional automations, by the terms and formulas, the scientific style is exact, its exactness being characterized by the carefully defined and codified automations.

In the acts of speech of the practical and scientific style we find a tendency toward a relative uniformity of the composition and a considerable stabilization of the marked stylistic means. The chief tendency of the technical style can be followed in the lexical-stylistic sphere and in the syntactical-stylistic sphere.

In the lexical sphere, the uniformity of the terminological system, which makes possible the adaquacy of what the author wants to communicate and what is perceived by the reader or by the listener, is very important (this feature is usually called the intellectualization of

[1] O. Müllerová, 'K syntaxi nepřipravených souvislých mluvených projevů—přídatné výrazy a konstrukce' (The Syntax of Unprepared Continuous Spoken Utterances—Additional Expressions and Constructions) *SaS* 27 (1966) 118.

[2] The Czech technical style is studied especially in the following articles: J. Filipec 'Rozbor odborného stylu a jeho vnitřní diferenciace' (Analysis of the Technical Style and its Inner Differentiation) *SaS* 19 (1955) 37; K. Hausenblas, 'K specifickým rysům odborné terminologie' (Specific Features of the Technical Terminology) *Problémy marxistické jazykovědy* (Problems of Marxist Linguistics) (Prague 1962) 248; M. Jelínek, 'Odborný styl' (Technical Style), *SaS* 16, 1955, 25 and 'Syntaktické tendence odborného stylu (Syntactical Tendencies of the Technical Style) *Československý terminologický časopis* 2 (1963) 65; L. Kopeckij, 'O lexikálním plánu hospodářského jazyka' (The Lexical Plan of the Language of Commerce and Economics) *SaS* 1 (1935) 120; Z. Peška, 'Jazyk zákonodárcův' (The Language of the Legislators) *SaS* 5 (1939) 32. About studies of the technical style in English, French, German or Spanish cf. the bibliography to J. Pytelka's contribution to this volume.

the devices of expression). As for the specific devices of expression, it is important to establish a difference between technical terms (i.e. the words which have an exact unequivocal meaning in the technical style and which even in another functional style, such as in the colloquial style, are felt to pertain to the sphere of a technical style, e.g. 'volt', 'turbine', 'foreign exchange' etc.), the automized words, which can have a second meaning or a less exact meaning in other functional styles (e.g. 'course', 'extraction' etc.),[1] and the cliché words or sentences, especially frequent in business or administrative letters (e.g. in Spanish 'acusamos recibo de su grata carta', in French 'nous accusons réception de votre lettre' = we acknowledge your letter).

The terms may be explicit or implicit, general or specific to a certain school or working group, incidental and even individual. They are incorporated in the text in the following ways: the meaning of the term is assumed, explained or delimited (the delimitation may be done by way of definition, explanation, example, antithesis or comparison).

Synonyms are rare in the scientific style (compare, e.g. 'dichromate/bichromate', 'inorganic/anorganic/unorganic', 'tungsten/wolfram', 'pedology/soil science' etc.), but they are frequent in the practical technical style (compare, e.g. in Spanish business letters the synonyms of the terms 'to negotiate': 'negociar', 'hacer negocios'; 'operar' to operate, 'manejar' to manipulate, 'trabajar', to work, etc.; 'to pay': 'pagar', 'hacer el pago' to make a payment, 'atender' to attempt, 'cubrir' to cover, 'liquidar' to cancel, 'satisfacer' to satisfy, 'solventar' to solve, etc.); whilst the scientific style prefers neutral technical terms, the practical technical style (for example, that of business letters) and the spoken form of the technical style prefer synonymous terms which are functionally marked (e.g. in the Spanish business letter, the term 'cart' = letter is substituted by a functionally marked synonym 'su grata').

However, we generally find in the technical style the desynonymization of the terms or the differentiation of the words which were originally synonymous (e.g. the differentiation of economic terms such as 'bill', 'account', 'invoice').

'Lexical condensation' is frequent and it denotes the transition of the motivated types of denomination into the non-motivated ones[2] (such

[1] Cf. R. Kocourek, 'Synonyma v terminologii' (Synonyms in Terminology) *Tři příspěvky z oblasti odborné lingvistiky* Three contributions to the Linguistics of Technical Register (Prague 1966) 15.
[2] Cf. A. V. Isačenko, 'K voprosu o strukturnoj tipologii slovarnogo sostava slavjanskich literaturnych jazykov' (Questions of Structural Typology of the Lexical System of Slavonic Standard Languages) *Slavie* 27 (1958) 334–52.

terms are also called 'context terms' and have the form of simplified syntagmas, e.g. 'insurance policy'—'policy', 'insurance premium'—'premium', 'milking machine'—'milker', 'crawler tractor'—'tractor', 'subsurface irrigation'—'subirrigation', etc.). On the other hand, the substitution of a monocentric expression such as 'to measure' by a verbal-nominal syntagma 'to take measurements' corresponds to the tendency of the technical style to perceive the action, the process, as a substance: the conception of the action as a substance is connected with the possibility to terminologize more easily the substantives of action than the verbs, and leads to the decomposition of an idea of action expressed by a verb into substantives of action and auxiliary or semiauxiliary verbs.

In the syntactical plan of the technical style, the stress is laid on the compactness of the complex sentences and paragraphs, and on the clear arrangement and formal division of the utterances (of great importance are the conjunctions, demonstrative or relative pronouns and adverbs, and other means which serve to connect an utterance with the preceding one).

The compactness of the utterance is directly proportional to the so-called 'syntactical condensation',[1] i.e. a tendency to use non-verbal members of the sentence in those circumstances that could be expressed generally by a dependent clause. This tendency, which requires often more attention from the reader, is realized by using adjective, nominal and other condensors. Instead of a dependent clause there appears, for example, a substantive of action (Si 1959 a été une année de reprise économique, 1960 a été une année d'essor pour l'économie belge.' If 1959 was a year of economic advancement, 1960 was one of prosperity for the economy of Belgium), a gerund or infinitive construction ('. . . le financement d'un déficit budgétaire, méme réduit par l'amélioration des recettes . . .', '. . . the financing of the budget deficit, even when it is reduced by the increase in revenue'), etc.

The principal scales of stylistic compactness are:[2]

(a) the paratactic constructions,

(b) the hypotactic constructions,

(c) the gerund, participle or infinitive construction or even the attribute constructions,

(d) the nominal verbless constructions.

[1] Cf. J. Vachek, 'Notes on the So-called Complex Condensation in Modern English', *SPFFBU*, A 3, (1955) 63.

[2] J. V. Bečka, *Vybrané kapitoly z české stylistiky* (Selected Chapters of Czech Stylistics) (Prague 1966) 65.

IV.5. In his principal study on the functional styles, B. Havránek also defines the main features of the aesthetic or poetic style. They are the following: the variety of forms of the semantic plan, the determination of the relation of lexical units to what is being expressed and to the completeness of the utterance by the structure of the artistic or poetic work and by its foregrounding, and, finally, by the clearness of the discourse, determined by the structure of the work.

Various treatises of J. Mukařovský[1] deal with the aesthetic style in particular. This scholar defines the function of the language or the style of the poetry from the point of view of the maximal foregrounding of the utterance. In the poetic utterance the foregrounding pushes the communicative purpose into the background and becomes autonomous, accentuating the act of speech itself. The questions of the artistic style are more complicated than the problems of other areas of functional stylistics, because stylistics of language itself cannot solve the general problems of literary theory which must be linked with the analysis of the style of works of art.

In the discussion concerning the questions of style, two aspects of the relation between the proper style of works of art and the general category of functional artistic style can be distinguished: (a) some authors only admit the existence of an individual artistic style and reject its generalization, (b) other authors admit the possibility of the generalization in the area of the artistic style as well and the existence of general norms or tendencies, which form the substance of the artistic style. There is no doubt of the existence of a certain coherence of the style of literary works, nevertheless a great variety can be observed, and this is the reason why artistic style cannot be placed on the same level with the other functional styles.

The basic tendencies of the artistic functional style are: the prevalence of a subjective factor, the specific function of the artistic scenes, a constant necessity for the regeneration of the style, the variety and abundance in the selection of the means of expression. In regard to the unity of the artistic functional style, it can be said that all artistic acts of speech have their own aesthetic function.

V.1. One of the important general consequences of the theory of

[1] J. Mukařovský, 'Jazyk spisovný a jazyk básnický' (Standard Language and Poetic Language) *SČJK* 126 (see fn. 1, p. 113); *Kapitoly z české poetiky* (Chapters from Czech Poetics) (Prague 1948), German transl. *Kapitel aus der Poetik* (Frankfurt a.M. 1967); cf. also L. Doležel *Knížka o jazyce a stylu soudobé české literatury* (A Book about Language and Style of Contemporary Czech literature) (Prague 1962); 'Vers la stylistique structurale' *TLP* 1 (1964), 257; 'The Prague School and the Statistical Theory of Language'. *Prague Studies in Mathematical Linguistics* 2 (1967), 97, etc.

functional differentiation of standard language is the question of the norm and the codification of the standard language.[1] We can distinguish three periods:

(a) In the old period the standard language is identified with the literary language. Its chief characteristic is the conservativeness of the literary devices of expression and their norm.

(b) The second period, that of the programmatic proclamations of the Prague Circle in 1932, stresses the functional aspect and considers the standard language as a polyfunctional system with several stylistic layers. The problem of the literary norm (standard language norm) is now being treated within the standard language, and not simply within the opposition of the standard and colloquial languages. The language norm differs from the codification of the means of expression, but the process of differentiation of the means of expression within the norm of the standard language is considered a perpetual process.

(c) At the present time the question of varieties conditioned by regional differentiation also involves the question of the functional differentiation of the standard language. These varieties are taken as a form of balance between the static codification and the dynamic norm. Of great importance for the character of the contemporary norm of the standard language is the place of the spoken act of speech in contemporary public language communications and in the dialogues as presented in the utterances of mass language communication (TV., radio, interviews, etc.). This allows for penetration of the regional elements into the norm of the standard language. This conception of the norm is also reflected in the approach to works of art and to different functional styles. Its consistent application is based on the principle that an utterance must be evaluated according to the adequacy of the means of expression used to serve the given purpose.

PRACTICAL APPLICATIONS OF THE RESULTS OF FUNCTIONAL STYLISTICS

VI.1. The regard for practical requirements can be observed in the theory of the functional styles, especially in the practical activities of specialists who are versed in the field of the particular technical terminology, in that of training of new interpreters and technical translators, and in the teaching of the mother tongue and foreign languages.

VI.2. In foreign language teaching, the consistent application of the functional differentiation of the standard language does not only

[1] Cf. A. Jedlička, 'Zur Prager Theorie der Schriftsprache' *TLP* I (1964), 47. Cf. also the present position as outlined in *Kultura Českéwojazka* (the Culture of the Czech Language), collected volume (Prague 1969).

include the recognition of the fact that the foreign language teachers should know the language in question as a whole, i.e. the style of literary works, the technical and scientific functional styles, the practical technical style and the style of the spoken language,[1] but also that they should be aware of methodical considerations: the specification of the most important varieties of the modes of expression and a scientific description of the principal features of the different functional styles, from the point of view of their constant or terminological components and their potential or non-terminological elements. It further facilitates the choice of material which is to be taught at the different levels of foreign language teaching, and at the same time it helps to establish adequate methodical measures in the course of teaching. These are the main principles which have already been dealt with, at least partly (e.g. the frequency statistics of different functional styles, outlines of a methodology of commercial correspondence teaching, and advice on how to work with a technical text in language teaching, etc.); the rest are now being applied in foreign language teaching.

[1] Cf. E. Beneš, 'Syntaktische Besonderheiten der deutschen wissenschaftlichen Fachsprache', *Deutsch als Fremdsprache* 3 (1966) 26. Cf. also E. Beneš's contribution to this volume.

8 The Morphological Features of Technical English and Their Presentation in Teaching

Karel Bareš

At present, we are witnessing a considerable interest in technical English. There are several reasons for it. On the one hand, technical English represents a variety of English that, in consequence of the rapid development of technology, exhibits great lexical changes and a steady vocabulary expansion. From the point of view of linguistic theory, this domain of research has been rather neglected. On the other hand, due to the incessant growth of science and technology, specialists feel more and more urged to acquire quick information on the latest state of affairs in their fields on an international scale. This is primarily done through the medium of the English language. Consequently there arises the need of finding the most appropriate way in which individual specialists can be most quickly and most economically taught to acquire a sound and practical knowledge of English even though restricted to serve the aims of their specialized fields. However, we feel that it is necessary not only to prepare the technologists to study English technical literature, but also to instil in them a knowledge of how to express themselves about their specialized fields exactly and with high linguistic standards. To make teaching in this respect really efficient, a preliminary theoretical analysis of the problems of typical communications in individual branches is required.

A linguistic investigation of technical English, to which attention is paid both in Great Britain and in other countries, is a substantial contribution to the aim indicated above. This covers theoretical works primarily relating to the principles and wider problems of 'functional languages (styles)'—to use the terms of the Prague School of functional linguistics, on whose grounds the theory of functional languages was elaborated as early as in the 1930s by the members of the Cercle Linguistique de Prague as it then was.[1]

[1] Cf. B. Havránek, *Úkoly spisovného jazyka a jeho kultura*, *SČJK* (Prague 1932) 32–84.

In recent years, considerable results in linguistic theory have also been achieved by British scholars who have adopted a structuralist approach to describe the characteristics of standard English and its functional varieties, and who have elaborated such concepts as 'register, style, mode, field and role of discourse'.[1]

Those members of the present younger generation of Czech anglicists working along structuralist lines who devote their energies to a study of the problems of technical language have already narrowed their interests to the detailed questions of specific functional style, such as technology, agriculture, commerce, etc. This also seems to be the line in the linguistic efforts of younger workers in Great Britain.[2] It is also only fair to mention an array of works on this subject by Soviet anglicists, mostly unpublished dissertations.

The aim of this article is to present a linguistic analysis of the morphological features of technical English. Its results may serve as a basis for a scientifically grounded approach to the teaching of English as a second language, in particular to engineers.

The following analysis is based on contrastive principles and is effected by confronting current English and technical English. Underlying this study theoretically are the principles of the morphological analysis of English formulated by B. Trnka in his works.[3] The material analysed here and the examples used in this paper are terms taken from various regions of technical language, mostly from engineering and its related branches.

Differences between current English and technical English can be found at all linguistic levels and they manifest themselves in a different way both qualitatively and quantitatively.

The focus of the present paper is the morphological level and its two main parts, 1. grammatical morphology and 2. word-formative morphology.

1. Grammatical morphology (accidence) is almost compact in character in its relation to the English language as a whole, and, consequently,

[1] See a number of recent works by M. A. K. Halliday, R. Quirk and their collaborators. Cf. also the results of research work of the Communication Research Centre, University College London.

[2] Cf. the monograph *English in Advertising* by G. N. Leech (London 1966).

[3] B. Trnka, 'Some Thoughts on Structural Morphology' *Charisteria Gu. Mathesio* (Prague 1932); 'Principles of Morphological Analysis', *PP* IV (1963) 129–37; 'Rozbor nynější spisovné angličtiny, díl II, Morfologie slovních druhů (částí řeči) a tvoření slov.' (The Analysis of Present-Day Standard English, Part II, Morphology of Parts of Speech and Word-Formation) (Prague 1954, mimeographed university lectures) etc.

only very few divergencies in this respect can be found in technical English. Some of them are given below.

There are, for example, foreign morphological features in the exponents of the plural, for example: *focus/foci*, *radius/radii*, *criterion/criteria*; the original Greek and Latin exponents of the plural continue to exist here in the technical style in spite of levelling tendencies, which occur in some cases (*formula*, pl. *formulae/formulas*).

Another instance of difference is represented by morphologo-syntactic peculiarities within the category of number, such as the concord of verbs used in the singular or plural with the names of sciences ending in *-ics* (*dynamics is/are*), which reflects a corresponding differentiation of meaning.

Also the terminological use of some less frequent forms of irregular verbs which are of rather rare occurrence in current English (*wrought steel*), and also the double comparative (*lesser bindweed*, *lesser spearwort*, etc.) may be regarded as morphological deflections from current usage.

Sometimes, on the contrary, but also for terminological reasons, the morphological comparison of adjectives is replaced either by derivational gradation using the prefixes *extra-*, *hyper-*, *super-*, *ultra-* and others, or by using words as determiners in compounds (*low-carbon steel*, *medium-carbon steel*, *high-carbon steel*) to achieve greater precision of expression.

The latter instances suggest that there is no sharp boundary between the two parts of morphology, i.e. between grammatical and word-formative morphology. Overlapping by the exponents of purely grammatical categories and word-formative exponents also bears witness to this effect.

The suffix *-s*, which mostly performs the function of a grammatical suffix to denote the plural of nouns, may be given as an example. We leave aside the use of the suffix *-s* forming adverbs of the type *hence*, *perhaps*, etc. What we have in mind are frequent technical terms of the type 'work' (doing or making something) and 'works' (a factory, as, for example, a steel-works); or 'strength' (quality of being strong, used both of animals and of materials) and 'strengths' (the term denoting the engineering theory of 'strength of materials' as a subject of instruction).[1] The term 'strengths' used in its specialized meaning of the 'science of strength of materials' may be apprehended as an

[1] See С. И. Кречетников, Англо-русский словарь по металлообработке и по деталям машин. (English-Russian Dictionary for Machine-Shop Terms and Machine Elements) (Moscow 1949).

example of a tendency in word-formation and name-giving analogous to that applied in many already existing names of sciences ending in *-ics*; the suffix *-ics* itself is, in its turn, also explained as the original plural. The plural exponent *-s* becomes here a derivational suffix and the opposition in number disappears.

Another group of examples includes the names of tools and instruments of the type of *pluralia tantum*, such as *clippers*, *jointers*, *shears*, *dividers*, *compasses*, *trammels*, etc., which are very frequent in engineering. Let us examine, for example, the term 'shears' in more detail. The corresponding entry in Webster's Dictionary states that 'shear' denotes 'one blade of a pair of shears'; this is to say that 'shear', putting aside its other meanings, denotes only a part of the tool, so that the suffix *-s* covers two functions here: it expresses the category of number, and thus it is the exponent of the plural, but, at the same time, it acts as the exponent of a process of semantic transformation of this word which results in meaning the complete tool called 'shears'. Consequently, an overlapping of functions is at work here. However, a certain inconsistency in this area should be noted as some of the cited names of tools also admit the singular form, which is a well-known fact.

2. A greater difference between current English and technical English may, however, be found in word-formation.

The very core of word-forming morphemes contains a number of special morphemes used only (or predominantly) in technical language. This refers both to the basic and to the derivative morphemes, as may be seen in the basic morphemes in terms such as: *silicate*, *trochilics*, *dimerisation*, *osculatrix*, *heptode*, *sigmoid*, *serpiginous*, etc. and in some derivative morphemes in the same words (*-ics*, *-trix*, *-ode*, *-oid*) and many others of the same character, e.g. *-tron* (*Eyetron*, *Flashtron*, *ignitron*), *a-* (*atechnical*) *bicro-* (*bicrofarad*), *epi-* (*epiposition*), *peri-* (*pericycloid*), etc.

Insofar as the origin of morphemes used in coining terms in technical language is concerned, it should be considered whether the examined expression belongs to the sphere of theoretical or of practical technical language.

Technical language as used in the theoretical sphere contains far more foreign elements than the language of the practical sphere, whose typical feature is a much larger percentage of Anglo-Saxon lexical elements, thus making the latter type of language more closely connected with current language.[1]

[1] Of course, affixal morphemes are largely elements of foreign origin assimilated by the English language.

For instance, if we examine the functional language in the field of engineering theory, we find that word-formative elements loaned from Greek and Latin prevail in its terms. On the other hand, technical language as used in production engineering in factories and workshops is more accessible and comprehensible to the layman because it contains a high percentage of terms formed from purely native elements and thus stands closer to current English.

However, in spite of many technical terms which continue to be alien and incomprehensible to the layman, a certain number of new technical terms (both theoretical and practical) are gaining wider general importance and penetrating into the vocabulary of current English from narrow specialist use.

Human life is becoming ever more permeated by technology and its inventions, so that many technical terms have become indispensable to us in every-day life. Thus the boundary line between the current and technical language is becoming fluent; this is reflected in turn in the changed attitude toward the linguistic exclusiveness of those morphemes that are frequently used to coin such terms which are thus getting closer to current language. A certain ever-growing number of terms can already be regarded as a part of colloquial English.[1]

Another very significant difference in word-formative morphology is found in the semantic content of formally identical word-forming morphemes used in current and in technical English alike. The words borrowed from the vocabulary of current English to be integrated in the stock of terms of some technical branches are identical in form in both varieties of English, but their meanings are different. The new precise meanings of the terms that have originated in this way are stated for each branch by the definitions offered by official 'Standards'; cf. terms such as *resistance*, *squirrel cage*, *terminal*, *excite*, etc. in electrical engineering, or *force*, *strength*, *stress* and *strain* in mechanical engineering, or *power* in mathematics, etc.

This may be observed at the level of full words.

A completely analogical situation arises when a morpheme generally used in current English acquires terminological meaning. The meanings of deriving morphemes are also clearly described by precise definitions for their specifically technical use. The validity of such definitions is sometimes broadly extended to several branches though it is frequently restricted just to one, cf. *-ance* in the names of quantities in electrical engineering (*capacitance*, *impedance*, *inductance*, *leakance*, *reactance*, etc.),

[1] Cf. Jiří Nosek, 'Některé významové rysy moderní hovorové angličtiny'. (Some Semantic Features of Present-Day Colloquial English) *PP* 6/46 (1963) 155.

-ate used in chemistry to denote salts of a specific valence, as in *carbonate, chlorate, nitrate, silicate, sulphate*, etc., or *micro-* which conveys the exact meaning of 10^{-6} when used in the systems of physical units, etc.

As may be seen, a salient feature of morphemes employed in the sphere of technical language, in contrast to those used in current language, is a deeper semantic intensity. This statement applies particularly to derivative morphemes. The difference in semantic intensity of affixes in current English is mentioned by B. Trnka[1] and also by O. Jespersen.[2] This property, however, becomes more conspicuous in technical language. Owing to their deeper intensity of meaning, the terminologically used derivative morphemes shift in character closer to basic morphemes; in this respect, the boundary between the basic and derivative elements is comparatively hazy. Nevertheless, these derivative morphemes do not cease to be dependent, synsemantic elements. The semantic depth of a terminologically used derivational affix exceeds that of general word-forming affixes, such as *-ed, -ic, -ive* commonly denoting property. Thus the terminological affix helps to name quite new concrete concepts, see, e.g. in chemistry, in the names of substances belonging to a given series of chemical compounds. In such a case the derivational morpheme is a relevant element of the given name and is almost equal to the basis of that word because both of them are equally semantically important for the newly coined word; for instance, *silic-* (*ium*) plus *ate*, *alumin-* (*ium*) plus *ide; -ium* = here suffix denoting 'chemical element', *-ate* = here suffix denoting 'salt', *-ide* = here suffix denoting 'a kind of compound with metal'.

Among the other specific properties of morphemes used in technical language we must mention the possibility of a readier rise of new morphemes and their quick establishment and integration in technical terminology if adopted by an acknowledged terminological authority. As an example see the influence exercised upon the development of chemical terminology by the organization of IUPAC (International Union for Pure and Applied Chemistry).

The shift of the word-formative function of morphemes is also connected with the rise of new deriving morphemes. A great number of them are at different stages of transition from the status of basic morphemes (or words) towards derivative morphemes.

[1] B. Trnka, 'Fonetický a fonologický vývoj slova v nové angličtině.' (The Phonetical and Phonological Development of the Word in Modern English) (Prague 1962, mimeographed) 104.

[2] O. Jespersen, *A Modern English Grammar on Historical Principles*, Part VI, *Morphology* (London 1946) 533.

Considering the fundamental word-forming methods, we find that they are basically shared by both current English and by the functional varieties of English (technical English), insofar as the general principles operating at a given stage of linguistic development are concerned.

Thus the vocabularies of individual regions of technical language differ from current language from the semantic and formal viewpoints, but the general laws (principles) of word-formation used in the current and technical languages are basically much the same. It is in some of their concrete applications that they are, obviously, different, e.g. the occurrence of certain word-forming patterns, such as the over-long multi-word terms, for instance: 'a liquid filled bellows type differential pressure measuring element'. A difference may also be found in proportional quantitative utilization of individual methods of word-formation.

From the above it follows that in technical vocabulary we also encounter terms and specialized expressions:

(a) formed by compounding (*crankshaft*, *wheelbase*, *gearbox*, *herringbone gear*, *differential pressure type specific gravity measuring instrument*, etc.);

(b) shortenings of several types, e.g. *psi* = 'pounds per square inch', *Tech* = 'Technological Institute', *prefab* = 'prefabricated', *prop* = 'propellor', *Alnico* = 'an alloy of aluminium, nickel and cobalt', *D-H rail* = 'double headed rail', etc.

(c) blends, such as *trunnion* $<$ *trunk* $+$ *union*, *traxcavator* $<$ *tractor* $+$ *excavator*, *lubritection* = *lubricant protection*, etc.;

(d) terms formed by affixal derivation, e.g. *countershaft*, *electrifiable*, *deenergization*, *subsubmicron*, etc.

(e) words arising by conversion: *to blow out*/*with blow-out of fuses*, *the valve*/*to valve*, etc.

In trying to enumerate the most important word-forming methods applied in technical English, (f) such terms should also be mentioned as acquire their new specialized meaning through a change in the original meaning (semantic transfer)[1]—e.g. *dog*—'another name for the stop (machine part)'; *cow-mouthed chisel*, *killed steel*, *to dovetail*, *eyeing*, etc.

In introducing these most important word-forming processes in English, we state them in an order suggested by E. M. Mel'cer in his analysis of the productivity of word-forming processes in present-day

[1] The term 'transfer' is used by G. Stern in his *Meaning and Change of Meaning* (Göteborg 1931).

English.[1] He has based his investigation on neologisms coined in the period of 1930–1953, i.e. mostly on technical words.

The order of importance of word-forming methods is, however, subject to changes due to the period of development of the language and to the branch investigated. For instance, an analysis of English terminology of the rubber industry (in a volume of 1285 terms) has revealed the following order: 1. compounds, 2. derivatives, 3. metaphorically formed terms, etc.[2] Taking into account that the rubber industry is a young branch and its terminology has developed only recently, the above treatment may give an idea of how the word-forming methods are represented in present-day technical English.

However, first place belongs to compounding, which according to all analyses and statistics is recognized as by far the most widespread and productive word-forming process in English.

In this article special attention is drawn to the process of derivation by prefixes and suffixes in technical English, and, in view of the extent of the technical branches as a whole, our investigation is chiefly based on examples from the sphere of engineering and its related branches, as already previously mentioned.

The opinion that the derivation of words is a process of a binary nature is shared by all scholars. A derived word falls into two parts, its base and the derivative element, no matter whether these parts are morphologically further divisible into smaller meaningful units or not.

Also in the process of deriving technical words there are morphemes which are (a) basic and deriving (affixes), (b) independent or bound, (c) from the viewpoint of origin either native (Anglo-Saxon) or foreign, and finally (d) real (independent or bound, e.g. in the term *bevelment*, *bevel* is a real independent morpheme, *-ment* is a real bound morpheme) and only virtual (residual), which are bound morphemes.

Affixal elements occurring in the terms of technical English may be classed into three groups.

The main group of affixes (type A) is represented by traditional affixes. These are stable, long-established and generally recognized affixes, such as *-er*, *-ish*, *-ness*, *-oid*, which form the basic stock of deriving

[1] Е. М. Мельцер, 'К вопросу о процессах словообразования современного английского языка' (On the Problem of Processes of Word-Formation in Present-Day English), Иностранные языки в школе 4 (1957) 17–18.

[2] See unpublished diploma thesis 'Some English Technical Terms from the Rubber Industry Examined from the Onomatological Point of View', by M. Vrážel (Brno 1959).

affixes. This is where the least difference in affixes between technical English and current language may be observed. A number of terminological affixes used here are common in form with those of current language. Apart from them there are affixes typical only of technical style. This is the region of least theoretical controversy on the status of affixes in the linguistic system. Synonymy can be seen at work even among traditional affixes used to coin terms, for instance, *monophase/uniphase*, *bipolar/dipolar*, *multicore/polycore cable*, etc. The polysemy of affixes is not suppressed in terminology either. Affixes are also employed in terminology to replace a multi-word term by a shorter one (the so-called univerbalization—cf. the terms in production engineering, such as *drilling machine* > *driller*, *planing machine* > *planer*, *shaping machine* > *shaper*, etc.). Some exclusively specialized affixes preserve a relative unambiguity of meaning, but an absolute homogeneity of meaning is rare.

The next group consists of affixes and affixal elements the morphemic build-up of which is in some respects unusual, and often disputable when gauged by the criteria of general linguistics. On the other hand, these elements are stylistically very characteristic especially of technical English.

Here they are labelled 'unstable affixes' (type B). By this term we mean such morphemes as are in gradual transition to affixes, or have already belonged to the category of affixes for a short period of time, so that their ties with the words from which they have arisen are still alive in our linguistic consciousness; e.g. shortened elements *-matic* < *automatic*, *-tron* < *electron*, *-trol* < *control.*[1] They have a deeper intensity of meaning, a feature typical of the affixes in technical style.

It is the area of unstable affixes in which the word-forming methods of compounding, blending and affixal derivation—which in many respects show parallel features—come closely together. Particularly salient is a certain genetic and structural relationship of compounding and blending to suffixation. Quite a number of terminal components of compounds and (even sub-morphemic) elements of blends in technical English tend gradually to acquire the status of suffixes in a similar way as, e.g. the suffixes *-dom*, *-hood*, etc. have arisen from full words through the categorial shift in current English over a long span of time.

The ease of this process of transition from the function of terminal

[1] For a detailed treatment of this phenomenon see K. Bareš, 'The Elements -MATIC and -TROL in Technical Terms', *Acta Polytechnica*, Práce ČVUT v Praze, Series II, No. 1 (Prague 1967) 55–66.

components of compounds towards suffixes varies. It is influenced by the character of the word-final component, which may be an independent word of native or foreign origin, a clipped word, or a loan-word which exists in English only as a bound morpheme. After the categorial change has taken place, the new affix and the independent word from which it has developed sometimes continue to exist alongside one another. This circumstance is responsible for varying views on the classification of such linguistic elements and on the structure of words which are formed with them. The large number of transitional stages between compounds and derivatives, or, better, between word-forming components of compounds and affixes, makes some linguists introduce the category of semi-affixes.[1]

The transition of final components of compounds, clipped compounds and blends to suffixes is a productive way in which the stock of English suffixes is enlarged with new morphemes particularly in technical language. These new deriving morphemes also become established in technical language much faster than in current English.

We come now to the third group (type C) which includes the so-called quasi-affixes, unreal affixes, dubious morphemes. We shall narrow our discussion to the problem of suffixes and quasi-suffixes in order to be more specific.

Suffixes carry defined and definable meanings. Alongside of them, however, there exist monophonemic or polyphonemic terminations of words which are analogous to suffixes in their word-final position and external shape but without any definite semantic content (leaving grammatical meaning aside).[2] They possess a number of characteristic features which are frequently interlaced but need not be represented all at once in the given type. These elements seem to aim at suggesting an outward formal completeness of a word in its graphical, structural and phonic forms.

[1] Cf. H. Marchand, *The Categories and Types of Present-Day English Word-Formation* (Wiesbaden 1960). For 'semi-affixes' see pp. 156 and 158. Likewise D. S. Lotte uses the terms of 'prefixoid' and 'suffixoid' in Russian: Основы построения научно-технической терминологии. (Basic Concepts of Scientific and Technical Terminology) (Moscow 1961). The term полусуффикс (semi-suffix) is also used by M. D. Stepanova in her analysis of the system of word-formation in German, Словообразование современного немецкого языка (Moscow 1953).

[2] Their capacity for distinguishing frequently individual parts of speech can hardly be denied; it is, however, not this kind of meaning that we have in mind. It must also be admitted that they are able to denote a very wide class of concepts (e.g. a 'trade mark'). With respect to the great number of terminations used in this manner and to the fact that the notional class denoted by them is vast, it is possible to say that they possess practically no (or almost no) communicative value (semantic content). Cf. a detailed treatment of this subject: K. Bareš, 'On the Transformation of Morphemes in Present-Day English', *PP* VIII 2–3 (1965) 124–31.

As can be seen in the material examined, they chiefly occur in trade names and trade marks, and consequently also aim at being impressive and attractive. They have a conative function.[1] We subsume the terminal elements already mentioned under the term of quasi-suffixes.

As typical English quasi-suffixes in technical language we may consider, for instance: *-a* in such expressions as *Galtona*—serrated blade cutters produced by R. Lloyd Ltd., Galton House, Birmingham, *Alina*—alignment apparatus (trade mark); *-ex* in the expression *Kendex*—milling cutters produced by Kennametal Inc., Latrobe; *-o* in the trade marks *Chaso* (chasers and self-opening die-heads), *Miraclo* nylon core belts, The *Producto* Machine Co., etc. In these instances *-o* is purposely attached to the word-basis the lexical meaning of which does not, however, reflect any subsequent change. In this way *-o* seems to have acquired the function of a word-final signal, i.e. it has a quasi-suffixal and distinguishing power. Its purpose is to expand the phonemic word and to set it more sharply against the others.

The boundaries between the quasi-affixes, traditional and unstable affixes are fluent, and transition from the category of quasi-affixes to the category of affixes is possible. It is, of course, necessary that the originally meaningless termination should not remain isolated, but new words in the same notional sphere should be formed with it. These new coinages may be grouped into a semantic series in which the original quasi-suffix can attain a fuller semantic content.

The terminological meaning of affixes can be observed both in individual isolated words, and in self-contained terminological systems. In the sub-systems based on affixation the carrier of terminological meaning can be a prefix, a suffix or both. The formation of terminological series, which are far more neatly cut than semantic series of words derived with prefixes or suffixes in current English, and which are of several types, is a characteristic feature of the cited sub-systems. Having this systemic force, the affixes assume a semantically distinct function of the common characteristic feature for the whole semantic series constituting (a) horizontal series with all members of the series having the same affix of identical meaning, (b) vertical series in which each member of the series has the same basis and a different affix, but the affixes class all the members into a self-contained sub-system; and (c) antonymic series, where the antonymy of the series is expressed through the antonymy of applied affixes.

[1] Cf. K. Bühler's notion 'Appelfunktion' /i.e. conative function/ in his *Sprachtheorie* (Jena 1934).

The application of prefixes to derive the names of higher and lower ranks of units offers an illustration of a terminological sub-system in the onomatological field of numerical and quantitative relations. As used here, the prefix *tera-* denotes 10^{12} of the basic unit, and in an analogous way *giga-* denotes 10^9, *mega-* 10^6, *myria-* 10^4, *kilo-* 10^3, *hecto-* 10^2, *deka-* 10^1, *deci-* 10^{-1}, *centi-* 10^{-2}, *milli-* 10^{-3}. *micro-* 10^{-6}, *nano-* 10^{-9}, *pico-* 10^{-12}. Examples: *megadyne* = 10^6 dyne, *decibel* = 10^{-1} bel, *microinch* = 10^{-6} inch, *picofarad* = 10^{-12} farad, etc. Systems of this type are created particularly in modern technical branches, which no longer admit a spontaneous development of terminology, but build up their terminologies systematically.

However, the use of affixes in technical language has also some drawbacks. One of their negative features in this domain is, for example, polysemy, especially if it occurs within the same branch. It cannot be entirely uprooted because this would destroy the tolerable limit of the number of morphemes used. Thus the loss of polysemy and narrowing to one specialized meaning is an ideal requirement for the use of an affix in technical style.

Semantic unambiguity, which is demanded for affixes as the means contributing towards establishing terminological systems at least in the 'micro-vocabulary' of a certain branch, is supported by standardizing measures. By this means, not only words but also individual deriving morphemes are assigned exact terminological meanings as a result of standardizing tendencies in terminology. Thus the discussed morphemes assume a special function and become an important factor in building up the English technical vocabulary.

In the previous pages we have introduced a number of typical morphological features of technical English which differ from current English. Differences appearing in word-formative morphology are of primary importance among them.

It is possible, on the basis of this brief linguistic description of the morphological features of technical English, to arrive at scientifically grounded conclusions concerning the most efficient and methodically adequate presentation of the above stated facts to the students of technical English.

Theoretical statements in the area of word-formation in technical English can be applied in the practical teaching of English as a second language to Czech technologists.

This application has several aspects. Two of them, the linguistic and pedagogically methodical, are of greatest concern to us. The linguistic aspect may be presented as a confrontation of word-forming processes used to coin English terms with corresponding morphological processes in the mother tongue, i.e. in Czech. This is to say that, in order to be taught English terminology, the students are supposed to have a knowledge of Czech terminological word-formation or they must acquire it first. In teaching we have to stress the occurrence or non-occurrence of the univerbalization, the frequent use of affixes, their systemic force in terminology, the structural side of compounds and other features parallel in the technical styles of both languages. In other words, to gain a reliable starting point it is necessary to work out a short contrastive linguistic characterology of technical English and of technical Czech. Herein the diverse items offering the most reliable starting point for confrontation will be compared with concurrent ones.

The methodically pedagogical process develops and at the same time narrows the aspect of language teaching by selecting the most suitable vocabulary and linguistic material organized in utterances. To begin with, the technical texts of simple grammatical structure should be selected in order not to distract the attention of students from terminological problems. At the more advanced stages of study the terminologo-lexical and syntactical components should be put on the same footing from the pedagogical viewpoint: a more difficult text is presented as an organic fusion of both components in one utterance. Methodics of this type will demand not only a list of technical terms in the form of independent words and compounds, but also a list of affixes of all types with corresponding Czech equivalents. This catalogue of morphemes will have to be set into structural relations with other linguistic means, i.e. the use of its items must be practised within sentences where the word or morpheme in question is duly transformed or filled in.

The instruction in technical English based on the contrastive study of the Prague School supports the theory which says that the corresponding English and Czech technical texts are not and cannot be mechanical item-for-item translations, and that it exists to explain their relations adequately and this means that one must begin with the systemic knowledge of structural peculiarities in both the languages.

This article presents a selection in several directions: it singles out technical linguistic elements from the broader sphere of English taken as a whole; it puts forward the demand for a confrontation of groupings of English and Czech linguistic features, and, finally, it sketches the way of selecting linguistic units to serve teaching purposes, i.e. it distinctly aims to go beyond the limits of linguistic analysis itself. This article has tried to avoid being constrained to only a narrow practical level, but it assumes that notional relations must be built up both at the level of English and Czech technical terms and at the level of practical instruction in languages. The language teaching process is conceived by us as a limited transposition of linguistic relations into the network of methodical relations on the basis of complete technical utterances and their adapted parts and segments.

In starting in the present paper with linguistic analysis, we are aware of the fact that the application of linguistics to language teaching does not find linguistic material ready to be applied but such that must first be linguistically processed and analysed to serve the given purpose. Such an application of linguistics, however, requires the mastering of, and an organic fusion of, the two processes—linguistic and methodical—and a blend of theory and practice.

9 The Syntax of Scientific German in Foreign Language Teaching*

Eduard Beneš

The present increasing importance of the study of foreign languages is largely due to the fact that it is necessary for a continually growing number of people to read scientific and technical literature written in foreign languages, to understand lectures on subjects in their field given by foreign lecturers, to speak and even to write papers on scientific and technical subjects in a foreign language. In order to meet these demands foreign language teaching has to take into account the style of scientific and technical texts; in some cases the language of science is the sole objective of instruction. If the organization of such instruction is to be expedient and efficient, it is necessary to elucidate the linguistic peculiarities of scientific style. We shall attempt to do so on German material.

In the conception of the Prague School, scientific style is one of the four basic functional styles of the standard language. This question is treated at length by J. Dubský;[1] here it is sufficient to emphasize only certain points relevant to the subject of the present study. By functional style we mean the linear organization of a text in a particular sphere of communication characterized by specific aims and conditions. To meet the requirements imposed upon it, a functional style selects, modifies and suitably arranges the means of the language system, and, if necessary, even develops specific devices of its own (frequently on an international scale). This applies also to scientific style, for the needs of which a special 'language of science' (i.e. a non-linear subsystem of linguistic means) develops within the range of individual national languages, but nevertheless according to identical international principles of style.[2]

* This study is a revised and extended version of a paper published under the title: 'Syntaktische Besonderheiten der deutschen wissenschaftlichen Fachsprache' in *Deutsch als Fremdsprache* 3, 1966, Heft 3, pp. 26–36.

[1] Cf. J. Dubský's contribution to this volume.

[2] K. Hausenblas, 'Styly jazykových projevů a rozvrstvení jazyka' (The Styles of Language Utterances and the Stratification of Language) *SaS* 23, 1962, 189–201.

The Prague School usually distinguishes the following functional styles of the standard language: colloquial, literary and technical (in addition to these sometimes also a publicist style).

Technical style is further divided into practical working style (e.g. official style or commercial style) and theoretical or scientific style. The two styles have a great deal in common; yet each has its specific features. Here we shall confine ourselves to scientific style.

Like the standard language itself, even scientific style reveals considerable internal differentiation according to the general purpose of the discourse, the manner of its realization and its subject.[1] In spite of its many variants, there exists a relatively homogeneous central area, the impersonal standard style, now commonly used, for example, in textbooks. In a synchronistic study of scientific style it is profitable to start from this central area, the standard scientific style of today. Owing to its relative uniformity it lends itself to distinctive characterization. On its background it is then possible to study the diverse peculiarities of scientific style, due both to individual and inter-individual causes (e.g. the genre, subject, purpose etc.). In particular, we can study its various transitional and peripheral variants (such as essays, polemics, popular scientific lectures or radio or television discussions of scientific questions, and the like). For the purposes of foreign language teaching a knowledge of the neutral standard scientific style is of special importance since it is this particular style that is the objective of learners endeavouring to acquire either a reading or a productive knowledge of scientific German.

The basic functions of scientific style are as follows:

(a) Completeness of linguistic expression with regard to the thematic plan and a tendency towards maximal parallelism (attainable in a given language) between linguistic expression and the gradual development of the subject;

(b) accuracy of expression, given by defined or codified automations.[2]

Besides these, the last few decades have been characterized by the development of a subsidiary function, which manifests itself in a tendency towards economy and compactness, in increased intellectualization and finally in standardization of expression.

In studies of scientific style, more attention is usually paid to lexis

[1] J. Filipec, 'Rozbor odborného stylu a jeho vnitřní diferenciace' (An Analysis of Technical Style and its Internal Differentiation) *SaS* 16, 1955, 37–52.

[2] B. Havránek, 'Úkoly spisovného jazyka a jeho kultura' (The Tasks of the Standard Language and its Cultivation) *SČJK* (Prague 1932) 32–84, especially pp. 68–70; in part translated by P. L. Garvin under the title 'The Functional Differentiation of the Standard Language', *PSRE*, pp. 3–16.

than grammar. This is not surprising, since an indispensable component of the language of science is its terminology, which constitutes a special lexical area that does not belong to the common stock of words. Syntactical peculiarities of scientific style, on the other hand, consist not so much in the use of special linguistic means as in the specificity of their selection, and the measure and manner of their utilization. Consequently, in studies aiming at finding out the distinctive features of scientific style, proper attention should be paid to frequency counts. A functional-structural linguo-stylistic analysis of the syntax of scientific style, which draws also on frequency counts, can determine:
(a) which syntactic devices enable scientific style to fulfil its function,
(b) how these devices are interconnected.

A detailed analysis of excerpts from the period of the last twenty to fifty years has shown that scientific German of the present day is characterized by the following syntactic features:

1. Scientific German of the last fifty years displays a pronounced tendency towards *shortening of the total sentence length.* If the average number of words in a sentence from a nineteenth-century work on natural science was 28·5 (for social science 34·4), the present sentence length is about 20 words.[1] In connexion with this shortening, there has been a decrease in the number of complex sentences; the proportion of complex sentences does not as a rule exceed 35 to 50 per cent of all sentences, a complex sentence rarely containing more than two subordinate clauses.

Obvious *preference* is given *to the simple sentence,*[2] which, however, is considerably expanded and otherwise amplified (e.g. by parentheses, additions and the like, which are distinguished graphically since the prevalent mode of discourse in scientific style is the written language). Above all it is the verbal nucleus that is expanded by a number of various complements, the most important being adverbial modifiers. Further, considerable amplification is shown by the individual parts of the sentence, which are either variously multiplied (often in the form of extensive enumerations), or are themselves further expanded, frequently in several ways, which in turn gives rise to complex attributive clusters. The average length of an individual sentence in a scientific text is thus still considerable, particularly in comparison with colloquial

[1] C. F. Sladen, *The Approach of Academic to Spoken Style in German,* Philadelphia 1917; W. Fucks, 'Unterschied des Prosastils von Dichtern und anderen Schriftstellern. Ein Beispiel mathematischer Analyse. *Sprachforum* 1, 1955, 234–44; H. Eggers: 'Zur Syntax der deutschen Sprache der Gegenwart', *Studium generale* 15, 1962, 49–59.

[2] R. Große, 'Entwicklungstendenzen in der deutschen Sprache der Gegenwart', *Deutsch als Fremdsprache* 1, Heft 2, 1964, 1–6.

style. Whereas a sentence (both principal and clausal) in the stylized colloquial speech in a play contains an average number of seven words, a sentence from a scientific work usually has ten to eleven words.[1]

2. In contrast to complex sentences, a simple sentence always contains only one fully expressed predication, to which everything else is related. It is characteristic of scientific style that the predicative relationship is largely expressed by *verbs with weakened meaning*, which semantically approximate the linking verb, whose function—besides being the carrier of the verbal grammatical categories (person, number, tense and mood)—is merely to connect the subject with its complement. The semantics of these verbs can be characterized as an *expression of certain logical relations*. The number of logical relations to be expressed in scientific style is limited and their expression is considerably standardized. It might be useful to examine the various clichés used for the expression of these relations, e.g. identification, qualification, quantitative, temporal and spatial, causal and final relations, relations of general dependence, etc. Although a particular logical relation can be expressed by quite a number of synonymous verbs, the needs of scientific style are met on the whole by a relatively small number of different verbs as compared with other styles. Thus for example the proportion of verbs in the total of lexical items counted in Czech plays amounts to 32·23 per cent, while in scientific texts it is only 20·91 per cent.[2] This is likely to apply to German as well. Besides, 70 to 80 per cent of all verbal forms in scientific style are represented by verbs with weakened or abstract meaning. The results of a study of German medical texts have shown that only a quarter of all the different verbs counted that are of the highest frequency and altogether empty of meaning constitute 75 per cent of all verbal forms.[3] Apart from verbs with weakened meaning scientific style of course also employs verbs with specialized meaning approximating technical terms, since they absorb into themselves the predicative complement (so that we are actually faced with verbalization of nouns), compare for example, *röntgen*, *verstädtern*, *entkirchlichen*, *einwaggonieren*, etc. The more technical a text is, the more pronounced is this dual character of its verbs. In comparison with the total proportion of verbs of these two types the proportion of concrete, non-technical verbs is comparatively low. On

[1] W. Winter, 'Relative Häufigkeit syntaktischer Erscheinungen als Mittel zur Abgrenzung von Stilarten', *Phonetica* 7, 1961, 193–216.

[2] J. Jelínek, J. V. Bečka, M. Těšitelová: *Frekvence slov, slovních druhů a tvarů českém jazyce* (Frequency of Words, Word-Classes and Word-Forms in Czech) (Prague 1961).

[3] R. Baumbach, 'Das Verb in der deutschen medizinischen Fachliteratur', *Metodické rozhledy k vyučování cizím jazykům* (Methodological contributions to Foreign Language Teaching); mimeographed. (Palacký University Olomouc, 1966, No. 3.)

the other hand in everyday narrations of events, both in colloquial and literary style, the largest number of verbs in German have an actual, concrete meaning (whether or not specialized) and only a smaller number have an abstract or weakened meaning. This is true even of narrations in scientific style.

3. Semantic emptiness of verbs and the preference for simple sentences is connected with the next typical feature of scientific style, its *tendency towards nominal expression.*

If nominal expression is regarded as a facultative variant of verbal predication, it is possible to distinguish the following types of nominal expression:[1]

I. Verbal predication is *dissociated* (polarized) into a *verbo-nominal* phrase, which can be represented by:

A verbo-nominal phrase containing a *substantive of action* or—more generally—a verbal or adjectival abstract noun; there are two subtypes:

(a) the agent is expressed: *er nimmt eine Überprüfung vor;*

(b) the agent is not expressed: *eine Veranstaltung fand statt;*

B a verbo-nominal phrase containing a *substantive of agent* (nomen agentis): *keiner war so sehr der Fortsetzer des Kampfes . . . /=keiner setzte so sehr den Kampf . . . fort/;*

C a verbo-adjectival phrase: *krank werden, deutlich machen*;

II. Verbal predication of a facultative clause (or principal sentence) is *transposed* into a nominal phrase, which can be represented by:

A a verbid (infinitive or participle), e.g.:

In der Ruhe vom Retinaculum festgehalten, wird sie bei Beunruhigungen abgeschnallt.

Um Reizwirkungen zu vermeiden, zieht man Zinkpaste vor.

B a noun (a verbal or adjectival abstract), e.g.:

Zur Vermeidung von Reizwirkungen zieht man Zinkpaste vor.

(As a result of transposition the number of verbal predications in sentences is reduced.)

III. Verbal predication is *concealed in apposition* (attribute), which can be treated as an equivalent of a facultative parenthetic sentence or clause: *Sein Verfasser war Vendelin Hippler, der Führer der Odenwälder Bauern.*

IV. Verbal predication is *entirely suppressed* even in the independent principal sentence: a verbal sentence is replaced by a nominal sentence:

[1] Cf. M. Renský, 'English Verbo-Nominal Phrases', *TLP* 1, 1964, 289–99.

Äthiopien: Staat in Nordostafrika, konstitutionelle Monarchie, Föderation von Ä. und Erithrea ; . . .

If we examine to what extent and in what manner these different types of nominalizations are employed in scientific style, we find that some of them are on the whole rare, e.g. type I.B, which occurs mostly in publicist or essayist discourses. The utilization of other types, e.g. I.C, is on the whole the same as in other styles.

Of higher occurrence are types III. apposition (see below in Section 5.(f)) and IV. nominal sentences. In scientific style, nominal sentences are not at all rare, as is sometimes erroneously believed. Compare, e.g., the following cases: the abbreviated style of encyclopaedic dictionaries; descriptions of substances and organisms (often in tabular form); standardized forms of anamneses, diagnoses and various findings in medicine, etc. According to Eggers[1] nominal sentences represent 2·5 per cent of all sentences contained in continuous scientific texts.

In order to achieve sentence condensation scientific style utilizes to a large extent infinitival and participial phrases, i.e. type II.A (see below Section 5.(c)–(d)). These verbids, however, are transitional phenomena between nouns and verbs and their shift to nominalization is not so pronounced.

Scientific style is characterized primarily by the two remaining types: I.A and II.B.

Until recently type I.A, i.e. dissociated predication, was in practical manuals of German style indiscriminately rejected. Whereas the Prague School asserted a functional conception and evaluation of these constructions as early as the 'thirties, in Germany, a decisive step towards recognition and a sound evaluation of the specific function of these verbo-nominal phrases has been made only now in the works by K. Daniels[2] and P. von Polenz.[3]

From the semantic point of view, these verbo-nominal constructions sometimes fill in a gap in the German system of word-formation; they provide means of expressing various shades of meaning, such as Aktionsart—cf. *in Schwung geraten*, *in den Besitz gelangen*, *zur Abstimmung kommen*, etc.; they may replace an extinct or missing causative verb, e.g.: *zu Fall bringen*, *zum Sinken bringen*, *zur Verantwortung ziehen*, etc. Sometimes their employment may be motivated by the fact that they possess other syntactic properties than the corresponding simple verbs, e.g. they can be used without an object, cf. *Bedeutung haben—etwas*

[1] H. Eggers, op. cit. fn. fig. 1, p. 44.

[2] K. Daniels, *Substantivierungstendenzen in der deutschen Gegenwartssprache*, Düsseldorf 1963.

[3] P. von Polenz, *Die Funktionsverben im Deutschen*, Düsseldorf, 1963.

bedeuten. In other cases they may compensate for the rigid position of the German finite verb, if it is required by the needs of the functional sentence perspective (see below).

Dissociation of simple predications into a verb (without any concrete meaning of action) and a noun (expressing the actual action as a concept) is typical of scientific style; in fiction, it is not so common and is often limited to phraseological constructions such as: *einen Rat geben* etc. The specificity of its utilization in scientific style consists in the fact that it provides means of expression on a more abstract level, on the level of defining concepts, i.e. on a level not of mere description of verbal actions, but of their conceptual fixation, evaluation and logical value-judgement. Fittingly expressed by P. Hartmann:[1] 'Wenn jemand verbal z.B. eine Fliege totschlägt, dann ist das noch lange kein nominaler (juristisch-fachsprachlicher) *Totschlag*. Und deshalb kann auch der Jurist fur sein hauptwortliches "Totschlag verüben" nicht ohne Fehler "totschlagen" setzen, wie Sprachpfleger dergleichen verlangen.'

In this respect type I.A is in agreement with type II.B, i.e. noun transposition, where predication is transposed into the substantive. In the latter case a potential clause becomes a sentence part, whereas in type I.A, sentence predication remains preserved. In both cases, however, we are concerned with the fact that the semantics of the verb proper (or predication) are expressed by a noun of action or an adjectival abstract.

This results in a significant shift in meaning: if an action is denoted not by a verb, but by a noun, it is not grasped in its temporal aspect, but is interpreted as a substance (object), removed from the passage of time and strictly isolated.[2] The formation of abstract nouns, which took place at an early period, was a great achievement in the development of human speech and human thought. Abstract nouns which have originated or originate through transformation of original verbal predications, reflect the ability to summarize what is expressed by sentence predication as a particular event or intellectual content.[3]

If we regard nominal expression as a variant of predication, then under nominalizations of type II.B we may include not only verbal abstracts but also adjectival abstracts. Cf. *Im Bild ist die Messung*

[1] P. Hartmann, '"Lebendige" Sprachformen. Zur Frage des nominalen Ausdrucks.' *Sprachforum* 1, 1955, 223–33, quoted p. 229.

[2] M. Sandmann, 'Substantiv, Adjektiv-Adverb und Verb als sprachliche Formen', *Indogermanische Forschungen* 57, 1940, 81–112.

[3] W. Porzig, 'Die Entstehung der abstrakten Namen im Idg.' *Studium generale* 4, 1951, 145–53.

eines Stabdurchmessers gezeigt (= *Im Bild ist gezeigt, wie ein Stabdurchmesser gemessen wird*). (Here verbal predication is transposed into a substantive of action.)—*Auffällig ist die häufige Zweikernigkeit der Zellen* (= . . . *daß die Zellen zweikernig sind*). (Here the predication consisting of copula and adjective is transposed into an adjectival abstract noun.)

Substantival transposition is realized in German partly by substantives of action (especially nouns in *-ung*, foreign words in *-ion* and others) and substantivized infinitives, partly by adjectival abstracts in *-heit/-keit*.

Scientific thinking finds it convenient to denote even actions (or certain qualities, abilities etc.) as concepts, often by established terms (both native and foreign), some of which can hardly ever occur as verbs. This is particularly the case in natural sciences, but also in legal style and the like. Even if we are not concerned with technical terms, nominal transposition of predications is convenient, e.g. in enumerations, etc., owing to its compactness.

The most suitable verbs for connecting intellectual contents expressed by substantive-transposed predications are such as have acquired the character of almost formula-like signs for particular intellectual contents. They form a basis for convenient clichés into which substantival denominations of diverse actions and events may be easily inserted as variables. Substantival transposition may be employed for manifold expansion of the sentence as well as its parts, thus facilitating the inclusion of several transposed predications in one sentence and relating them to the primary (nontransposed) predication.

Employment of the types of nominalizations I.A, II.B that lead to highly abstract expression is in agreement with the basic function of scientific style, i.e. the tendency 'for discourses to be as abstract as required and capable of expressing intellectual relationships and complexity', 'for discourses to give a true picture of the accuracy of objective (scientific) thought, for word-terms to approximate concepts and for sentences to approximate judgements.'[1] At the same time sentence structure exhibits a modern tendency towards standardization.

4. Even the widespread *predilection for the passive voice* in scientific style is functionally conditioned: it is in agreement with the tendency to formulate a sentence not as 'agent—action' but as 'a theme and the events relating to it.'[2] The passive voice as the marked correlate of the unmarked active voice enables us to express an action in such a way

[1] B. Havránek, op. cit., p. 45.
[2] V. Mathesius, 'O passivu v moderní angličtině (On the Passive Voice in Modern English), *Sborník filolugický* 5, 1916, 220.

that the agent is weakened (i.e. does not operate as subject) or is not expressed at all (the 'valence' of the verb being thus reduced by one degree). Therefore passive predication is used especially in such cases where the initiator of the action is not known or is vague or unimportant or is to be intentionally disguised, or if attention is to be focused on the action itself. In scientific style it is suitable primarily for impersonal, objective statements of actions which take place beyond the sphere of activity of any human agent, being called forth by objective causes. This manner of description is suitable especially for natural events, but often even for social events if they are due to objective causes.

Apart from the passive voice, there are other possibilities of weakening the agent. If we are concerned with the expression of actions whose initiators are persons or social institutions, we can use the *man* construction. This construction provides a transitional means towards the passive voice; the agent is considerably weakened (since it is generalized and indefinite), but it retains the function of the subject; its suppression or elimination is thus not so complete as in the passive.

With verbs that do not form the passive voice or where the formation of the passive voice is impeded by lexical-syntactic restrictions, the *man* construction is the only means of weakening the agent (cf. *man ist, man weiß, man bekommt*).

Most verbs, however, form the passive voice as well as the *man* construction, the two variants appearing both with intransitive and transitive verbs (*man tanzt—es wird getanzt; was spielt man—was wird gespielt*). The difference in grammatical meaning between the two means of expression is often negligible, the two variants being freely interchangeable, e.g. in descriptions of working operations or recognitive procedures. Cf. *Einfacher gelingt es, wenn man das Vorderende vorher in Kalilauge mazeriert/wenn das Vorderende vorher . . . mazeriert wird.— . . ., die man als Cistothecien bezeichnet/die als Cistothecien bezeichnet werden.*

In some cases, however, the difference between the two variants is more appreciable. The *man* construction, although stylistically neutral, is less bookish and more colloquial than the passive voice. On the other hand, expression by the passive voice is stylistically marked and this stylistic feature may be actualized. A stylistically motivated use of the passive voice suggests impersonal objectivity, general, indisputable validity, even expression of unalterable laws. Therefore it is the favoured way of expression in legal style; cf. e.g. *Der Ehrentitel wird verliehen an Lehrer, Lehrmeister und Erzieher.* (*Gesetzblatt*).

The use of the passive voice may be actuated by other motives. The passive voice enables us—if need be—to choose as subject an object affected by various actions, which leads to greater compactness of expression (than e.g. if the *man* constructions were used): *Das gepreßte Papier wird auf Maß geschnitten, sorgfältig von den restlichen Quellmitteln gereinigt, getrocknet und geglättet.*

If the finite verb is in the active voice, it is sometimes difficult to distinguish the subject and the object, the only signal of the function in ambiguous cases being the word order subject—object. In the passive voice, on the other hand, it is possible to distinguish precisely the agent and the patient, both types of word order being possible in agreement with the needs of the functional sentence perspective.[1] Cf. *Die Richter werden von den Landtagen gewählt.* In the active voice the word order object—subject, required by the functional sentence perspective, would be hardly intelligible and practically impossible: *Die Richter wählen die Landtage.* The word order subject—object in turn would conflict with the needs of the functional sentence perspective: *Die Landtage wählen die Richter.*

In addition to the passive voice as a regular morphological verbal category there exist other possibilities of expressing the passive perspective: e.g. the so-called possessive passive (cf. *sie erhalten das bezahlt*) or various verbo-nominal constructions (such as *eine Wandlung erfahren, Bestätigung finden, in Vergessenheit geraten, zur Darstellung gelangen, unter dem Schutz stehen* etc.).

On the whole, passive expression—both verbal and verbo-nominal—is sometimes more adequate to the logical structure of scientific thought than the active;[2] consequently it is a fully functional and indispensable means of scientific style.

5. Scientific style endeavours to express the thematic plan as fully and explicitly as possible, being at the same time linguistically very brief and economical. This tendency towards *linguistic condensation* results in a predilection for *connecting the parts of the sentence as closely as possible.* If for the expression of a particular content we can choose between two variants, one being a closer and the other a looser construction, then scientific style gives definite preference to the closer construction. This general tendency may be accounted for by more frequent employment of several syntactic phenomena, which are typical of scientific style, viz:

(a) The so-called *contracted sentences*, in which a sentence part is multi-

[1] Cf. J. Firbas's contribution to this volume.

[2] M. Dokulil, 'Morfologické kategorie passiva ve spisovných jazycích severských ve srovnání se spisovnou češtinou' (The Morphological Categories of the Passive Voice in Standard Scandinavian in Comparison with Standard Czech), *Hrst Studií a vzpomínek*. Brno 1941, 81.

plied. They are often construed with correlative conjunctions (*sowohl—als auch*, etc.); sometimes they are elliptical, e.g. *Bei weiter sinkendem Außendruck nehmen sie zuerst an Intensität zu, dann wieder etwas ab.*

(b) *Pseudo-relative clauses* and *während* clauses (denoting a contrast) are also common, although both can be replaced by parataxis; e.g. *Das feste Metall wird in Tiegel eingesetzt, wobei zunächst die Hüttenmasseln schmelzen.*

(c) *Infinitival constructions* of all types. Great predilection for them is witnessed e.g. by the findings of W. Flämig,[1] which show that in present-day scientific style infinitival constructions with *um zu* occur in 95 per cent of cases, while final clauses only in 5 per cent; in popular prose, on the other hand, the ratio of the *um-zu* constructions to the final clauses is 58 : 42.

(d) *Participial constructions.* They do not occur so frequently as infinitival constructions, but still, they are fairly common, e.g. *Das Produkt aus . . . heißt Drehmoment, oft kurz Moment genannt.*

(e) *Manifold amplification of the attributive.* An amply expanded attribute in presubstantival position, whose nucleus is a participle (or an adjective), is still characteristic of German scientific style, though not to such an extent as in the nineteenth century. Also attributes in post-substantival position often display considerable expansion of various kinds, attributive genitives being combined with prepositional phrases (see below (g)).

(f) *Appositions.* Scientific style is characterized both by explicative or enumerative, and classificatory appositions.

(g) *Prepositional phrases,* which in the function of an attribute, object or adverbial modifier represent a closer syntactical connexion than the corresponding facultative clause. (The means of expression listed here, sub (c)–(g), equally represent different types of nominal expression.) In order to determine as precisely as possible the dependence of the substantive of the prepositional phrase on its head, scientific style fairly often employs the so-called secondary prepositions (e.g. *mittels, hinsichtlich*) or collocations approximating prepositions (such as: *auf Grund, mit Hilfe, im Verlauf*). These prepositions and quasi-prepositions denote explicitly a definite clear-cut meaning, which though involved in the meaning of the primary preposition as well, is not conveyed by the latter with sufficient distinctness. In scientific style, these secondary prepositions provide more precise, specialized and finely differentiated denominations for various intellectual relationships (expressed explicitly by lexical devices).

[1] W. Flämig, Untersuchungen zum Finalsatz im Deutschen, Berlin 1964.

(A similar tendency to express different relations explicitly by lexical devices, in preference to the implicit grammatical means, appears in scientific style in the expression of modality as well.)

(h) *Relative adverbs.* They represent an even closer mode of expression than the corresponding prepositional phrases, since syntactic constructions are considered the closer, the more completely predication is suppressed; or more generally, the fewer grammatical elements are contained. Cf.: . . . *so daß . . . zwei Stunden für Rechtschreibung . . . stundenplanmäßig festgelegt werden können.*

In recent time the occurrence of relative adverbs in scientific style has become especially frequent. They undoubtedly represent a functional means, even if their frequent employment often meets with the disapproval of purists.

6. Since the sentence in modern scientific style is 'loaded' with content, it is imperative that it should have a *clear and well-organized structure.* Thus on the one hand sentences form *self-contained, architectonically balanced and lucidly composed wholes,* on the other hand, however, they are *clearly and closely interconnected.*

As for the semantic organization of scientific texts, it is convenient if the communicative value of the individual parts of the sentence gradually and continuously increases from the theme to the rheme of the utterance, i.e. if it is arranged in agreement with the objective order required by the functional sentence perspective.[1] (Some investigators have called this type of word-order arrangement 'social', 'pedagogical' or 'matter-of-fact', since it pays regard to the listener.)[2]

In German word order the principle of free arrangement of words according to their growing communicative value operates in the non-verbal sphere, while the verb itself is governed by the grammatical principle (fixed order of the finite verb and the obligatory sentence frame). On the whole, however, German word order adapts itself to the needs of scientific style fairly plastically, since there are a number of possibilities which can compensate for its rigidness (Stellengebundenheit) in the sphere of the finite verb and the sentence frame.[3] One of these means is the so-called *Ausklammerung* (i.e. exemption from the sentence frame), which in some cases has become fully grammatical. It is possible (in agreement with the needs of the functional sentence perspective) to take out of the frame and place at the end of the

[1] Cf. J. Firbas's contribution to this volume.

[2] E. Lerch, 'Typen der Wortstellung', *Idealistische Neuphilologie*, 1922, 85–106; E. Richter, 'Grundlinien der Wortstellungslehre', *Z. f. rom. Phil.* 40, 1920, 9–61.

[3] E. Beneš, 'Die Verbstellung im Deutschen, von der Mitteilungsperspektive herbetrachtet', *PP* 5, 1962, 6–19 (reprinted in *Muttersprache* 74, 1964, 9–21).

sentence, e.g. an enumeration, a comparison, a clause, an infinitive with *zu* etc., if this component is to become the proper, though secondary, rheme of the sentence. Cf.: *Die Berufung zum Schöffenamt dürfen ablehnen:* (1) *Ärzte*, (2) *Personen über 65 Jahre*, (3) . . .

Similarly the subject, whose fixed position in the sentence is only imaginary, is often shifted further to the end, especially in scientific style, if it is the rheme of the utterance, e.g.: *Beim Anprallen der Moleküle . . . ensteht hier durch die Summe aller Stoßimpulse ein Druck.*[1]

The theme (the 'basis') of the sentence in scientific style is usually not a mere '*Ertrag*' of the preceding sentence; it often moves the communicated content forward in such a way that it contains data from a potential sentence that might have been omitted: e.g. *Diese Reformbewegung griff bald auf die anderen Länder über. In Deutschland schlossen sich . . . etwa 150 Klöster der Reform an.*—Here the theme of the second sentence may be replaced by a whole sentence: . . . *über. Sie kam auch nach Deutschland. Dort* . . . In this way scientific style becomes highly condensed (in contrast to the style of e.g. fairy tales).

At the same time the first position in the sentence is occupied by an element which is somewhat emphasized, so that the entire sentence is intonationally balanced as a homogeneous, closed whole. (In connexion with this is the fact that in scientific style the first position is much more occupied by another sentence part than the subject, most commonly an adverbial modifier.)

The close construction of sentences in scientific style rests not only on the close linking of the content elements; it is often explicitly expressed by formal linguistic means (the so-called *Satzverflechtung*).

It would be desirable to investigate further how sentences compose paragraphs and longer contexts. These questions, however, are beyond the scope of sentence syntax; they are the subject matter of the science of composition, which belongs rather to the sphere of *literary* stylistics.

In a study of the syntactic peculiarities of scientific style account should be taken of the close interrelations between syntax and lexis. Whole classes of lexical devices (e.g. secondary prepositions or nouns in *-ung* or adjectives in *-mäßig*) owe their origin and development to the needs of syntax while syntactic means may in turn fill in gaps in the lexical system (e.g. when denoting Aktionsart).

The means of word-formation in present-day German allow remarkable linguistically economical condensations of the content and extraordinarily close syntactical-lexical connexion of words. Thus it is

[1] E. Beneš, 'Die funktionale Satzperspektive (Thema-Rhema-Gliederung) im Deutschen', *Deutsch als Fremdsprache* 4, 1967, 23–8.

often possible to express by one word, especially a compound, what otherwise would have to be expressed by a collocation or a clause. The tendency towards higher condensation of expression (particularly by means of compound words) can be convincingly demonstrated, e.g. by a comparison of two editions of Brockhauslexikon. The earlier (1935) version: *Bach im Gebirge, der zuzeiten viel Geröll führt* has been replaced (1957) by: *Gebirgsbach mit starker Geröllführung.*

Scientific style can be examined not only in contrast to other functional styles of the same language, but also in relation to the scientific styles of other languages.[1] Modern European languages display remarkably identical international style norms and tendencies. A multilateral contrastive linguistic study provides a more general and objective picture than a mere bilateral comparison, which may lead to antithetically onesided and subjective distortions.[2]

Insight into the functionally conditioned peculiarities of the different styles of the standard language is a prerequisite for scientifically based cultivation of the mother tongue. Until recently, German purists entirely lacked this understanding, thus condemning indiscriminately—with little effect, however—everything that distinguishes scientific style from 'natural' (usually popular) speech. Only recently there have appeared the first signs of German language critics who have adopted more modern standpoints and conceded scientific and technical style the right to functionally justified linguistic peculiarities. The task of modern practical stylistics will be to establish style norms by which the adequacy of a particular stylistic means could be judged in actual cases.

Until such manuals of style based on modern conceptions and detailed documentation are available, it is necessary in teaching scientific German to rely on the linguistic reality, actual usage, which is quite different from the prescriptions of purists.

Scientific style is characterized by so distinct features in the choice and arrangement, employment and adaptation of linguistic devices that it differs essentially from the colloquial and the literary style. Here we have outlined a survey of its most striking syntactical features. Let us now briefly mention its lexis. We can distinguish the three following layers: 1. words common to all users of the language; 2. general scientific words; 3. special scientific words.[3]

[1] Cf. M. Renský's contribution to this volume.

[2] K. R. Bausch, 'Der Nominalstil in der Sicht der vergleichenden Stilistik', *Muttersprache* 75, 1965, 223–36.

[3] *L'Initiation des Étudiants et Chercheurs Étrangers à la Langue Scientifique et Technique.* CREDIF, Paris, 1966.

The lexical differences of scientific style as compared with colloquial and literary style consist not only in terminology, but also in the general scientific words, which constitute the connecting links of scientific expression. This layer comprises words denoting more or less abstract concepts and intellectual relations; to some extent these words also occur in colloquial and literary style, but their occurrence is rare or exceptional, while in scientific style, their frequency of occurrence is strikingly high and their distribution in all fields of science uniform. Such words are, e.g.: *bedingen, Ergebnis, beträchtlich, erfolgen* etc.

In the region of special scientific words we can further distinguish lexical items (not only terminology!) occurring in several scientific disciplines and those restricted to one science or even one of its branches.

In foreign language teaching the linguistic specificity of scientific style should be taken into account. If the objective of instruction is partial or exclusive command of scientific style, it is necessary to select quite different teaching materials than are commonly used in traditional instruction in courses aimed at general language training (in colloquial and literary style).

In the selection of teaching materials in instruction of the scientific style it is not sufficient—as is often done—to confine oneself to technical terminology. Special attention should be paid to the general scientific words and phrases. Experience from actual instruction has shown that internalization of the special scientific words (including terminology) is not so difficult as that of the general scientific words.

It appeared that a restricted list of 2,200 words rationally selected for reading German scientific literature[1] covers, directly or indirectly, on the average about 95 per cent of all words (including technical terms) in samples from different sciences. Of the remaining 5 per cent about half is accounted for by technical terms which are neither contained in the list nor derivable from it. Internalization of an additional 500–1,000 technical terms would allow the learner to read scientific literature without a dictionary.[2]

Furthermore, particular emphasis should be laid on internalization of those productive types of word-formation which are important for the language of science; this enables the learner to extend easily both his receptive and productive vocabulary by a considerable number of

[1] *Uchebnyj slovar po nemetskomu yazyku*. Moscow 1961.

[2] V. Stehlík and V. Rejtharová, 'Lexikální minimum pro četbu odborné literatury' (A Minimum Vocabulary for Reading Technical and Scientific Literature), *CJvŠ* 6, 1962–63, 247–52.

words. (The number of words in *-ieren* given in Mater[1] is 2,000, of adjectives in *-bar* about 800, the actual numbers being of course much larger.)

In the selection of grammatical means, attention should be focused on the syntactic constructions typical of scientific style. At the same time the study of lexis and phraseology should be organically connected with the study of grammar, the two components being integrated in such a way that general scientific words should be practised in collocations and sentence patterns typical of scientific style.[2] Thus it is possible to substitute different typically scientific expressions into given sentence patterns, e.g. in drills practising government; or given lexical material may in turn be variously transformed into grammatical constructions characteristic of scientific style, e.g. the so-called 'gerundive' with *zu*, participial constructions, nominalizations, etc.

If the teaching materials are selected in this manner it is possible to teach scientific German to learners working in different fields at the same time and with the use of one common textbook. Instruction is first concentrated on the general features of the language of science, which are common to all fields. Later it is differentiated according to branches of study.[3] If the learners are advanced students in their field, they can internalize technical terms themselves by extensive reading of suitably chosen texts.

This conception has a number of advantages and is justified both linguistically and pedagogically, as well as from the point of view of contemporary science: owing to its fundamental opposite tendencies, integration and specialization, and owing to its rapid development it is very difficult to select for the different scientific disciplines restricted lists of technical terms containing everything indispensable and nothing superfluous; moreover, considering the huge number of terms of the many fields of science, this task would be hardly feasible. It is obvious that every specialist will have to continue his linguistic studies, as far as technical terminology is concerned, in order to keep pace with the development of his field of study or in accordance with his later specialization or orientation to border disciplines; anyway, in many cases, he will have to resort to a technical dictionary.

It should be kept in mind, however, to what extent the learners of a foreign language are familiar with their field of study: a different

[1] E. Mater, *Rückläufiges Wörterbuch der deutschen Gegenwartssprache*, Leipzig 1965.

[2] I. Schilling, 'Gestaltungsfragen im Fremdsprachenunterricht an Hochschuleinrichtungen', *Deutsch als Fremdsprache* 3, Heft 1, 1966, S. 15–20.

[3] E. Beneš, 'Eine Sonderform von Lehrbüchern für den Fremdsprachenunterricht: das Lehrbuch für Wissenschaftler', *Deutsch als Fremdsprache* (Leipzig) 5, 1968, 45–50.

approach to technical terms is to be expected from students of technical schools or university students who are only beginning to gain insight into it, and from university graduates and research workers who have a good command of their field and its native terminology (if working in new scientific disciplines they are even obliged to coin new terms).

In general, instruction aimed at scientific style should be differentiated according to the actual objectives and conditions of study. As to the objective of study, it is important to pay regard to the required *extent* of knowledge, i.e. if the knowledge of scientific style is the exclusive or partial objective, if productive or only reading knowledge is aimed at, etc. Further, it is important to consider the required *degree* of achievement, i.e. whether reading with or without a dictionary is aimed at, etc. As regards the conditions, a great deal depends on how much time is allotted to instruction, as well as on the age, education, intellectual level, preparation and performance of the learners.

Accordingly, textbooks should be suitably differentiated. In Czechoslovakia research workers and post-graduate students are now provided with special language textbooks conceived differently from those for university students. These textbooks[1] are considerably more exacting both from the linguistic and content point of view, impose higher demands on the working effort and lead to a higher degree of mastery of the foreign language than textbooks for university students. Moreover, they are uniform for students of all fields, since in our experience research workers internalize the necessary terminology of their field (often very narrow or only originating) without appreciable difficulties, individually outside the language course.

In the universities, on the other hand, it is useful to have textbooks differentiated according to the branches of study (e.g. for technical disciplines, social disciplines, etc.), containing essential terminology.

A special problem arises with respect to whether productive or receptive knowledge of scientific style is aimed at. Even though the written and spoken form of discourse in scientific style is essentially the same, even so certain differences do appear. There are different stylistic genres that occur as a rule only in the written form, e.g. a report, review, article, summary, etc., and others that usually appear in the spoken form, e.g. an inquiry, answer to an inquiry (giving information), address, discussion, lecture, etc. The needs of a research

[1] Cf. E. Beneš, V. Stehlík and J. Baloun, *Němčina pro vědecké a odborné pracovníky* (A Textbook of Scientific German for Postgraduate Students and Research Workers), Prague 1965; L. Dušková and L. Bubeníková, *Angličtina pro vědecké a odborné pracovníky* (A Textbook of Scientific English for Postgraduate Students and Research Workers) Prague 1965.

worker are usually met by the ability to produce (in speech or in writing) only some of them, with a varying degree of urgency. This should be taken into account in textbooks for research workers in the choice of texts and exercises aimed at developing the individual skills. Another complicated question is how training in the receptive and productive skills and training in the written and spoken form of scientific style should be integrated and how different components should reinforce each other; and finally, in what mutual relation and order training should be organized.

Closely connected with this is the question as to what relation training in the general stylistically neutral language should have to training in scientific (or technical) style.

There are evidently quite a number of solutions, varying in their dependence on the given objectives and conditions. In general, however, good results seem to have been obtained if instruction is organized in such a way that at the elementary stage teaching materials contain undifferentiated texts composed of structures, words and collocations common both to the spoken and the written language, while at more advanced stages texts for training in speaking and reading tend towards distinct differentiation.

The linguistic knowledge that the scientific style in agreement with its special functions, essentially differs from the colloquial style, both in lexis and in syntax, induces us to differentiate accordingly foreign language teaching. This should be reflected not only in the selection of teaching materials, their arrangement, presentation, and manner and intensity of practice, but also in the so-called *Textgestaltung* from the stylistic and content point of view in the sense that instruction should concentrate on stylistic genres characteristic of the particular scientific discipline and filled with adequate content.[1]

[1] E. Beneš, 'Zur Typologie der Stilgattungen der wissenschaftlichen Prosa', *Deutsch als Fremdsprache* (Leipzig) 6, 1969, 225–33.

10 Some Principles of Stylizing a Dialogue for Foreign Language Teaching

Irena Camutaliová

It is generally acknowledged that any text for the purposes of foreign language teaching should be stylized. By stylizing a teaching text (in our case a teaching dialogue) we mean two things: compiling it as an original text or adapting some text (a fictional dialogue in the widest sense: from a work of fiction, from a drama, a film, from a broadcast or a television play) or other suitable language material (a dialogue of everyday life) according to certain criteria for teaching purposes. Different textbooks and manuals show in stylizing teaching texts a marked predominance of non-linguistic aspects (they are chiefly pedagogical, psychological, didactic, methodological) whereas the linguistic approach has been so far practically limited to simplifying the teaching dialogue stylistically and neutralizing it emotionally. This state of things cannot be considered satisfactory as it obviously does not make use of important linguistic investigations. One of the tasks of the present paper is thus to try—after having briefly analyzed various criteria applied up till now to the stylization of a teaching dialogue—to concentrate on various aspects of the purely linguistic approach, applying some of the main principles of the Prague Linguistic School, and in this way to stress the need for introducing more linguistics into language teaching in general. The practical result of this analysis should be to find the optimal way of presenting a teaching dialogue to the language-learner so that he may learn to take part in a conversation, which comprises the abilities to start or to enter a conversation and to sustain it.

It is obvious that neither a real dialogue of everyday life (hereafter 'an everyday dialogue') nor a fictional dialogue can be included in a textbook as such. The reasons are different: we cannot possibly take an everyday dialogue because of its purely communicative function and its rudimentary character which would conflict with pedagogical, methodological, as well as linguistic aspects[1] (by analogy, it would be

[1] K. Hausenblas characterizes everyday spoken utterances as unprepared, informal, emotional, free and easy, giving simple spontaneous information in the condition of

equally incorrect—except in a few special cases—to introduce an everyday dialogue in a work of fiction):[1] but, on the other hand, we cannot take a fictional dialogue either because its stylization is determined by various factors which as a complex have *aesthetic function*, So we first establish the basic opposition between an unstylized and a stylized dialogue and in the latter the secondary opposition of fictional dialogue to teaching dialogue. A more complex opposition is then triangular:

x fictional dialogue

unstylized dialogue
(i.e. everyday dialogue)

x teaching dialogue

What interests us in particular are the oppositions in which one member is the teaching dialogue, i.e. everyday dialogue versus teaching dialogue (which will be the chief concern of this paper) and fictional dialogue versus teaching dialogue. The special criteria of stylizing fictional dialogue according to the multilateral functions it has in a work of *belles lettres* have to be discussed elsewhere[2]—here only a few aspects closely connected with our problem will be mentioned. An author chooses only those elements from an everyday dialogue which, according to his artistic intention, are not superfluous (as for instance some components of everyday situations like greetings, thanks, apologies etc.) or commonplace (for example, a dialogue on shopping), avoiding at the same time unduly long dialogue. We can say that the principle of choice and condensation is applied in this case. Another aspect of choosing a certain manner of stylizing a fictional dialogue is that it corresponds to the literary movement and taste of the day (classical, romantic, realistic). Further, it is important that the spoken language in a fictional dialogue corresponds to the epoch depicted, to the social milieu and to the character of the fictitious persons portrayed. For aesthetic purposes it is quite possible to stress or even exaggerate

---

a direct contact between interlocutors (speaker and listener). See his paper, 'O studiu syntaxe běžně mluvených projevů, '(The Study of the Syntax of Everyday Spoken Utterances), in *Otázky slovanské syntaxe* (Problems of Syntax in the Slavic Languages) (Prague 1962) 313 ff.

[1] This opinion was expressed in K. Koževniková's paper К вопросу художественного воспроизведения высказываний повседневной устной речи в литературном произведении (The Artistic Reproduction of Spoken Utterances of Everyday Life in the Works of Fiction), *ČsR* X/2 (1965).

[2] See the paper by K. Koževniková in this volume.

some traits of the spoken language of one person and to neutralize them in the case of another person; such asymmetry is regarded as an appropriate means of plastically depicting life. Such are the aspects of stylizing a fictional dialogue. In view of some of them there are only a few instances when the fictional dialogue should be recommended in teaching a foreign language: when it is instructive (that is, when it acquaints the learner with the way of life abroad, with a different attitude of the people abroad to an important intellectual problem, with an eminent author or a remarkable work of belles lettres, etc.) or for linguistic observations (for example, when it contains marked phenomena of the spoken norm of a foreign language). Owing to the oral production and the audial perception of spoken language the optimal form of acquainting the student with fictional dialogue (particularly with that kind that is made not to be perceived by eyes but by ears, for example, a dialogue in a drama) should be listening to it recorded and making observations on the slightest shades of intonation and the authentic normative pronunciation. The students may be asked then to repeat some of the sentences from the dialogue, choosing those that could be used in a real conversation. In such a way the fictional dialogue should be expected to serve rather as a means of instruction and an object of linguistic observation than as a practical means of teaching the language-learner to talk.

The teaching dialogue, on the other hand, should be stylized in such a way as to become the main device of developing the learner's speech abilities. The present paper is an attempt to single out some of the non-linguistic and linguistic principles of stylizing a teaching dialogue; we make no pretence of providing a complete list or establishing any hierarchy. By analysing each of the principles separately we cannot always avoid artificially divorcing related topics, or occasionally joining aspects that deserve autonomy. It will, however, be a success if the analysis shows that the intuitive and empirical approach to stylization results in a complex of principles. But the chief aim of the analysis is that it should serve to put the stylization of a teaching text on a rational basis—at least from the linguistic approach.

Let us analyse different principles of stylization critically, showing the approach of the author to the object of this stylization. The first are general pedagogical principles.

1. The principle of *up-bringing*

It determines the choice of certain situations and topics (for example, a quarrel, or gossip are excluded), it restricts the content of the dialogue and means of speech used in it to such phenomena that may be imitated, that are positive in every respect. Consequently, such dialogues often show abstract, ideal persons without any individual feature, without any problem. But what is still worse—and contradicts the principle itself—is the suppression of emotionality and the lack of humour in the teaching dialogue. The result is that the dialogue has no dynamics, no conflict, it becomes lifeless. In addition, this principle should imply the consideration of the learner's age (which has not always been fully done in teaching dialogues for children and young people). Even less attention has been paid to the professional or individual interests of the learner. On the other hand, political views are sometimes unnecessarily stressed in the teaching dialogue.

2. The principle of *generalizing*

When stylizing a teaching dialogue the author tends to reduce all possible concrete situations of everyday life that may arise, chiefly in the case of the language learner meeting a foreign-language-speaker, to one generalized situation with typical features. This generalization can be explained by the fact that the teaching dialogue should be applicable to any place, any time and any interlocutors.

The principle of generalization affects the contents of the teaching dialogue, too. But at the same time there should be one particular element in it at least—an idea, a problem, an interesting piece of information, an original or indisputable point of view that would stimulate the student to speak of his own experience or provoke him to express his own attitude. The task of the teacher in such a case is to organize and help his students make of the somewhat abstract teaching dialogue a living thing. It is to be used as a sort of a spring-board for a relatively independent and individual compilation of a whole series of concrete dialogues dealing with the topic in particular, considering certain concrete conditions (a concrete place, time, situation) and persons with certain traits of character and certain inter-relations. As to language study this kind of work serves to transform speech habits acquired by intensive training (we prefer this term to the word 'drill') into secondary speech abilities[1] and leads on to the acquisition of a certain skill in foreign language conversation.

[1] This kind of work has a creative character which requires complex secondary speech abilities from the students (and from the teacher as well), i.e. to be able to react to some unexpected utterances or to some new situation in an individual manner. The term 'complex secondary ability' is used and explained in the book: A. A. Mirolyubov, I. V. Rakhmanov and V. S. Zetlin, Общая методика обучения иностранным языкам (Principles of Foreign Language Teaching Methods) (Moscow 1967) 140.

3. The principle of *imparting information*

This principle actually makes up a part of the general didactic principle of instructing the learner. It may be for instance giving information on the economy, politics, history and culture of the foreign country; but this kind of information can be as easily imparted in a monological form. What can best be included in a dialogue is adequate information on the discord between two ways of life and the differences between conventions of behaviour and conventional speech-forms of social intercourse. The particular problem now is who should take part in the teaching dialogue and where it should take place. It is unnatural if for instance Dick and Carol speak Russian together, i.e. if the persons having one common language (in this particular case English) use in the teaching dialogue a language which is foreign to both of them. On the other hand, if only dialogues between foreign-language native speakers are introduced their topics become limited (centred chiefly around family-life) and they are, as a consequence, of little interest and use to the language-learners. As to the setting of the teaching dialogues the action should take place not only in the foreign country but should be situated in the country of the language-learners as well. In this way an opportunity of naturally varying the generalized situation arises. Thus one part of the teaching dialogue takes place between a foreigner arriving in the learner's country and talking to different people, another part of the dialogue introduces a language-learner having difficulties when coming to the foreign milieu and having to speak with different native speakers of the foreign language. Both basic varieties will then quite naturally bring forward a series of problems (with questions and answers), misunderstandings (with necessary explanations), confrontations of attitudes and opinions, even 'conflicts', arising from the varying amounts and quality of information and different manners of life and behaviour of the language learner and the foreign-language native speaker—all giving an opportunity of supplying the required information or explanation of the fact.[1]

[1] Not far from this conception is C. E. Eckersley's *Essential English for Foreign Students* (Warsaw 1955); in it the author introduces dialogues of an English teacher and students coming from different countries, and the dialogues of the students among themselves, English being their common language. There is only one thing this book lacks: dialogues situated in the student's home country. Some of the dialogues in a textbook of Russian introducing dialogue between a foreigner and native speakers can be considered a definitive success, e.g. the dialogues of an American student called Phillip studying Russian in the USSR and talking with his Russian friends on various occasions. See: C. L. Dawson, CH. E. Bidwell, A. Humesky, *Modern Russian* I–II (New York 1964, hereafter referred to as *MR*). As the present book is intended for teachers of different foreign languages, we have decided to give examples and

This principle (as well as the previous one) helps the language-learner in the milieu of the foreign country to overcome social and psychological difficulties. Even being aware of the fact that a language-learner is not expected to act, behave and talk like a native speaker, he may find himself in an awkward situation when he is misunderstood or when he fails to understand the native speaker. This may have an unfavourable effect on him, in spite of the fact that native speakers as a rule forgive a language-learner for making mistakes and are patient enough to repeat things if the latter does not understand them.

Secondly we must take into consideration general methodological principles: some of them have already been applied in foreign language teaching, others are new and are discussed here:

4. The principle of *respecting a particular standard of knowledge and language skill*

Practically, the application of this principle means a simplification (graded from maximum to a lesser degree) of the contents of the teaching dialogue, of its structure and language. The most difficult task is to compile a dialogue for beginners: it ought to be neither too difficult nor too primitive in its contents and in its language form. The gradation of difficulty is of the utmost importance not only in textbooks where dialogues are a part of the teaching material but also in special conversation-books (manuals) where this aspect has not been taken into consideration. These manuals are usually conceived as an informative booklet for tourists with a fairly high standard of general knowledge.

5. The principle of *saturating* the teaching dialogues with a maximum of *teaching units*

The teaching dialogue usually deals with a narrow topic but there is a tendency to give in condensed form all the language material (mainly the vocabulary) pertaining to a particular but comparatively wide topic. This, on the one hand, makes a teaching dialogue into a kind of film-shot torn out from life (which is not undesirable); on the other hand, however, it is charged with a number of quite different syntactic structures and overloaded with too much and too varied

---

quotations from Russian textbooks—Russian being our material of investigation—in footnotes. We have chosen several textbooks and conversation-books of Russian published in recent years in different countries to illustrate some of our points. These quotations—with positive or negative evaluation—are not meant to be a critical analysis of the books as a whole.

vocabulary. It would be more correct if a certain amount of lexical and grammatical material were repeated in the same dialogue, then systematically in several dialogues (see below, point 7. on repetition) and the most effective included in exercises in the form of dialogues.

6. The principle of *including teaching units only for active mastery*

This principle is closely connected with the two above-mentioned methodological aspects. The authors of textbooks as well as the language teachers, evidently assume that students should learn to use actively all the components of speech contained in the teaching dialogues. This conclusion can be drawn from various types of exercises attached to the dialogue and from the teacher's assignment to learn the dialogues by heart. But examining the function of the teaching dialogue we see that this principle is altogether faulty. It is indispensable that the student be taught to understand a foreign language in its spoken form. As is generally known, the acquisition of this skill is for various reasons much more difficult than learning to understand a written text. Now, a language learner is usually being trained to read newspapers, works of fiction, or scientific literature in the original by being given texts containing material intended both for active use and passive knowledge in a certain reasonable proportion. Would it not be logical to apply the same principle in teaching spoken language, i.e. in stylizing a teaching dialogue? According to this principle the teaching dialogue should also contain a certain amount of language material only to be acquired passively,[1] i.e. just to be understood; the application of audio-visual aids is also highly recommended and some types of exercises should be introduced just for this purpose. Thus the new principle of introducing elements of the spoken language as teaching units both for active and passive mastery would quite justifiably substitute the older, one-sided aspect which ignored the fact that a participant in a dialogue also has the role of an addressee and must be prepared for it.

7. The principle of *repetition*

The form of a dialogue is very suitable for this methodological purpose because one of the characteristic features of spoken language

[1] The idea that the student must know much more about and of the spoken language to be able to understand it at all and take part in a conversation—as well as the idea of introducing some elements of spoken language into teaching dialogue for passive knowledge only—were suggested by V. Kostomarov in his paper: 'К итогам дискуссии о разговорной речи' (On the Results of the Discussion on Spoken Language), Русский язык в национальной школе 6 (1966) 17.

as such is the recurrence of its certain components and their variations in certain communicative situations. It becomes more and more evident that recurrence is not arbitrary but is regulated by rules or tendencies (a few of them have already been discovered). This is, of course, recurrence in normal speech, but language teaching can well make use of this linguistic fact and choose forms of speech for repetition in the teaching dialogue that are at the same time objects of recurrence, e.g. the word which is to be repeated should be included in a rejoinder where its recurrence is organic.[1] Then the repetition will not look unnatural, and will be a part of the actual teaching and not restricted to outside exercises and revision lessons. By combining the linguistic fact of recurrence and the methodological device of repetition we heighten the significance of the principle of repetition considerably.

Finally we are concerned—and that is our chief task—with the linguistic approach to stylizing a teaching dialogue. Until now its part in stylization seems to have been a very limited one and its manifestation could be called:

8 The principle of *maximum simplification with stylistic and emotional levelling*

This tendency in linguistic approach is obviously connected with the above-mentioned pedagogical principle of generalization and in the hierarchy of values even seems to have been inferior to it. A brief observation of language-teaching texts shows that they tend to simplify the language, to neutralize style and to suppress emotion. These tendencies which are common to both monologues[2] and dialogues are not so explicit in the former because:

(a) Most monologues in teaching texts are taken from written sources. In linguistics the written aspect of the language has been investigated quite systematically, and various language devices are seen to come from different levels of the language. These levels, as well as their function in speech, have been described, and the result of these investigations can well be applied to stylization of a monologue.

(b) Various genres of literature are being included as teaching texts, e.g. extracts from works of popular science, from the press, from fiction, from folklore. Along with various genres different styles of language are being introduced which alone warrant stylistic variety.

[1] See the dialogue on p. 38 in the new textbook by V. N. Vagner and Yu. G. Ovsyenko, *Russian* (Moscow 1967).

[2] By 'monologue' we mean a text which has a monological form (a description, a narration, a letter), and not a dramatic monologue (e.g. Hamlet's monologues).

(c) A larger number of more complicated styles may be introduced without fear of misunderstanding as the perception of written texts is easier, since it is visual and the text being fixed in letters can be re-read. The simplification of the text is thus not felt so urgently.

On the other hand—it must be admitted—stylizing teaching dialogues has many disadvantages: it has no solid objective rational basis since no linguistic description of spoken language exists, of its dialogue form and of its stylistic varieties; moreover the perception of spoken language, which is done audially, is much more difficult. In consequence the authors of teaching dialogues cannot be blamed for using the simplest and most neutral language devices and avoiding carefully those which have a conspicuous stylistic or emotional colouring. They, quite naturally, prefer to use such devices as will be met in spoken utterances as well as in written ones, in a monologue as well as in a dialogue, in casual conversation as well as in business letters. The simplification is also seen in the structure of the teaching dialogue, the prevailing type being: A asks simple questions, B answers them using simple sentences. An utterance consisting of more than one or two sentences is rarely included. The sentences are as a rule simple and short (but syntactically complete) lacking elements that seem superfluous. But these elements (as we see from the most recent investigations) serve to relate utterances of different interlocutors (as to their content, the present situation or another person) as well as to show the attitude—more or less rational or emotional of the speaker to his topic. Thus the absence of these important structural components deforms the dialogue turning it into a series of disconnected independent utterances instead of being a sequence of interrelated, or connected rejoinders. As to the participants in teaching dialogues they are usually 'generalized' (see the principle of generalization, above) and consequently all their national, social and individual features are levelled (note too that they are usually distinguished by letters or numbers only). What must be considered most faulty is that no difference, chiefly from a linguistic point of view, is made between the speech of a language learner (acting in the dialogue) and various native speakers—all of whom use the same colourless expressions and simplified sentence-patterns.

One of the consequences of simplification is slight (or very often lack of) gradation of difficulty in a sequence of teaching dialogues.

Sometimes the tendency to stylistic neutralization is substituted by keeping to one level—not neutral stylistically—which cannot be considered correct either: this kind of one-sidedness is even more debatable, since the choice of the stylistic level is entirely subjective and may mislead the language learner.

This analysis shows that simplification and levelling of the language in the teaching dialogue contains a serious danger: the very complex problem of teaching the spoken language is being solved in an over-simplified way by neutralizing specific features of spoken language (and the dialogue as such) which in fact means deforming it and consequently giving the language-learner an inadequate and distorted notion of the spoken forms. Another point—which should not be underestimated—is that such dialogues beome lifeless and cannot affect language-learners emotionally (which is important from the psychological point of view, see also the above-mentioned principle of upbringing).

To sum up, this principle as such cannot be considered incorrect or unsuitable, but doubts and objections are to be expressed as to the inadequate quantity and the dubious oversimplified quality of its realization in practice, which leads to some undesirable results.

It therefore seems reasonable to modify this linguistic principle according to some aspects of the basic linguistic theories of the Prague School with which as a result of more recent investigations some Czechoslovak and Soviet linguists and methodologists agree.

First of all it is necessary to be consistent in distinguishing between the *spoken and written norms* (standards) of the language.[1] It seems quite natural to use the spoken norm in conversational parts of a textbook or in any dialogue included in some other text; but as teaching experience shows there is always a great deal of material in teaching dialogues that is not typical of the spoken language. Among other reasons this is due to the fact that some authors of textbooks compile their dialogues in written (graphic) form and seem not to have read them aloud. Thus the influence of the written norm becomes very strong. Besides, this is the form of speech that has always predominated in textbooks, both in the teaching of one's mother tongue and of foreign languages. We should, therefore, not be surprised to find this tendency manifesting itself[2] as soon as an author puts pen to paper.

[1] The term 'spoken norm' is used by J. Vachek for the spoken language within the limits of the standard. His interpretation of the terms 'written and spoken norm', 'written and spoken utterances' has been given by him in many of his papers and summarized in his book on *The Linguistic School of Prague* (Bloomington and London 1966) 101 ff.

[2] This tendency is observed for instance in translations of fiction, where the dialogues sometimes tend to be bookish, and even in the dialogues in original works of some authors who do not find the right level of style. Cf. I. Camutaliová, 'K otázce stylizace autorské řeči a dialogu v beletrii' (A Contribution to the Problem of Stylizing an Author's Language and a Dialogue in Fiction), *ČsR* 2 (1962) 98 ff.

But this basic distinction between spoken and written utterances does not seem to be sufficient for our purposes. In order to stylize a teaching dialogue we need to utilize still another finer approach.

We can use one of the theses of the Prague Linguistic School[1] which speaks of four stylistic functions of the standard language: the communicative function, the technically practical function, the technically theoretical function and the aesthetic function. The relation of this classification to the former one is as follows: In the written norm we have three functional styles corresponding to the three latter functions whereas the spoken norm has a purely communicative function. But in the textbook various elements of the more highly developed functional styles penetrate into some topics of conversation (e.g. at the post-office, transport, shopping) because the author wants to make the student familiar with extensive material which the student may encounter in this area (cf. various incriptions, names of the shops, instructions etc.). Indeed, all this material pertains to the topic, but this is not sufficient reason to include it in dialogues or conversational phrases since it is rarely found in spoken utterances unless as a quotation. Such material in teaching dialogues distorts the uniformity of style; and these phrases, belonging to journalese or an official style, that not only sound but look bookish and stiff, infiltrate spoken utterances.

But even restricting ourselves to the spoken norm and underlining its communicative function does not yet solve the problem. There exists a wide range of various elements of speech within the spoken norm which have different stylistic values. But the differentiation of these elements within the spoken norm is highly complicated. There have been some investigations of the problem but there has been no definite classification made as yet.[2] The terms 'spoken language'

[1] The theory of the stylistic functions of the standard language was outlined by B. Havránek who formulated it for the first time in 'Théses', *TCLP* 1 (1929). See also the explanation of this theory in J. Vachek, *The Linguistic School of Prague* (Bloomington and London, 1966) 96.

[2] The differentiation within the spoken norm differs basically from that in the written norm. In the latter it is chiefly the function (or the aim) of the utterances which determines its style, whereas in spoken manifestations it is the different conditions of communication that are reflected. From this point of view it is even dubious whether the differentiation of the spoken norm should be called stylistic. See I. R. Galperin's view of the problem in his Очерки по стилистике английского языка (Treatise on Stylistics of English) (Moscow 1958) 27. See also O. Lapteva's theoretical opinion of the rich variety of levels of every cultivated standard language and of the difficulties in classifying these spheres of spoken language which she calls uncodified: 'О некодифицированных сферах современного русского литературного языка' (About uncodified spheres of modern standard Russian), Вопросы языкознания 2 (1966) 40 ff.

and 'colloquial speech' are used in a very wide sense. In different languages the stylistic characteristics of this formation, its relation to the standard literary language and to the written norm, differ considerably.[1] Within this spoken norm some 'neutral' level must be found which can be recommended to the language-learner. But the following difficulties arise: the neutral (or middle) level is a rather vague term and can be found only intuitively by educated native speakers (who actively use functional styles in the written norm as well). Another point is whether this neutral level is ideal for language-learners: in general they should keep to a little higher level than the middle level owing to their special position. But even this solution seems to be an oversimplification of the problem. Applying the linguistic criterion of the type of dialogue (see below) and the methodological principle of respecting the standard of knowledge and language-skill of the learner, we must insist on a further differentiation. Advanced learners should know that in a certain type of dialogue ('thematic', see below) where especial or abstract topics are discussed, it is quite appropriate to use the 'higher' i.e. the formal, level of the spoken norm, whereas in certain recurrent situations of everyday life the neutral, i.e. the colloquial, level is preferable. The practical conclusion to be drawn by a language-learner is that his choice may oscillate between these two levels.[2] Even when in friendly company or with a family where the intimate style is used he should be—owing to his particular social position—very careful about using this style himself; what is intimate for the native speaker may sound

[1] In a more detailed analysis of modern spoken Russian T. Vishnyakova makes an attempt to classify its stylistic varieties. She distinguishes three of them: (*a*) the formal style—which is used by people talking about business or to strangers, in situations where only distant or official contacts exist; (*b*) the colloquial style—which is neutral (inside the spoken norm), informal, used in recurrent situations of everyday life; (*c*) the intimate style used within a family and among friends. See her paper: 'О некоторых проблемах обучения разговорной речи' (On Some Problems of Teaching Spoken Language), Русский язык в национальной школе 3 (1965) 15–18. All the above mentioned varieties belong to the standard language. Outside the classification remain the non-standard spoken utterances, the elements of the 'low' style social and regional dialects, slang, etc.

[2] This is a conclusion which may be drawn from the practical recommendation made concerning spoken Russian by V. Kostomarov in his paper 'Разговорная речь: Определение и роль в препоЃавании,' (Spoken language: Its Definition and its Role in Language Teaching) Русский язык в национальной школе 1 (1965) 15. He recommends a book which is consistent and reliable from the stylistic point of view Пособие по развитию навыков устной речи для иностранцев (An Aid to Develop Russian Speech Abilities of Foreigners) (Moscow 1964, 1; 1967, 3). Another book worthy of recommendation is: S. Chavronina, *Russian As We Speak It* (Moscow 1962, 1) hereafter referred to as *RWS*.

improperly familiar when used by a foreigner. By no means should he ever drop lower, i.e. outside the standard language—though he certainly should be made acquainted with some of its elements. A brief characterization of various formations (slangs) and elements (vulgar expressions) of non-standard language should be included in footnotes to the teaching text. The language-learner (even a very advanced one) should be warned that even if he uses expressions of this kind appropriately—which he is not certain to do—he may be considered funny, laughable, ironical, ill-mannered, too familiar or even vulgar. The learner can be warned of this by including a dialogue in the text in which such a situation occurs. The less advanced the learner, the more likely difficulties of this sort will be.

Taking into account all the above-mentioned factors the methodological solution of the problem may be represented as follows: at the beginner's stage only elements generally used both in the written and spoken norms, i.e. stylistically neutral, should be introduced. During the second stage a basic distinction between the written and spoken norms at the colloquial level should be drawn, but to be perceived only passively. This distinction then becomes accentuated and activated in the third stage. In the fourth stage finer distinctions within the spoken norm should be made: besides the colloquial level some elements of formal speech should be introduced (passively at first) and contrasted with the former ones whenever possible so that the student learns first to distinguish and then—in the fifth stage—to use them consciously. This concerns some situations of differentiated social intercourse: there are some dialogues in everyday life which have a tinge of formality (e.g. meeting a group of foreign delegates) and on the other hand a larger number of informal dialogues on a colloquial level (e.g. meeting a friend returning from abroad). In such instances the two opposed stylistic variants should be introduced and confronted in teaching dialogues more consistently than has been done up till now. Owing to the complexity and the importance of the fifth stage it should last at least twice as long as the others. After the distinction of the two levels in the spoken norm has been actively mastered, some elements on the intimate level can be introduced (for passive perception only), the two levels of the spoken norm remaining constantly predominant, and that is the sixth stage.[1] Later on, in the seventh stage, formal dialogues on

[1] Such a confrontation has been attempted, for instance, in a conversation-book with programmed training 'Mluvte s námi rusky' (Speak Russian with us) compiled by members (V. Barnet and others) of the Department of East Slavonic Languages of the Caroline University of Prague in 1964. In Lesson One of the book a student called Kostya first meets his friend Igor and chats with him in a free and easy way on

interesting or special topics may be included. In the eighth, ninth, and tenth stages the learner should be told about some elements of non-standard language used in spoken utterances by native speakers: elements of 'low' style, social and professional dialects, slang, etc. This order of introducing certain stylistic levels—formal and colloquial—to be mastered actively, and demonstrating only some elements of other levels (intimate and non-standard) intended just for passive knowledge, may be presented in the form of the following diagram:

SPOKEN LANGUAGE		Stages of language learning										
		Language devices	1	2	3	4	5	6	7	8	9	10
	Standard	Stylistically neutral	━	━	—	—	—	—	—	—	—	—
		Formal style				···	━	━	━	—	—	—
		Colloquial style		···	━	━	━	━	—	—	—	—
		Intimate style						···	···	···	···	···
	Non-standard	Low' style								···	···	···
		Social dialects, professional dialects, slang									···	···
		Regional dialects										···

(*Note*: The thin solid line means that the learner should actively use the elements of the particular level; the thick solid line means emphasizing a certain level at a certain stage, the dotted line means receptive knowledge. The scheme shows the emphasis on the two levels of the spoken norm—the colloquial and the formal—which the learner should feel entirely competent to use. The scheme does not include a differentiation within the written norm).

In order to emphasize the many levels of language the characters in each teaching dialogue can be of different stylistic levels. As the basis for this finer distinction the speakers may be contrasted according to their mother tongue: it should be the native speaker who uses a more varied syntax and a richer vocabulary including idioms and words of various stylistic colourings. In other words, besides using the most frequent, automatic elements of the spoken norm (from both the colloquial and the formal level) they may express these same elements in an unusual, 'de-automatized' manner, and also draw on elements

the colloquial level (with some elements of spoken Russian at an intimate level). Then he visits his mother's friends and some formal elements are introduced. In Lesson Eighteen a wholly formal dialogue takes place when a delegation from abroad visits the director of a scientific research institute for the first time.

from the periphery of the standard language or even non-standard elements. The use of these stylistically marked features of speech, especially the non-standard ones, requires a commentary with adequate translation where possible. Sometimes an explanation can be included in the dialogue itself (e.g. after having used an obsolete word the speaker may say, 'My grandmother liked this word,' or after an idiom from student slang he might add, 'As my son would say,' etc.). The differentiated linguistic approach to the stylization of the teaching dialogue is very close to the 'foregrounding'[1] in poetic language (which a fictional dialogue comprises, too). But it should not be forgotten that the inclusion of foregounding elements into the teaching dialogues should not be purely ornamental and uncontrolled. It should be strictly regulated by the predominant teaching function.

At the same time this wide range of stylistic elements of speech can serve to characterize the speaker socially and individually, i.e. to show the speaker's age, sex, occupation, social standing, character, temperament, etc. Many differentiations of this sort can be reflected when stylizing a teaching dialogue, and a wide range of persons whom the language learner is likely to meet can be shown. Different social groups should be represented (workers, peasants, shop-assistants, intellectuals, students), persons of different ages (old, middle-aged, young, children), people with different traits of character (optimists, pessimists), persons of different moods (grumbling, sad, gay, joking), etc. If these aspects were properly realized in the stylization of the teaching dialogue the present wide gap between it and a fictional dialogue would be diminished and the teaching dialogue would be or approximate a work of art—in the terms of the Prague Linguistic School, it would acquire an aesthetic function.

Now that we have dealt with the different aspects of the problem of compiling a teaching dialogue using various stylistic elements of speech we shall pass on to the question of constructing it as a whole. For this purpose the theory of the semantic structure and function of a dialogue,[2] i.e. the dialogue form of speech in general can be applied. The semantic structure of the dialogue is determined by three factors:

[1] This is the English translation of the Czech term 'aktualizace' (from the French 'actualization') used in the *Prague School Reader in Esthetics, Literary Structure and Style* (Washington 1964) edited by P. L. Garvin.

[2] This theory is explained by J. Mukařovský in his paper 'Dialog a monolog' (Dialogue and Monologue), *Kapitoly z české poetiky*, (Chapters from Czech Poetics) vol. 1 (Prague 1948) 129 ff. (German transl. *Kapitel aus der Poetik*, Frankfurt a.M. 1967). He develops and draws conclusions from some of the ideas which the Soviet linguist L. P. Yakubinsky expressed in his paper 'О диалогической речи' (About Dialogue Speech), сб. Русская речь 1 (I'etrograd 1923) 96–194.

the actual objective situation, the relation between the 'I' and 'you', i.e. between the persons taking part in the dialogue ('psychological situation')[1] and the interaction between their 'contexts' (i.e. verbally manifested attitudes) and the common object of conversation.[2] A conversation (a dialogue, speech in the form of dialogue) presents thus a chainlike sequence of utterances of two or more speakers the connexion of which is based on the relation between 'I' and 'you' (the speaker and the addressee). Any two neighbouring utterances by different participants in the dialogue may (usually) be chosen to see this connexion manifested more or less explicitly. The first of the utterances serves as a stimulus, the second as a response[3] thus forming a paired combination which can be considered the minimal elementary, more or less autonomous language unit in a dialogue.[4] There are special language devices to make the connexion between the two (usually) neighbouring utterances (the stimulus and the response) explicit so that they may then be called 'paired utterances'. These are the same devices of speech that cement a chain of paired utterances into a dialogue. They are of various kinds: *lexical*—some of them are used to maintain contact between the speaker and the addressee (verbal formulas such as 'you see' видите-ли or using a person's name or title); others serve to show logical connexion between utterances ('consequently' . . . and could also be used in monologue speech); and some express a subjective (personal) attitude to a fact (or to the preceding utterance)—'I think', 'as it seems to me', по-πо-μоеμу, как мне кажется; *syntactic*—ellipses, variations of the word-order (conditioned by the context or the situation of the dialogue), recurrence of components, parallel syntactic constructions. The methodological consequence to be drawn from this kind of analysis is that since

[1] Cf. also J. R. Firth's ideas about the 'set' of a person and about the context of situation, as explained in his work *The Tongues of Men* (London 1964, 2).

[2] These ideas are related to K. Bühler's theory of the three functions of language (based on relations of the members in the triangle: speaker—listener—object of speech) as explained in his fundamental work, *Sprachtheorie* (Jena 1934).

[3] These are linguistic terms and should not be given behaviouristic interpretation.

[4] The chainlike arrangement of paired utterances in the dialogue is the reason why this unit does not have a segmentary character and is dubious as a language unit. See C. Bosák, I. Camutaliová 'K výstavbě dialogu' (On the Structure of the Dialogue), *SaS* 3 (1967), where an attempt is made to find the segmentary units of the dialogue. The idea of seeking language units in the dialogue has been inspired by N. Yu. Shvedova's dialogue units (based on the principle of syntactical structure and consisting of a number—usually two to four—of rejoinders), see her monograph Очерки по синтаксису русской разговорной речи (Treatise of the Syntax of Spoken Russian) (Moscow 1960). Even if the existence of paired utterances and dialogue units is debatable from a purely theoretical point of view, methodologists recommend them as very practical teaching units (cf. fn. 1, p. 163, above).

paired utterances are a fact of the speech process they can be considered a practical unit of language teaching. For this purpose the dialogue elements of the speech should be used systematically and somewhat emphasized to make the paired utterances more autonomous. In order to bring this idea to life it is of the utmost importance to determine typical elementary and at the same time simple (i.e. consisting of one sentence) paired utterances and typical devices used to connect the stimulus and the response in a dialogue.

Now, we can more easily pass from this elementary unit of dialogue speech to a complex of paired utterances, i.e. to a dialogue (a conversation) as such. According to the degree of presence of one of the three semantic factors (the actual objective situation, the psychological situation, the interaction of 'contexts') the following three types of the dialogue[1] are distinguished:

1. *A situational* dialogue—where the actual situation dominates the dialogue (e.g. talking about the weather when it is bad or when it suddenly changes, making some remarks about common work, asking a person to do something);

(2) *A personal* dialogue—where personal relations are expressed (chiefly from the viewpoint of evaluation—positive or negative—of either partner in the dialogue) and emotions experienced—often mutually—by speakers (hatred or love) the extreme case of this being a quarrel or a declaration of love etc. Some conventional formulae of social intercourse belong here as well. J. Mukařovský does not include them here because they do not show personal relations but are used just to maintain contact—be it formal or intimate—between the interlocutors e.g. forms of address, calls for attention, various formulae of politeness.

3. A dialogue which may be called '*thematic*', in some cases '*conversational*' (although Mukařovský does not name it at all)—where some particular topic is chosen deliberately both for its distance from the situation and its irrelevance to the personal relations between the partners in the dialogue. Conversation centres round this topic (important or unimportant) and reveals the partners' different attitudes towards it. An extreme case of this type is for instance, a conversation as one of the forms of social entertainment (conversation for conversation's sake).

It should be remembered here that speech devices of certain stylistic levels are used in different types of dialogues respectively: the formal

[1] See also Mukařovský, op. cit. fn. 2, p. 174.

level in thematic dialogues, the intimate level in personal dialogues. For situational dialogues the colloquial style is typical, but there are some situations of social intercourse where all three levels are possible under different social conditions.

In real life, in an everyday dialogue, we should scarcely find any of these types in their pure form. The most common instance of the everyday dialogue is a 'complex' dialogue containing elements of all three types. All these elements are involved in a conversation and become intertwined, their functions not being sharply delimited. Only in some cases (in shorter dialogues)—which are rather exceptional—does one of the factors with the clearly definable function become dominant. But in stylizing a dialogue for teaching purposes the above mentioned typological classification might be very useful: A teaching dialogue should concentrate the attention of a language-learner on one object—a certain communicative situation, a certain topic (problem) or certain relations between (or among) the participants in the dialogue. As to the proportions in which different types should be introduced it seems advisable that the majority of teaching dialogues should be purely situational, some of them thematic, just a few personal. 'Complex' dialogues could well be used for revision work.

Having this distinction in mind a further differentiation of exercises and teaching devices can be carried out. If a language learner wants to get to a foreign country as a tourist, he should undergo a complex training in all the possible situational dialogues that he is likely to encounter in the course of his travels. If a waiter learns a foreign language he should get a training in recurrent situational dialogues connected with his occupation as well as in thematic dialogues about meals (explaining what this or that kind of dish is), food in general, about restaurants and the different ways of service in different countries etc. The language-learning of an expert, a scientist, (excluding a philologist) or a business man is usually motivated by the need to read in a foreign language, to speak and correspond with foreign experts about their common professional interests, regardless of whether the learner goes to the foreign country or not. For this purpose such a learner has to be trained in thematic dialogues pertaining to his respective occupation. The conversation-books we now have at our disposal contain mainly situational dialogues and a series of sentences and phrases which should meet the tourist's requirements. Thematic dialogues are rare (even in textbooks, not to mention conversation manuals); this can be partially explained by the fact that a greater amount of factual knowledge and a better command of the language are necessary in order not to be superficial but to keep up the appropriate intellectual level of the interchange of observations and opinions on the chosen subject. As to the language, a basic stock of special expressions must be acquired to be able to make a longer utterance (or a short monologue).[1] Incidentally this situation does not differ to any appreciable extent from that when people have to talk more profoundly about some special or serious subject (sports, motor-cars, music) in their native language: they must know something about the subject as well as some special expressions. As for the personal dialogue it is obvious that the aims of foreign-language teaching cannot include the requirement of teaching the learner to keep up this kind of dialogue in its pure form especially since close personal relations between peoplc from different countries are not typical. What should actually be taught are some of the above mentioned conventional structural elements of a dialogue which serve to keep up the contact between partners in a conversation.

But even the application of each general principle and the consideration of the linguistic aspects do not make a teaching dialogue perfect. The best teaching dialogues have some additional qualities:

(a) The teaching dialogue is an autonomous unit but it is carefully connected with all the other teaching material in a textbook (considering the general didactic principle of complexity).

(b) The teaching dialogue is appropriate to the chosen situation (cf. also the principle of generalization), so that if, for instance, the teaching dialogue is about people sitting in a train they talk about trains, transport, or travelling in general but not about the problems of education (which could of course happen in real life).

(c) The people in a teaching dialogue do not just chatter about nothing in particular (which might also be the case in real life): their dialogue has some sense, some logic, brings some new information of special interest (appropriate to the age, profession, etc. of the learners), or presents some important problem. But this stressing of the intellectual standard does not mean that a teaching dialogue should be devoid of humour. The learners

[1] Interesting material of this kind for study is to be found in dialogues on aeronautics and cosmonautics in the book by G. Makarova, I. Melnitchenko and Z. Lomakina: Смотрите, слушайте, говорите! вып. 1, В1. космос (Look, Listen, Talk! Into Space), (Kiev 1966) 72, 131–2.

should never get the impression that it is conversation for conversation's sake or, which is perhaps still worse, conversation for teaching purposes only.

(d) The length of a teaching dialogue corresponds to the chosen communicative situation as well as to the contents of the dialogue which means, in practical terms, that it leads to some end in the shortest possible way and contains nothing superfluous from the teaching point of view (cf. the aspect of condensation in a fictional dialogue). There must certainly be a difference in the number and length of utterances between two situational dialogues: buying cigarettes is an everyday trivial affair of two or three stereotyped utterances whereas buying a motor-car is a situation involving many discussion points and can be only adequately portrayed in a longer dialogue. Apart from the subject of a dialogue the learner's standard of knowledge should also be taken in account. At the beginner's stage only short dialogues (consisting of two to four utterances) should be introduced otherwise they tend to be unnatural and boring.[1]

(e) The teaching dialogue is dynamic which means that it is constructed according to the basic rules of dramatic action. It contains either a clash of ideas or a conflict of persons or—what is most typical—it brings to the fore widely differing opinions, which reflect the diversity of life and habit of different nations. The dynamics of the teaching dialogue add to its aesthetic function as well.

(f) And last but not least, a good teaching dialogue is suitable for training purposes. It offers the opportunity of making many variations—appropriate at a certain stage of language study—which means primarily that it contains some elements that may be easily substituted. The language-learner—especially the beginner—enjoys (as a rule) this kind of simple play with words, imitating real conversation. For the teacher the possibility of substituting some elements in a dialogue allows him to check the students ability to use new words or constructions and to create analogical situations themselves.

Having shown and critically analysed the main general principles and linguistic aspects of stylization of a characteristic teaching dialogue

[1] This happened for instance in the dialogue on page 23 in *The Penguin Russian Course*, compiled by J. L. N. Fennel (1961). This dialogue, which consists of ten utterances, ought to be divided into three 'microdialogues' (utterances 1–4, 5–6, 7–10). The third of them would be the most suitable for further training.

we must look for the common denominator: the teaching function of this kind of dialogue. Thus the principle of functionality should be predominant, all the rest are simply facets of this one extremely complex aspect.

Summary

The dialogue is the chief form of a teaching text which introduces typical phenomena of spoken language into foreign language teaching, and it should be stylized as relatively natural dialogue set into a typical communicative situation, having a certain structure, containing in some logical thematic connexion the most frequent types of spoken utterances which serve as speech stimuli and speech responses in an unambiguous, monosemantic, 'favourable' context which helps the learner understand and memorize it as a whole and its particular elements.[1] Then it can be considered functional. But to bring such a dialogue into existence is no easy task.

To meet the manifold demands of functionality extensive linguistic research should be made into every language that is to be taught. This will reveal, first of all, the frequency and distribution of components of speech in the spoken norm of the standard language in general and in its dialogue form in particular. The first steps have been made in the sphere of lexicology—where stylistic colouring is most notable—showing the most frequently used, stylistically neutral words in different languages.[2] But there still remains much to be done—the peculiarities of pronunciation in the flow of speech, lively speech activity with its rhythm and dynamics, new tendencies in word-formation in spoken language, all have to be described and analysed. But it is in syntax where most problems arise. It is no easy task in any language to find the syntax generally used in spoken utterances, since such syntax lies somewhere between the standard literary syntax and the seemingly irregular, chaotic syntax of spontaneous speech.[3]

[1] This point of view coincides with the opinion expressed by K. Koževniková and O. Kafková, in their paper, 'Лингвистическая и педагогическая проблематика разговорного стиля' (Linguistic and Pedagogical Problems of Spoken Style), Русский язык в национальной школе 2 (1966) 24.

[2] Cf. Yu Markov and T. Vishnyakova, 'Русская разговорная речь: 1200 наиболее употребительных слов' (Spoken Russian: 1,200 most frequent words), Русский язык в национальной школе 6 (1965). Another attempt is that of N. P. Vakar, 'A word count of spoken Russian. The Soviet usage' (Columbus, Ohio 1966), based on materials of contemporary drama and fiction.

[2]The syntax of spoken Russian has been investigated primarily by N. Yu. Shvedova who showed diverse types of rejoinders according to their syntactic structure (as, for instance, repeats) in her monograph op. cit. fn. 4, p. 175.

The result of the investigation of these diverse problems will help to create a rational basis and to find the best linguistic approach to the optimal stylizing of a teaching dialogue. Then in compiling a teaching dialogue—just as in compiling a fictional dialogue—the attention of the author will be concentrated not only on what is communicated but also on how it is communicated. Under these conditions the language of the teaching dialogue will become differentiated and variable, escaping the danger of schematization and—even more—making foreign language learning an exciting discovery.

11 A Semantic Study of Terminology and its Applications in Teaching Technical Language

Rostislav Kocourek

Technical language occurs in utterances by specialists *qua* specialists. The lexical units of technical language tend to be differentiated into three distinct semantic types: auxiliary undefined, autosemantic undefined, and defined. Autosemantic undefined lexical units are sufficiently clear in the environment of a technical utterance (situation and the defined units in context). Defined lexical units, that is those used in utterances in a sense defined by users, are here called terms, or, collectively, terminology.

Terminology is made up of field terminologies, corresponding to the needs of groups of specialists, studying a given subject matter by specific methods for particular purposes.[1] A field terminology can be stratified into intellectual layers, according to the average intellectual achievement of users, e.g. the secondary-school, undergraduate, postgraduate layer of a field terminology.[2] Technical language and terminology can therefore be understood in a very broad to a very narrow sense according to what sense we decide to impose upon *specialist*, *field*, and *define*. Our decision will be made in conformity with the aim we set ourselves in our study.

The aim we have in mind in the present paper is to teach the semantic aspects of L_2 field terms to advanced undergraduate or to postgraduate specialists whose mother tongue is L_1, who have a working knowledge of L_2 grammar, general-service vocabulary and general scientific vocabulary, and who want to extend this knowledge so as to be able to communicate in L_2 on the subjects of their field. For the readers' convenience the field has been left unspecified, although the

[1] Cf. *technical languages* in Z. Vančura, *Hospodářská linguistika* (Economic linguistics) (1934) 48.

[2] Cf. Havránek's *special languages* in: J. Vachek, *Dictionnaire de linguistique de l'Ecole de Prague* (1966) especially *langue spéciale et style fonctionnel* (p. 44), *intellectualisation de la langue* (p. 38) *styles fonctionnels* (p. 70).

choice of examples is influenced by the author's previous research.

In order to treat a complex subject in a few pages, a number of interesting problems have had to be sacrificed. Among these are: differences between spoken and written language, diachronic semantic phenomena, morphosemantic fields, content of grammatical categories, terms not constituted by noun phrases, differentiation between the task of the classroom teacher and that of the author of teaching materials. Regrettably space only permits a brief mention of the author's detailed account and bibliography of Czech and Slovak terminological studies in the thirty years following 1934.[1]

It is interesting to examine the methods of foreign language teaching from the viewpoint of the language used by teachers. The basic constituents of this language seem to be sentences presenting the facts to be assimilated (presentation sentences) and those eliciting verbal response (conative sentences). So what has been called the linguistic function of appeal, or conative function, is of great importance in teaching, if we agree, that is, to consider as conative any linguistic manifestations which are orientated toward an active reaction on the part of the listener.[2] It is a little surprising that most classroom verbal activities of learners can be very simply grouped as either answering questions or executing requests.

It has been maintained with justice that technical language is primarily referential, cognitive. It is no less true that technical utterances frequently combine cognitive and conative ends. Specialists hold discussions, debate in working parties, communicate while working, put and answer questions, issue and receive orders. They write and get technical letters, have telephone conversations, give interviews in papers, on the radio, for the television. Cognitive-conative communication in L_2 also takes on various shapes in the teaching of the field of specialization concerned. The teacher of the semantic aspects of foreign terminology will find it useful to examine technical utterances of this kind. In so doing he will be able to formulate his own questions and requests in those syntactic structures and by means of those lexical units that are actually encountered in technical utterances.

Notice incidentally that metalinguistic utterances also appear in

[1] 'Termín a jeho definice' (The term and its definition) *Československý terminologický časopis* (Czechoslovak Terminology Journal) 4 (1965) 1–25. A nearly forgotten but still modern document may be added: J. Čada, L. Kopeckij and Z. Vančura, *Teoretické základy studia cizích jazyků na obchodních školách* (Theoretical foundations of foreign language study at commercial schools) (1935) 12 pp. Its authors sought and outlined an application of linguistic theory to technical language teaching.

[2] A. V. Isačenko, 'On the conative function of language' (1948) reprinted in *PSRL* (1964) 92.

technical discourse. So metalinguistic L_2 exercises seem to be legitimate if the semantic problems they are about and the vocabulary they employ are currently encountered in utterances of the field.[1]

The meaning of a term can be explained in a number of ways. How do we, for instance, answer the question *What is a computer?* or the request *Explain the meaning of 'computer'?* The following are a few typical examples of what we might do:

(a) We point to a thing such as the Leo 360 computer produced by English Electric. We usually add a sentence, e.g. *This is a computer.*

(b) We point to a picture, for instance to the diagram of a computer layout or to a photograph of a computer. We may accompany the gesture with a presentation sentence as in (a).

(c) We explain by means of a paraphrase or a definition in L_1 or L_2. We say for example that *a computer* is *any device capable of automatically accepting data, applying a sequence of processes to the data, and supplying the results of the processes.*[2]

(d) We explain by means of another term in L_2 or L_1, e.g. by saying that *computer* in English is *ordinateur* in French.

(e) We explain the meaning through longer utterances dealing with computers. The presentation sentences are then contained in the utterances in the textbook or on the tape.

In example (a), a relation is indicated between a term and a thing. Meaning is explained by pointing to one of the things that the term denotes. Case (b) is one where a relation between a term and a picture is shown. Meaning is explained by pointing to a picture. In (c) and (d), the term is translated by means of other words: in (c) by a definition, in (d) by another term. The last case, (e), shows the meaning indirectly by indicating more complex relations between a term and other lexical units appearing in the context. These relations (a) to (d) are reciprocal. Instead of asking *What is a computer?* we could reverse the procedure and say *What's this?*, *What is the name for any device capable of automatically accepting data . . .?*, etc. or employ the corresponding requests. Let us keep in mind that both the from-the-term approach (*What is a computer?*) and the toward-the-term approach (*What's this?*) are possible, each having numerous interrogative and imperative

[1] For everyday legitimate metalinguistic sentences see H. E. Palmer's and F. G. Blandford's questions and requests about language in *Everyday sentences in spoken English*, section 'Asking for linguistic information'.

[2] British Standards Institution, *Glossary of terms used in automatic data processing* (B.S. 3527: 1962) No. 10007, p. 7.

variants. Each of the procedures (a) to (e) has its advantages and its shortcomings. The meaning of a term will best be explained to a foreign terminology learner if as many of the above types of procedures are employed as are feasible.

Pointing to things, (a), is very suggestive and is a part of such effective methods as are teaching through actions, look-and-say, and activity teaching. Not all terms, however, can be shown to denote something yielding visual data. The percentage of such terms varies from field to field. Besides, the thing denoted may be practically inaccessible in class. On the other hand, pointing to things makes use of only one type of sensory data. Even though visual data are the most important, not only sight could be resorted to in explaining denotation. Hearing would help to explain some acoustic and musical terms, smell to explain olfactory terms, taste for gustatory ones, touch for tactile terms in the broad sense, etc.

Explanations by pointing to things are often unnecessary if pointing to pictures, (b), can be used instead. Unlike a beginner in chemistry, who hears about sulphuric acid for the first time, our learner of, say, German terminology already knows what *sulphuric acid* is, has seen and smelled it and avoided tasting or touching it. What he wants to know is what to call that acid in German or, conversely, what *Schwefelsäure* means. The picture can therefore stand for the thing provided it makes the learner think of *BOV*, the substance in question.

Pictures (including slides, films, diagrams) are more frequently used in the classroom than things. Pictures are made by man and can therefore be easily adapted to the aim we set ourselves in teaching, which cannot always be said of things. We can, too, obtain pictures of things that are inaccessible in the classroom. We can also construct pictures that show only certain properties of a term, for instance only those we intend to talk about with our students. To say nothing of the notorious unicorn-pictures, which, unlike unicorns, can be said to exist. This makes pictorial explanations elastic and useful.

The use of pictures in teaching is based on the fact that reciprocal translation is possible between linguistic signs and extralinguistic signs such as pictures. In using pictures as visual aids we have been indulging in what for instance Jakobson called intersemiotic translation, or transmutation.[1] This takes on a new importance in technical language teaching where interlingual translation methods have been so frequently employed.

[1] R. Jakobson, 'On linguistic aspects of translation', in: R. A. Brower (ed), *On translation* (1959) 233.

I have found it helpful to examine every single term for demonstrability, i.e. for the possibility of explaining or suggesting its meaning by pointing to things and pictures. Demonstrable terms are set apart and treated differently from others. No opportunity should be missed to take advantage of the demonstrability of terms as often as possible.

Unless accompanied with verbal explanation, pointing is rudimentary and clumsy. If we simply show a Leo 360 to the learner and say that that is a computer, he might think that *computer* stands for *Leo 360* or *this room here full of electronic hardware*. Teachers know what amusing shapes erroneous interpretations of pointing can take on. That is why pointing is usually accompanied by verbal explanation. Needless to say that in foreign language teaching, our concern is with the verbal explanation, rather than with the thing or picture.

We can now go over to types (c) and (d). Considered together, they cover cases where the meaning of a term is explained verbally, in other words.[1] The explaining expression, whether it is a term or a phrase, is synonymous with the term explained. We say that the term is translated by a term or by a phrase. The translation can be either intralingual or interlingual. So a term in L_2 can be translated by means of a phrase in L_2, by a synonym in L_2, by a synonym (or equivalent) in L_1, or by a phrase in L_1.

Intralingual translation by a phrase is a procedure useful to the man in the street and scholar alike. How else could a monolingual dictionary find its way to a best-seller list in 1966? When asked by his son what *statisticulation* means, Father might perhaps offer an explanation of this sort. The semantic data available in good monolingual dictionaries have been appreciated, among others, by Hjelmslev[2] and Fodor and Katz.[3] Looking up, for instance, *solids-not-fats*, we find that it means *the constituents of milk other than butterfat and water*. What, semantically speaking, is this? A term is said to have the same sense as its definition. This must certainly be a semantic relation different from the term-thing or term-picture relations spoken of above. Whatever the labels used, linguistic meaning is frequently considered as a relation between form (name) and sense. However interesting sense may be, linguists seem to be unable to get at it unless sense is expressed by means of

[1] I use *word* in a broad sense including the following special cases: abbreviations such as *P.T.O.* (pee-tee-oh), numerals such as *1* (one), alphanumeric expressions as *L2* (el-two), symbols as p (pee), π (pi), $+$ (plus).

[2] L. Hjelmslev, 'Dans quelle mesure les significations des mots peuvent-elles être considérées comme formant une structure?', *Proceedings of the Eighth International Congress of Linguists* (Oslo 1957) 653.

[3] J. J. Katz and J. A. Fodor, 'The structure of a semantic theory', *Lg.* 39 (1963) 185, fn. 15.

words. Linguists are free to choose such a definition of sense as may be handled by linguists. Let us attempt to understand by sense of a term the defining phrase of that term. I mean such defining phrases as have been formulated by the users of the term and correspond to a class of occurrences of the term in technical utterances.

The term may, of course, have synonyms corresponding to the same defining phrase.[1] All members of a synonymic group are usually not known to one and the same person. The meaning of a term may then be explained to him through the synonym he knows.

In terminology teaching it is no less useful to employ visual aids for explanation or presentation of demonstrable terms, than it is to formulate definitions for all terms to be taught and to decide which synonyms, if any, will be admitted to the obligatory section of the field terminology, called here the term-list. Our term-list is restricted not only as to field and intellectual layer, but in accordance with the number of available teaching hours and other limitations. A tentative list is selected, in the first place, from the vocabulary obtained from a representative corpus of utterances.[2] Selection is primarily based on frequency and distribution of the term in the corpus. Definitions should not contain hidden terms not included in the term-list. So we can either include in the list certain terms needed for definitions or avoid using new terms in definitions. Flood and West's *Scientific and technical dictionary* is an example of how this problem can successfully be solved.

The tentative list should also be examined for synonymic groups and synonyms should be arranged according to frequency within the group. The decision to be made is which less frequent synonyms should be admitted to the term-list. It seems reasonable to accept less frequent synonyms that might be of help to learners, so that even if, for example, the abbreviated term *CAT* proved more frequent than its synonym *clear-air turbulence*, both would probably be considered together. The same goes for such pairs as *quasar/quasi-stellar radio source* or for the pairs *trivial name/systematic name* in chemistry, e.g. the herbicide *Dinoseb/di-nitro-ortho-secondary-butyl-phenol*.

If a less frequent synonym is introduced separately, it should invariably be explained by the principal term already known to the

[1] See my paper 'Synonyma v terminologii' (Synonyms in terminology), in: B. Trnka (ed.), *Tři příspěvky z oblasti odborné lingvistiky* (Three papers in technical linguistics) (1966) 23.

[2] Cf. this author's paper, 'K metodě zpracování dvoujazyčných terminologických slovníků' (A method of elaborating bilingual terminolological dictionaries) *Československý terminologický časopis* (Czechoslovak Terminology Journal) 5 (1966) 65–84.

learner. So *trunk* would be presented through the synonymous term *highway*, signifying in the field of automatic data processing a *major path along which signals travel from one of several sources to one of several destinations*. A special case of such explanations is the optional introduction of American synonyms for British terms or vice versa, e.g. *rutabaga* for *swede*, *alfalfa* for *lucerne*, *billion* for *milliard*.[1]

Whereas synonymity sentences will probably only occasionally be used in sense presentation, definitions seem to be more handy. The use of carefully worded definitions makes terminology teaching more profound. If a student learns, reproduces, formulates and discusses definitions in L_2, he gradually learns to be precise and matter-of-fact in using a foreign language. This is a virtue probably more vital in technical language than mere fluency. Teachers can employ definitions for a number of exercises. From the structural semantic viewpoint, the chief advantage of definitions is that they contain data on the semantic structure of terminology. In order to permit interesting discussion the precision of wording required from the learner should be on a level corresponding to his knowledge of L_2.

A variety of questions and requests elicit or permit answers in the form of definitions. Examples of variants of such questions taken from the field complex of agriculture: *What is header-harvester? What are fungi? What does weathering of rocks mean? What is meant by pF? What is the meaning of a three way cross? What is the definition of a plant food unit?* Examples of requests: *Define silt. Give the definition of S.E.* (starch equivalent). *Explain the meaning of parasitism. Give the meaning of Braford. Discuss the meaning of blackleg.* It is unnecessary to explain how analogous questions and requests are introduced into ordinary classroom activities and how they can become a starting point for or an outcome of a fruitful dialogue.

Of the numerous types of defining, one is particularly capable of being employed together with visual aids and can be presented in very early stages of instruction. It is the defining by examples and by enumeration. Modifications of the following types of questions and requests could be used to elicit answers approaching such definitions. Questions: *What cereals do you know? What types of drainage can you enumerate? What different classes of fertilizers can you name? What types of crop rotation are you acquainted with? What systems of ignition are used in tractors?* Requests: *Name all fruit trees you know. Name the most common*

[1] See my paper, 'Rozdíly mezi britskou a americkou zemědělskou terminologií' (Differences between British and American agricultural terminology), *Papers of the Agricultural University Prague* (1961) 403–7.

field crops. Name the best known perennial weeds. Name some garden tools. Make a list of farm implements. Give the classification of plant viruses. Give examples of selective herbicides. Give the expressions for the three inflorescences in grasses. List the leading dairy breeds of cattle. Thus instead of, or alongside with, questions and requests of the type *What are fungicides?* and *Explain the meaning of fungicides*, we can use those of the type *What fungicides do you know?* and *Give a list of fungicides.*

It would be possible to devise a classification of questions and requests according to the types of definition they elicit, or, which comes to the same thing, according to the types of presentation they require. The variety of questions and requests eliciting the same type of definition could be classified according to syntactic criteria.

Let us now consider another type of explanation, namely that of interlingual translation. In bilingual and multilingual dictionaries, meanings are explained by synonyms in another language, or foreign equivalents. For instance, the German term *Hubschrauber* and the Czech *vrtulník* are explained to English-speaking learners as *helicopter*. This is very often a very clear and quick explanatory procedure for terms that prove to have equivalents. Only unfounded feeling against any translating whatsoever or unwillingness to take the pains of looking for equivalents can make us neglect this procedure. When an English-speaking learner comes across the French terms *mazout* and *boutoir*, what a shortcut it is to be told that they are *fuel oil* and *bulldozer* respectively.[1]

Note that an interlingual translation method in the classroom is by no means what I advocate. I only hold that if the learner has a manual where terms are given equivalents in his mother tongue, then much vain effort in class is avoided. The time saved can be employed in extending foreign language exercises. Even when compared with pointing and definitions, exact equivalents in L_1 hold their ground as helpful tools of semantic explanation, particularly of the non-demonstrable terms. There are good reasons to avoid bilingual teaching in class. So corresponding questions and requests, such as *What is the English for 'mazout'?* and *Give the English equivalent of 'boutoir'*, will be resorted to only in very exceptional cases. But in doing away with interlingual semantic explanations we lose the assurance of semantic precision. It was, among other things, the abandoning of translation (one possible semantic aid) that led to the introduction of visual teaching methods (another possible semantic aid). Or, perhaps, the reverse.

[1] The Franglais term *bulldozer* was eventually permitted by the Académie Française in April 1967.

Existing equivalents or near-equivalents of terms should be known to the teacher and available to the student in the process of learning at home. An English-speaking student does not learn how to use the German *Rechenmaschine* or the Russian *vyčislitel 'naja mašina* if we tell him that they are *computer* in English. We only explain to him very quickly and fairly precisely the meaning of the term. And that, in itself, is no mean accomplishment.

In order to be able to tell the student what the equivalent is, we must first find out ourselves. And that is a difficult task if we are not easily satisfied with blunderbuss equivalents. Term entries in bilingual and multilingual specialized dictionaries are often of little help to a terminology teacher. The dictionaries may be outdated, the selection of included terms inadequate, the frequency of correct equivalents low. Professor Trnka was right in 1927 when he remarked that the very necessary improvement of dictionaries could be achieved by applying the results of semasiological study in lexicography.[1] We should not be surprised that the search for equivalents is time-consuming. Even the detection of geographical near-synonymy between terms of the same language is difficult. A considerable amount of effort had to be spent before, for instance, the crops grown in Guinea, North Africa, India, Malawi, South Africa, Sudan and China and called *Guinea corn*, *durra*, *Indian millet*, *kafir corn*, *great millet*, *milo*, *feterita* and *kaoliang* were all recognized as the complex *Sorgum bicolor*.[2]

The semantic comparison of terms belonging to different languages aimed at the eventual determination of equivalents is here called equivalence study.[3] Translation, glossing, merging, analysis, and comparison of a large corpus of field utterances, completed by questioning of specialists, seem inevitably to arrive at results that are sufficiently precise.

Two important properties of the term come into prominence in equivalence study. Firstly, being a lexical unit, a term may be constituted by a word or by a lexicalized word-group. That is why equivalence study does not compare individual corresponding words but complex lexical units as a whole. So for instance a simple comparison of Czech terms, containing the word *zemědělský*, with corresponding English terms shows that this Czech adjective is rendered by a number

[1] B. Trnka, 'Semasiologie a její význam pro jazykozpyt' (Semasiology and its importance for linguistics), *ČMF* 13 (1927) 132.

[2] Cf. my paper 'K anglické terminologii tropických plodin' (English terminology of tropical crops), *Papers of the Agricultural University Prague* (1962) 223–34.

[3] Cf. my paper Ekvivalenční průzkum anglického termínu soil conservation (Equivalence study of the English term soil conservation), *Papers of the Agricultural University Prague* (*School of Agronomy*) 1965, 451–59.

of adnominal expressions in various English terms: *farm* (machinery), *farming* (co-operative), *Farmers'* (Weekly), *agricultural* (engineering), *Agriculture* (Division of FAO).

Secondly, a term is a defined lexical unit, so that if the same form is used in other defined senses, it is considered as homonymous within terminology, and if it is used in undefined senses, it is considered as polysemic and outside terminology. This potential ambiguity of the form of the term results in the fact that, from the viewpoint of the whole lexicon, the term is often only one, defined sememe of an ambiguous form, corresponding to some, but not all its occurrences. So we do not simply ask what the equivalent of *digit* is. We ask for the equivalent of *digit* in the sense of, say, *occurrence of a character*. That is why terms in our term-list should be correlated with equivalents via defining phrases in L_2 and in L_1. Moreover, term occurrences in our texts ought to correspond to the definitions given in the textbook.

Not equivalents, but analogous terms accompanied by further explanation are often the only result of equivalence study. If we look for the English equivalent of the Czech *meliorace,* the one thing we can say with certainty is that, contrary to dictionary entries, the equivalent is neither the faux ami *amelioration,* nor *soil improvement,* nor *reclaiming of land.* Its individual occurrences could be translated by one of the following British or American expressions: *drainage and irrigation, land improvement, soil conservation, soil and water conservation.* Both *meliorace* and, e.g. *soil conservation,* are ambiguous and strongly influenced by the different etymologies (*melior* v. *conservo*) and by administrative, historical geographical and cultural factors. As such they belong to transitional lexical units between terms proper, and technical but undefined units. Only occasionally can such differences between a term and its near-equivalent be the subject of questions and requests eliciting the learner's explanation, e.g. *What is the difference between 'soil conservation', as defined by H. H. Bennett in 1947, and 'meliorace' as defined by K. Jůva in 1962,* or: *Discuss the difference between 'soil conservation' and 'meliorace'.*

Why should we care for equivalents if they are often hard to find or non-existent? The point is not to overemphasize the importance of equivalents, but to insist on a consistent and complete analytical comparison of corresponding L_1 and L_2 terms.[1] The author of the textbook and the teacher can take advantage of the phenomena that are similar and concentrate on the differences which bring about harmful interference from the learner's mother tongue.

[1] Cf. V. Mathesius's passage in: J. Vachek, *Dictionnaire de linguistique de l'Ecole de Prague* (1962, 2)) 22, see *comparaison analytique et point de vue fonctionnel.*

Interlingual explanation of a very special kind is what could be called etymological explanation. Let us imagine that we teach English terms to Tunisian undergraduate students who, being bilingual and diglossic,[1] have a good knowledge of French, literary and Tunisian Arabic, but for whom most European languages are little accessible. In teaching to them for example the English lexical units *pedology* (= soil science), *chernozem*, *gestalt psychology* (= configurationism), and *robot*, we shall not only give them the French equivalents, *pédologie*, *chernoziom*, *gestaltisme*, and *robot*. In preparation for a definition, we can impart to them etymological knowledge by means of French calques of the respective original Greek, Russian, German and Czech (K. Čapek's) forms.

Such simple explanations are with us to stay. The response to etymological asides is exceptionally lively. Perhaps because, even if historically biased, the learners feel intuitively that the core of such explanations are often present-day, if vague, semantic data. Not infrequently do such data exert a strong influence on the range of semantic postulates imposed by scholars on existing forms and on neologisms. In this respect, etymological explanations are not only of the past and present, but they point to the future.

The explanation of common, or popular, names by means of scientific names in botany and zoology is another special case. It is irrelevant here whether we class this phenomenon separately as explanation between a term of an international naming system and a term of a natural language, or as, say, Latin (or Greek)-English or as English-English explanation. Scientific names, such as *Drosophila melanogaster*, are international in that they tend to be used uniformly throughout the world, but substantial geographical or personal polyonymy[2] exists despite the strict rules of nomenclature committees. They are also Latin or Greek in some of their inflections and in a number of stem morphemes. And they are English or American, German, French, Czech in their phonemic aspect.

The teaching of botanical nomenclature[3] is considerably facilitated by the possibility of explaning common names by scientific ones and conversely. Much misunderstanding is avoided if *holly* is explained to a botanist as *Ilex aquifolium*.

[1] *Diglossic* in the sense given by C. A. Ferguson, 'Diglossia', in Dell Hymes (ed.), *Language in culture and society* (1964) 429.

[2] *Polyonymy* is here used in the sense discussed by O. Vočadlo, 'O polyonymii a desynonymisaci v angličtině' (On polyonymy and desynonymisation in English) *ČMF* 29 (1946) 46–58.

[3] Botanists differentiate between *nomenclature* and *terminology*. In this paper, nomenclatures are considered as part of terminology.

However necessary the preceding types of semantic explanation and of corresponding exercises may be, they are all insufficient in one major respect. Their concern is with the meaning of a single term. They can hardly show in detail how a term is used in utterances. With the exception of definitions and motivated synonyms, they are of little help if we want to teach to learners which other terms of L_2 the term in question is semantically related to and the character of these relations. So such explanations say little about the use of terms and about the semantic structure of terminology.

In the teaching of terminology, the meaning of terms has to be explained by showing how the terms work in longer utterances printed in the textbook or recorded on the tape. The text explaining the term computer will then deal with computers and discuss the classification description, characteristics, functioning, applications, etc., of computers. And the text will contain all relevant graphic, phonemic, morphological, and syntactic facts about the term. Besides, such texts contain use occurrences of *computer*, its collocations and the terms that are somehow related to it. A terminology teacher, or rather the author of the textbook, will hopefully not attempt to teach the semantic structure of a field terminology through theoretical talk about the complex lexicon structure. His knowledge of terminology structure will be imparted to learners through carefully worded texts and semantic exercises containing occurrences of terms whose place in the structure is to be shown.

If the linguist studies the different ways in which users of a field terminology express structural semantic relations and the ways in which they formulate questions and requests concerning such relations, he will find a number of questions and requests concerning such relations which are considered relevant by the users. Such questions and requests can easily be classed, simulated and adapted for use in terminology teaching.

The linguist will moreover have at his disposal citations of all sentences in which the terms occurred in the corpus used.[1] He will use these citations in the preparation of collocation exercises,the importance of which can hardly be exaggerated. Occurrences and collocations are, after all, concrete manifestations of what is often called use, as contrasted with definition or meaning. Definitions are worth anything only if they hold good in utterances. But if they do, as they indeed

[1] Cf. J. R. Firth, 'A synopsis of linguistic theory, 1930–1955', *Studies in linguistic analysis* (1957) 26–7.

should in the textbook, they contain valuable indications of the semantic structure of terminology.[1]

Let me now review the findings of the present paper. The question was how a semantic study of terminology can be applied in teaching the technical language. The core of such semantic terminological applications was found to be in existing types of semantic explanation. These types constitute the skeleton of the semantic presentation put forward by the teacher in the classroom or in the textbook or on magnetic tape. They can be expressed in declarative presentation sentences. A number of these have been discussed. A presentation sentence for pointing to things or pictures is: *This is a computer.* For defining: *Solids-not-fat are the constituents of milk other than butterfat and water.* For lexical intralingual synonymy: *'CAT' stands for 'clear-air turbulence'*, or: *The American equivalent for 'swede' is 'rutabaga'*, or: *The scientific name for 'holly' is 'Ilex aquifolium'*. For interlingual lexical synonymy: *The French for 'fuel oil' is 'mazout'*. The presentation sentences dealing with more complex semantic paradigmatic and syntagmatic relations of a term are included in the texts of textbooks or on the tape.

Presentation sentences are the basis of exercises consisting in the teacher's questions and requests eliciting the learner's answers or verbal execution. The learner's verbal response should in principle tend to be the same as the teacher's presentation. Each presentation sentence could be transformed into questions or requests. Besides, questions and requests can be directed either from the term to be studied or towards it.

So in pointing, we can use, for instance, the following sentences: *What is a computer? Show me a computer. What's this? Give the name for this.* In defining, we can say: *What's solids-not-fat? Define solids-not-fat. What's the name for the constituents of milk other than butterfat and water? Give the name for the constituents of milk other than butterfat and water.* As there are numerous ways of defining, there are numerous types of response to such questions and answers. When we use lexical synonymy, we can say: *What is the scientific name for 'holly'? Give the scientific name for 'holly'. What is the common name for 'Ilex aquifolium'? Give the common name for 'I. aquifolium'.* When we use interlingual lexical synonymy, we can say: *What is the French for fuel oil? Give the French equivalent of fuel oil. What is the English for 'mazout'? Give the English equivalent of 'mazout'.* Questions, requests, and other eliciting sentences concerning complex

[1] See this author's 'Synonymy and semantic structure of terminology', *TLP* 3 (1968), 131–46.

semantic relations will have to be worked out separately for each field of terminology and for each text.

The above types of questions and requests could not only be further differentiated, but each could be modified and organically joined to the preceding or following discussion. If distributed with adequate frequency in suitable places of the teaching process, they will render technical language teaching more efficient. They are sufficiently exact to permit utilization in tests, in the language laboratories and in the programmed procedures of teaching machines.

12 The Language of Literature and Foreign Language Teaching

Květa Koževniková

Stylistic investigations provide an ever more exact and detailed knowledge of the functional use of linguistic means. In modern theories of the teaching of foreign languages stylistics thus becomes an important subsidiary discipline helping one to orientate oneself critically in the multiform foreign language material and to solve appropriately the problem of both the content and methodology of language teaching according to concrete teaching aims. Within this scope of problems the relationship between the teaching of foreign languages and literary texts and, speaking more broadly, artistic expression in general, comes to the fore although it has generally been neglected from the theoretical point of view. Modern teaching methods with their strong inclination towards live spoken language no doubt 'dethrone' the literary text which has so far traditionally held the prominent place as, after all, written texts in general do. The great significance of literature for the culture of every nation as well as the culture of its language does not allow the artistic expression to remain outside the attention of the teaching process; it will, however, be necessary to find a new approach from the viewpoint of modern teaching methods. In this paper we shall try to show that it is not possible to reduce this approach only to the question of how to make correct and suitable use of literary texts in language teaching. We are concerned here with a much more complicated and, in its significance, a far more fundamental task, that is, how to create by the whole conception of foreign language teaching conditions under which the learner can actively master the basic functional forms of the language, so that in higher stages of his study he may be able to distinguish the basic aesthetic qualities of literary texts and thus enrich his knowledge of the cultural values created therein by the foreign language environment.

A very fruitful basis for the theoretical investigation of the stylistic qualities of artistic texts was provided by the studies of the members of the Prague School in the 'twenties and 'thirties studies in the field of linguistics as well as in that of literary science which were partly based on the endeavours of the Russian formalists[1] and which later influenced considerably even modern Western European structural trends. The theory of functional styles was perhaps one of the Prague School's greatest contributions: linguistic styles were interpreted for the first time as compact structures the main features of which are determined by their functional aims. Styles as 'structures' were thus studied from the point of view of the language-internal relationship between the partial units and the whole and were analysed at the same time from the viewpoint of their function; that is, the dependence of these structures on outside phenomena was being sought. It was this functional viewpoint that led to the artistic style being separated as a structure in contrast to all others since its dominant function is the aesthetic one (in other words, aesthetic intention, aesthetic orientation) whereas all the other styles are characterized by the communicative function modified in various ways. Linguists as well as literary scientists attached to the Prague School did not deny that even artistic expression has its communicative value; they emphasized the absolute domination of the aesthetic orientation of artistic linguistic expression, and it was this dominant feature that they regarded as a differentiating classifying characteristics justifying stylistic theory to distinguish between the artistic style and the other styles. The notion of the aesthetic value itself may, of course, be interpreted in many different ways as is documented after all by various older theories of art from the classics to the present. The Prague School conceived of this aesthetic function mainly as the intentional orientation of the perceiver's attention to the aspect of expression. J. Mukařovský has formulated it in the following way: 'The aesthetic function . . . concentrates attention on the language characteristics themselves—and is thus diametrically opposed to the orientation towards the objective, which is communication in language.'[2] In close connexion with this principle, the representative of the Prague School began to emphasize the so-called foregrounding procedures. To be able to impress the

[1] Cf. the views of B. Havránek, J. Mukařovský, V. Mathesius on the problems of stylistics, their Russian predecessors are G. Vinokur, J. Tynjanov, V. Shklovski, etc., cf. O. Sus, 'Предыстория чешского структурализма и русская формальная школа', *ČsR* 12 (1967) 229; R. Wellek, 'The Literary Theory and Aesthetics of the Prague School', in *Discriminations: Further Concepts of Criticism* (Yale U.P. 1970) 275.

[2] J. Mukařovský, 'O jazyce básnickém (On Poetic Language), *Kapitoly z české poetiky* (Chapters from Czech Poetics) I (Prague 1941) 82. German transl. *Kapitel aus der Poetik* (Frankfurt a.M. 1967).

reader, to create an active approach to the reader, linguistic means cannot have the character of usual automatized expressions. B. Havránek defines automation as 'such use of linguistic devices, in isolation or in combination with each other, as is usual for a certain expressive purpose, i.e. such a use that the expression itself does not attract any attention.' On the other hand foregrounding means (Czech 'aktualizace', French 'actualisation') the use of devices of language in such a way that this use itself attracts attention and is perceived as uncommon, as deprived of automation, as de-automatized, e.g. a living poetic metaphor, as opposed to a lexicalized one, which is automatic.[1] A peculiarity of 'poetic language' (this concept is now replaced by 'artistic style') is thus its active, creative relation to the literary norms of language, from which it often deviates and which it sometimes even deforms, as well as its relation to the conventions of the standard language, that is, to the aesthetic norm which is violated and surpassed in some way or other in every real work of art.

It is true that in its original conception the Prague School overrated the task of the aesthetic function in artistic expression, or rather it did not show due appreciation of the communicative function of every artistic expression. This conception may also be criticized for regarding the foregrounding and particularizing acts of speech as the dominant, ever present trait of artistic creation which is thus restricted to only certain types of literary works. Nevertheless, these basic observations opened up wide possibilities for further studies of works of art and became the fertile ground for modern concepts of stylistic theory. Contemporary Czechoslovak scholars developing further the tradition of the Prague School refer to the aesthetic communicative function of the artistic style and do not denote as its main trait a certain act of speech itself but rather a *potential internal stylistic variability* which is realized in different works by its more or less profound foregrounding relationship to the devices of language.[2]

The above-mentioned considerations of the Prague School about the 'poetic language' were not, naturally, intended to be of immediate use in the practice of the teaching of foreign languages; they have, however, become so much a part of the scientific awareness of modern linguistics that their influence can be distinctly recognized even in the present efforts to modernize the conception of foreign language teaching on scientific principles.

[1] B. Havránek, 'Úkoly spisovného jazyka a jeho kultura' (The Tasks of the Standard Language and its Cultivation) *SČJK* (Prague 1932) 52. Cf. P. L. Garvin, *PSRE*, 9.
[2] Cf. the studies by K. Horálek, K. Hausenblas, M. Jelínek, L. Doležel and others, referred to by J. Dubský in this volume.

If we first turn to the traditional method of teaching, we can see that the problem of artistic style was not being solved as an integral part of mastering various functional forms of language but that artistic style was treated mostly as a question of including artistic texts in the teaching process and of exploiting them. In this conception, literary texts are usually used in a three-fold manner:

1. First of all as *substitute models of colloquial expression* which the pupil is to master actively—here we are faced with dialogues in fiction and drama.

2. As *representatives of model cultivated expression* which the pupil is encouraged to imitate and as language material on the basis of which various linguistic phenomena are acquired.

3. As *initial texts for translation*, as a rule into the mother tongue.

Let us now try to consider the suitability of this use of literary texts with regard to the specificity of the artistic style as well as to the foreign language teaching aims. Speaking generally, the main aim is to attain an active command of a situationally suitable, *average*, *cultivated mode of expression* in all spheres of language contact and, particularly in the higher stage, to achieve receptive ability in distinguishing stylistic values of both the written and spoken norms of a language.

1. The first point to be considered in view of this aim is whether the dialogues of modern fiction and drama really represent those suitable models the learner is expected to imitate. It might seem that it is this part of literary works that is the closest to the extra-artistic language reality, that it is here that foregrounding and particularizing processes have the minimum possibility of application and that it may therefore well meet the teaching requirements if suitably selected. But a comparison of artistic dialogues with natural spoken communications,[1] which is a necessary and obvious test of the dialogue's suitability, shows above all that an artistic dialogue is always stylized whatever outward features of naturalness it might have and that this kind of stylization is extremely unsuitable for the aims of language teaching.

The differences between authentic spoken utterances and their literary counterparts (dialogues of fiction and drama) arise mainly from the fact that a literary dialogue does not spring up spontaneously but is created by only one speaker (author) in a complex formulating

[1] I base myself here on the findings of an investigation of Russian spoken utterances carried out by the Department of East Slavonic Languages of the Caroline University of Prague. The aim of this investigation was theoretical recognition of spoken utterances in dialogues; the results of this research served as basic principles according to which audio-oral teaching aids for the teaching of Russian to Czech students were prepared. Cf. I. Camutaliová's contribution to this volume.

process; the reception of individual replications in the dialogue is thus only seeming, in fact they are all directed at the reader (spectator, listener) to whom they always communicate partial elements of the authors' artistic message. At the levels of language this is reflected in several ways:

(a) The content of the replications in a dialogue always includes only what the author thinks suitable for a seemingly objective illustration: elements which are important from the viewpoint of the development of the plot, the characteristics of the atmosphere, the psychology of the dramatis personae and their general characteristics; they are, however, also elements which the author considers important from a compositional and sometimes even purely stylistic point of view. Therefore artificial replications originated in this way are usually much more definite and compact in content and therefore also more refined in syntax and lexis and more explicit in expression than the replications in natural dialogues. In their construction, they thus approach *written* utterances.

(b) Since direct utterances of the character nearly always reveal their personal characteristics or that of the atmosphere and should moreover enthral the reader and attract his interest, the replications in artistic dialogues are usually characterized by an increased *concentration of style*, i.e. an increased density of stylistically marked devices and of all other means which are striking in some way or other and go beyond the average level; they are emotionally not very engaged utterances especially in their expressiveness. In real life, it is for example more probable for a railwayman to say to a novice: 'Ты у нас работаешь еще недолго, и вот ты всему удивляешься' (You haven't been with us long and seem surprised by everything) than to use a metaphorical expression and a coloured, not very frequent phrase as is chosen in this situation by a character from Leonov's novel *The Russian Forest*: 'Нет, не хлебнул ты еще паровозной копоти, все тебе в диковинку'. (No, you haven't even taken a proper gulp of the engine smoke yet and gape open-mouthed at everything.) Similarly, hardly anybody could combine so masterly in real life strong vulgarisms with a sophisticated intellectual expression as Ostap Bender in Ilf-Petrov's well-known novel Двенадцать стульев (Twelve Chairs), 'Набил бы я тебе рыло, только Заратустра не позволяет.' (I'd like to slap you in the face but Zarathustra forbids it.) No doubt, hundreds of similar examples from all modern literature might be quoted. This feature of artistic dialogue strikes one especially in works whose intention is to demonstrate the way of speaking in a certain social environment. Here the hypertrophic occurrence of stylistically marked devices usually by far outdoes the reality. The impression of 'real life', 'usual and ordinary manner' and 'naturalness', which are the epithets usually employed in literary reviews, is aroused because the reader (recipient) primarily responds to the language and thought of the character and confuses extreme, only potentially possible features of some current spoken utterances with average current features.

The internal structural similarity to a written utterance on the one hand and the high concentration of stylistically marked means on the other hand are thus in contradiction to the ideal of a modern teaching dialogue. An artistic text certainly provides invaluable material for lexical, stylistic and other interpretations of the text but can seldom be a model of average, common, 'everyday' conversation. In teaching we often encounter conservative views which derive from the common use of literary texts for school purposes; this practice results in an over-emphasis on actively mastering the lexis, idioms and phraseological expressions, various sayings, proverbs etc., which, for psychological reasons as well, attract both the teacher's and the learner's attention far more than other less attractive linguistic devices. This is, however, a mistake which contradicts the modern conception of language teaching, especially of the audio-oral method the aim of which, in the field of independent spoken utterances, is to help the learner actively master and automatize the basic and most frequent dialogue constructions and their most common lexical-semantic content and thus enable him to express his thoughts, even their basic subjective, emotional and intellectual nuances, promptly, correctly and in proper relation to the context. Thus the point is not to master highly expressive means and an extensive 'thematic' lexis but rather to mechanize some habits in a certain simplified form of a spoken dialogue with 'mediocre expression'. Apart from the above-mentioned reasons, an artistic dialogue cannot also satisfy these demands because the very phenomena that must be stressed in the teaching process are dispersed, sometimes even absent, in such a text and their dependence upon situation is often far from clear. Thus we arrive at the conclusion that as long as we want to work with a text in some form or other when practising an independent spoken utterance in dialogue form, it is only proper to replace artistic dialogues by artificial ones, which should, however, be constructed in such a way as to have the greatest possible teaching effect in all respects. That means that such texts will represent for the learner some kinds of *general models* that are independent of the individual and unique situational coherence and simultaneously possess such a degree of artificial concretization that creates an impression of immediacy and relative naturalness that is attractive in content and provides at the same time methodological possibilities of becoming a starting point for various forms of audio-oral practice.[1]

2. The question of how *literary texts* can prove suitable as *models of cultivated monologue*, mainly written, requires a different answer. The criteria which will be used here for evaluating the suitability of individual texts in the teaching process can be developed mainly with the help of preliminary stylistic analyses. Such analyses will show first of all that artistic works are entirely heterogeneous in style. Apart from an external variability—individual works can differ distinctly from one another in the use of language devices and their organization—there often also exists a considerable internal variability realized sometimes in a very complex and striking form. Let us remain in the sphere of prose which is the most suitable for teaching. The variability in style is accounted for by some laws of the dependence of linguistic devices on certain types of structural background selected by the author. By his work every author evokes some fictionalized reality; in epic prose it will be a story the individual elements of which the author may either *review* (i.e. report about them in such a way as to create an impression of providing first-hand information for the recipient), or *reproduce* it, in the case of spoken utterances (the recipient then has the impression of reading an authentic text not originally designed for him), or he may finally *comment* on it (in information about those components of the passages reproduced that could not be made comprehensible by the reproduction itself, or he introduces evaluative and supplementary information about the reported passages).[2] It will therefore be necessary to look for models of cultivated monologues mainly within the scope of the *reporting procedures*. Nevertheless, very few texts selected in this way will have the character of average (in the positive sense of the word), aesthetically effective

[1] Dialogues constructed according to these principles are included in the partly programmed audio-oral course *Mluvte s námi rusky* (Speak Russian with us) on gramaphone records, by V. Barnet, D. Brčáková, K. Koževniková, I. Krjuková and others (Prague 1964). Cf. K. Koževniková and O. Kafková, 'Дингвистическая и педагогическая проблематика разговорного стиля', Русский язык в национальной школе, 2 (Mockba 1966) 18.

[2] Cf. in greater detail K.Koževniková, 'К вопросу художественного воспроизведения высказываний повседневной устной речи' (Artistic Reproduction of Common Spoken Utterances), *ČsR* 10 (1965) 74.

expressions that would be comprehensible to a foreigner. In choosing the reporting procedure the author has the possibility of making a further choice, namely from what point of view this procedure should be presented. The basic viewpoint may be personal, such as various types of first-person narrations; however, it may seemingly be quite impersonal. In either case it may then be shifted to various characters as well as to the author's subject in various ways. Thus the 'report' may be shaped in many ways; it may stick to the average language-aesthetic norm of a cultivated utterance, it may approach the stylistic principles of the language of the characters, it may also apply the principles of a creative treatment of the linguistic material and even try to be an exclusive, exotic particularization of current language conventions. The exclusiveness of the language need not necessarily be an indicator of the artistic qualities of the work. A literary work may strive to impress the reader not only in the first instance by its degree of expression but the weight of its impressiveness may also lie in such components of the literary structure as its contents, composition, etc.

A man with a more or less profound knowledge of a foreign language is not naturally able to perceive a foreign-language artistic text in all its plasticity and is not therefore able to make associations evoked by the expressive level of the work either. The first obstacle he comes up against is the fact that, unlike his mother tongue, he has not created a feeling for language convention, average, commonplace, for the dependence upon situation and context; he does not distinguish between stylistically marked and unmarked devices. He therefore cannot recognize the artistic shift of linguistic devices towards foregrounding and stylization and often applies stylistic criteria of his mother tongue to the foreign-language text, especially if the native and target languages are related. Those texts and works will therefore prove more suitable for the purposes of language teaching which do not appeal in too tricky a manner to the language awareness of the recipient; and, especially in the initial phase of mastering a language, it would be only proper to include artificial 'artistic' texts employing basic linguistic devices already mastered and using artistic procedures based on matter-of-fact object associations rather than on those of expression (e.g. simple comparisons, metaphors rather than quibbles).[1]

The whole complex problem cannot, however, be exhausted by the question of the selection of the texts. The knowledge of the stylistic

[1] Texts of a similar kind are also published by the Centre de Recherches et d'Études pour la diffusion du Français; cf. for example Pierre de Beaumont, *Du temps de la mère-Dame* and *A l'écoute de la mort* (Paris, Librairie Didier, 1962).

character of fiction, as well as every concrete didactic handling of it, leads to much wider problems concerning the whole conception of language teaching. If we want the learner to have a differentiated view of a foreign language, master its basic functional forms and thus learn the basic habits of cultivated written utterances, we must first of all guide him to establish for himself as soon as possible a solid *basis for evaluating* at least the ordinary situational and contextual linguistic devices. Is it, however, possible to create such a basis? The solution of this problem has so far attracted little attention[1] and thus we can present here only some basic conclusions concerning the stylistic problem of the teaching of foreign languages in general.

First of all, it is clear that a basis of stylistic cvaluation cannot be established by analysing artistic and other kinds of texts, since the analysis itself assumes the ability to differentiate and is in no way a safe method of mastering linguistic phenomena from the viewpoint of methodics. It will therefore be necessary to turn our attention to the whole *conception of language teaching* from the beginning and raise some specific demands concerning all spheres of learning a language. For the sake of illustration, we shall only mention here the practice of *grammatical* phenomena which under the existing conditions leads to the greatest levelization of the stylistic multiformity of language.[2] We might, of course, make the general demand that the phenomena practised be presented from such a didactic viewpoint and on such language material that the learner might be able to acquire the form of their most usual *situational* and *contextual* dependence as well. Thus:

(a) If possible, we must fill the structures (or forms) practised with typical semantic content or, in the case of structures with a wide range of contents, try at least not to select exclusive variants. For example, the Russian way of expressing approximate numbers by means of inversion ('Ему лет сорок'—'He is about forty' as opposed to the precise expression 'Ему сорок лет'—'He is forty') primarily concerns round numbers; and as it is a means mainly peculiar to the current spoken utterances it also concerns the stating of age ('Ему лет пятьдесят', 'Девочке года четыре'—'He is fifty', 'The girl is four'),

[1] An attempt at a solution of this problem has been made in *Linguistics and Style* by Nils Erik Enkvist, John Spencer and Michael J. Gregory (London, Oxford University Press, 1964).

[2] This is based on experience with the composition of audio-oral teaching aids in the Department of East Slavonic Languages at the Faculty of Philosophy of the Caroline University of Prague: 'Rusky se správným přízvukem' (Russian with the Correct Stress) by K. Koževniková, D. Brčáková, V. Nekolová, published in *Teaching Aids* (Prague 1967) and *Audioorální cvičení z ruské syntaxe* (Audio-oral exercises in Russian syntax) by P. Adamec, O. Kafková and S. Beková mimeographed textbooks (Prague 1967).

basic time relations ('Приду часа через два'—'I'll be back in about two hours', 'Лет пять я его не видел' 'I haven't seen him for about five years') and basic relations concerning payments ('У меня рублей двадцать'—'I have about twenty roubles', 'Дай мне рублей шесть'—'Give me about six roubles'). This enumeration of possible content is not exhaustive but if, however, the learner masters its basic semantic-situational devices, he will not only be able to use this construction correctly, in analogous cases, but he will also be able to recognize its special, uncommon use when for example he comes across foregrounding, 'Веков девятнадцать тому назад'—'about nineteen centuries ago or so', in Mayakovski's poem Владикавказ—Тифлис. He will then be able to appreciate the author's intimate treatment of history.

(b) Apart from this way of selecting the contextual-semantic content of the structures practised, it is of course necessary to continue establishing awareness of the stylistic level of the phenomenon in a quantitative way, i.e. by mastering a sufficient number of representative contexts (usually sentences in practice). It is, however, difficult to create an awareness of the stylistic level of a phenomenon where a grammatical phenomenon is, as it were, limited in its lexical space but touches simultaneously different stylistic strata of the language. For example, if the learner comes across sentences like 'Бросьте шутить' (strongly colloq.)—'Wind up your jokes,' 'Продолжайте маршировать' (P.T. command)—'Go on marching', 'Он начал читать' (neutral in style)—'He began to read', in a single exercise on the use of phrasal verbs with infinitives, it is clear that their stylistic level escapes the learner's attention or that they merge into a single, stylistically undifferentiated sequence in his view. The danger of the learner's stylistic levelization of the language is the greater, the more general the place in the given language structure the phenomenon practised occupies. A practical solution of this problem is to arrange more consistently the practised material according to stylistic homogeneity as well as in selecting broader contexts, which would enable the learner to recognize the situational dependence of every given context.

(c) Much depends naturally on the methodic presentation. Here we are faced first of all with the problem of audio-oral methods, as well as with pattern practice. If we are to consider the stylistic levels of linguistic devices, there are two relevant points: the audio-oral practice adequate to the utterance should be applied to only that material which is consistent with the usage of current spoken utterances in the language in question. Further, where the audio-oral methods or other modern techniques use transformations (e.g. put into the passive) or where they prescribe a certain model to be used in various ways in the learner's responses to a given stimulus (e.g. Answer in the negative using antonyms: 'Это новое платье?—Нет, старое.' 'You have a new dress, haven't you? No, that's an old one.') it is especially important that no stylistic tension should occur between the stimulus and the response or between sentences in their transformational relation. If we use in the stimulus utterances like 'Берегись поезда! Берегись машины!'—'Beware of the train! Beware of the car!' etc. and demand synonymic constructions in the responses as Осторожно, машина! Осторожно, поезд!'—'Look out, a car (a train) is coming!', we confuse crudely the stylistic levels and the situational dependence of both types of construction, since the learner has the impression that he is learning two possible ways of expressing roughly the same content. There are two styles used here: Берегись поезда etc.' is used exclusively as a warning in official notices whereas Осторожно, машина! can only occur in a dialogue, i.e. in a spoken utterance as a warning of an immediate danger. Constructions of the 'Берегись поезда' type are so closely linked to the written form that they are not suitable at all for audio-oral practice. (This raises the question whether such constructions should be mastered actively at all.)

In this connexion it is necessary to understand the limited possibilities of some modern methodic procedures, especially of exercises working with transformations. By merely practicing two constructions made up from the same lexical material, it is only possible to learn the given constructions and acquire an awareness of their semantic interrelationship, that of analogy in our case. But the differences in the dependence upon the situation and the stylistic colouring cannot be grasped by means of this type of exercises. From this point of view replicational fill-in exercises according to a given model are more suitable, because they enable the learner to acquire a better awareness of the approximate scope of the applicability of the practise constructions in which a certain type of stylistically and situationally instructive contextual relationship between the stimulus and the response is repeated.

(d) From this observation yet another principle may be deduced: it is necessary to avoid as much as possible material which is not independent or closed as far as the context is concerned. It is for this very reason that 'examples' from literary works, which are as a rule fully comprehensible only if we know the broader connexions given by the context (sometimes even by the whole work) and which are usually not well-balanced in style, can seldom provide suitable material. Here are a few examples of such situationally and stylistically uninstructive sentences practising the Russian conjunction 'пока' (while): Неизвестные злодеи, пока он любовался красавицей, утащили все, кроме контрабаса и цилиндра' (Чехов)—'While he was looking at a pretty girl, some unknown jokers took from him everything but the double bass and the top-hat' (Chekhov). 'Пока он пел, кот Васька все жаркое сьел.' (Крылов)—'While he was singing, the tom-cat Vaska devoured his chop' (Krylov). 'Пока закладывали лошадей, Ибрасим вошел в ямскую избу' (Пушкин)—'While they were harnessing the horses to the carriage, Ibrahim went into the room for the coachmen' (Pushkin).

Such materials have many disadvantages: to anybody who does not know the work or the extract in question the sentences may seem grotesque (this concerns the first two examples); it is further necessary to pay attention to the unknown words and thus distract the learner, which is useless because the narrow context and the complete lack of dependence upon a situation can neither support the idea of the expressive value of an element (for example, in the first case it is the jocose use of the word 'злодеи'—jokers, 'утащили' took) nor that of the stylistic colouring (e.g. the archaic elements 'закладывать лошадей' —to harness the horses to the carriage, 'ямская изба'—room for coachmen). A further danger lies in the use of an example in which the phenomenon practised occurs as part of artistic foregrounding: when, for example, illustrating semi-passive sentences by an example from Mayakovski—'Очень знать нам хочется, Звездная Медведица, как вам ночью ходится, как вам ночью ездится?' (We wonder, Mrs Bear, what you find walking at night like, what you find riding at night like?), we create the impression of a current semi-passive use of the verb 'ездить', 'ходить' (ride, walk). In fact, we are faced here with distinct foregrounding; the use of the semi-passive is common only in the case of a few verbs (дышится, живется, сидится etc.) and its aim in the above-quoted example from Mayakovski is a jocose personification of the constellation of the Great Bear.

Considerations about how to create a reliable basis for stylistic evaluation lead first of all to the negative demand of avoiding literary texts if they are not directly instructive in teaching the given phenomenon when individual grammatical phenomena are being mastered; and to the positive demand of endeavouring to achieve *stylistic homogeneity* of the material, including the individual exercises, as well as the highest possible *stylistic* and *situational* instructiveness which should be supported by a methodical presentation of the material. A suitably selected artistic text is certainly a necessary component of that phase of the teaching process which aims at the synthetic practice of independent cultivated utterances of the written type. A transition to authentic literary texts should obviously be represented by literary, not adapted texts of a simplified type based on grammatical and other language phenomena that have already been mastered and are supplemented by a system of exercises aimed exclusively at mastering the basic stylistic phenomena. In the initial phase of work with authentic artistic texts we find the following procedure to be ideal: first, exercises should be aimed at mastering those phenomena necessary for the comprehension of the artistic impression of the text. The introductory sentence of the well-known Song of the Stormy Petrel by Gorky is given as an example: 'Над седой равниной моря ветер тучи собирает. Между тучами и морем гордо реет Буревестник, черной молнии подобный.' (a literal translation: 'The wind is amassing clouds over the greyish plain of the sea. A Stormy Petrel is floating proudly between the clouds and the sea, similar to black lightning.— A literary translation: O'er the silver plain of ocean winds are gathering the stormclouds, and between the clouds and ocean proudly wheels the Stormy Petrel, like a streak of sable lightning. (M. Gorky, *Selected Short Stories*, Moscow, translated by Margaret Wettlin). Before reading the text the learner should be taught some common lexical units and their collocations, for example, 'Русская равнина' (Russian plain), 'равнины и горы' (plains and mountains) in contrast to 'поверхность воды, гладь, уровень ьоды' (surface of water). On the basis of these units, he will be able to understand quite easily Gorky's metaphoric use of the collocation 'равниил моря' (the plain of the sea). Similarly, he should learn the distinction between подобный—подобно (similar-like) as for example 'они сражались подобно героям' (they fought like heroes) or реять (флаг реет) (the flag is floating) etc. which would enable him to perceive the solemn emotion the text acquires by use of these devices. It is clear that there is never enough time to prepare the learner for the complete comprehension of every single literary text. However, a reasonable number of similar exercises will at least teach the learner how to approach the language of a foreign literary work.

3. The last method usually applied in the use of literary texts in the teaching of foreign languages is their translation into the mother tongue. What has been said above about the difficulty of determining stylistic

values of a foreign-language text without a prior solid basis for evaluation holds true in this respect too. Moreover, we force the learner to look for equivalents not only on the level of lexical-semantic relations in his mother tongue, which would still be a real task, but also on the stylistic and artistic levels which is usually beyond the capabilities of the average learner. The use of this technique as a means of mastering the language will undoubtedly be excluded from modern teaching methods. It can of course serve as a confrontation of the possibilities of expression in the foreign language with those in the mother tongue, thereby explaining the total system of stylistic devices, but this is obviously suitable only at the highest stage of foreign language teaching—at the university level. I do not consider translation itself to be a very advantageous procedure; I would prefer an analysis of good existing translations. This aspect of language teaching can easily be based on the modern theory of translation which in Czechoslovak linguistics is organically linked with the traditions of the Prague School. Contrary to other schools which deal either with the linguistic problems of translation or, with the problems of scientific literary interpretation, this theory of translation endeavours to embrace synthetically all three basic relationships between the original and the translation: (a) the relationship between the language of the original and that of the translation, (b) the relationship between form and content in the original (evaluating the aesthetic function of the foreign form) as well as in the translation (looking for equivalent forms in the mother tongue), and (c) the relationship between the resultant values of the original and the translation.[1]

A confrontation of the aims of modern teaching methods with the existing practice of including literary texts in the teaching process leads roughly to the following conclusions:

> Modern conceptions of the teaching of foreign languages stress as their aim the active ability of performing correct spoken dialogue utterances exploiting the mediocre spoken stylistic level, as well as the ability of performing independent written monologue utterances in a cultivated, stylistically higher form corresponding to a more difficult content. This aim presupposes a certain 'receptive preparedness' especially in the ability to understand more difficult spoken as well as written utterances and determine correctly their basic stylistic

[1] Contributions to the problems of the theory of translation may be found in the writings of the late Jiří Levý', (cf. i.a. J. Levý, *Umění překladu* (The Art of Translation) (Prague 1963); translated into German: Die literarische Übersetzung. Theorie einer Kunstgattung, Frankfurt am Main 1969.

levels. As a type of cultivated expression, the literary expression cannot therefore escape the teacher's attention, especially since by practising it broader cultural teaching aims are achieved. However, for the very reason that we are only concerned with one type of cultivated expression which has its specific feature (the duality of its aim—communication as well as aesthetic effect), the place of the artistic expression in the teaching process is rather complex.

What is common to all modern teaching methods is the effort to bring teaching as close as possible to the real conditions of the communicative functioning of the language in both content and method. Any exploitation of a literary text in the teaching process whether as a model of a spoken dialogue utterance or as material on the basis of which a phenomenon from a different plane than that of stylistics is to be acquired, is therefore directly contradictory.

A literary text belongs thus above all to that phase of the teaching process where a more refined expression is the object of the learner's practice. However, the variability of artistic style stipulates the criteria of the selection of literary works as well as of single texts in a rather complicated way: the main point is that the representative selections of artistic expression should lead the learner to an awareness of a certain medial position of artistic expression and its average level, in the good sense of the word, of aesthetic impression. To create this awareness is not, however, possible unless the learner has established and fixed for himself certain basic comparative stylistic criteria on the basis of other components and phases of language learning. Thus we arrive at the conclusion that the relationship between modern teaching methods and the artistic style is part of a much broader problem, how to make the basic stylistic characteristics of the single devices of expression an integral component in their acquisition and how to help the learner master the main functional styles of the foreign language concretely. We have outlined here several principles that might contribute to the attainment of this aim in the conception of the teaching of foreign languages. A more thorough elaboration as well as a practical realization of these principles may find suitable inspiration in the stylistic theories outlined by linguists of the Prague School.

13 The Prague School and Studies in the Language of Commerce

Josef Pytelka

I. After World War I at many Commercial Colleges, in particular in Germany and Holland, the theoretical study of the technical style of language in the sphere of economy, especially commerce, was encouraged. Since 1921 the Dutch periodical *De Handelscorrespondent* and its successor *De Spiegel von Handel en Wandel*, as well as some German commercial periodicals, especially *Zeitschrift für Handelswissenschaft und Handelspraxis* published many articles dealing with the language of contemporary commerce. Then at the First International Congress of Linguists, held at the Hague in 1928, E. E. J. Messing of Rotterdam read a paper entitled 'Methoden und Ergebnise der wirtschaftssprachlichen Forschung' in which he proclaimed the independence of this branch of linguistic study. Ten years later under his editorship the most significant papers on the subject which appeared in the above-mentioned periodicals were reprinted in the collective volume called *Zur Wirtschaftslinguistik* (Rotterdam, 1932) and at that time this name was generally adopted for this special branch of linguistics. Two main trends of thought can be traced in those papers. The first trend was a continuation of the historical method shown in the earlier works of A. Schrader,[1] B. Fehr[2] and A. Schirmer.[3] The adherents of the second trend, influenced probably by scholars such as Wundt or Vossler, either attempted to show the reflection of the character and customs of the respective nations in the language or they claimed that the study of the language of commerce is an aspect of the economic sciences and not a part of linguistics.[4]

Besides these theoretical studies a considerable amount of detailed

1 A. Schrader, *Linguistisch-historische Forschungen zur Handelsgeschichte und Warenkunde* I (Jena 1886).

2 B. Fehr, *Die Sprache des Handels im Altengland* (St. Gallen 1909).

3 A. Schirmer, *Wörterbuch der deutschen Kaufmannssprache auf geschichtlichen Grundlagen* (Strassburg 1911).

4 See e.g. E. E. J. Messing, *Die Sprachwissenschaft auf der Handels-Hochschule als Wissenschaft von der Nationalkultur der Völker* (1932) 116–23.

work of, e.g. the language of advertising, stock exchange dealing etc. has been accomplished. But research has failed to produce theoretical results in the form of a suitable methodology that could be applied to this field of study and to the study of style in other spheres of science and technology. It has also failed to yield a definition of the style used in the field of economy and commerce and to present 'Wirtschaftslinguistik' as a linguistic discipline.

Such was the general atmosphere when in the early 'thirties members of the Cercle Linguistique de Prague became interested in the study of the language of commerce. The Czechoslovak linguists were able to use some of the conclusions reached by foreign researchers, but from the very beginning they based their work on entirely different principles, i.e. on those of structural and functional linguistics, which they continued to develop in an original manner.

The stimulus to the study of problems dealing with the functional differentiation of the language was given by B. Havránek.[1] According to his formulation, the system of a given language splits into a number of special languages, which at that time were conceived as independent structures within a given language. The language of commerce was considered as one of these 'functional languages'. Z. Vančura in his book *Hospodářská linguistika* (Economic Linguistics),[2] a pioneering work in this field, conceived the 'language of commerce' as a more or less independent language structure within the standard language given by social environment and thematic basis. Under the influence of these views the term 'Wirtschaftslinguistik' (economic linguistics), quite common in Germany at that time, was adopted. However, from the onset, it was considered a linguistic discipline, not part of economic science.

As has been shown elsewhere in this volume, views of functional languages (dialects) were later reviewed and given more precise form. Today we no longer conceive of 'the language of commerce' as an independent structure and we have therefore also abandoned the term 'Wirtschaftslinguistik' (economic linguistics). Where it is still used, it applies only in the historical sense. In this paper we mean by the term 'the language of economics and commerce' the functional style of the standard language used in technical, colloquial or journalistic utterances in the sphere of economics and commerce.

[1] B. Havránek, 'Úkoly spisovného jazyka a jeho kultura' (Tasks of the Standard Language and its Cultivation) in the collective volume *SČJK* 32–84, and also in the book *Studie o spisovném jazyce* (Studies in the Standard Language) (Praha 1963) 30–59.

[2] (Praha 1934) 47–9; see also his paper 'The Study of the Language of Commerce' *TCLP* 6 (1936) 159–64.

Interest in research into the language of commerce was centred around the School of Commerce in Prague and partly in Bratislava. Discussions took place both in the Prague Linguistic Circle and the School of Commerce and led to a number of publications in this field. The authors concerned with this study, all of them members of the Prague Circle approached their problems synchronically and adopted one of the chief principles of the Prague School of Linguistics, namely that the devices of language form a purposeful system, i.e. that no linguistic phenomenon should be thought of in isolation but always in relation to other parts of the system of the language. They also established a consistent functional differentiation, i.e. they carefully distinguished the purpose of all linguistic means of expression, spoken and written, and they observed the suitability of the linguistic devices used for this purpose. They adopted the principle of the analytical comparison of functional and structural relations in the mother tongue and the language under observation, and they compared similarities and differences of individual technical styles, and the same style in different languages.

The application of these and other principles of the Prague School and the concrete research into carefully defined material helped to throw light on many general problems. For the first time in Czechoslovakia the study of technical style was carried out on a scientific basis. This stimulated further studies in related aspects of different languages and theoretical research into the language of science and technology, which, since the 'fifties, has been the centre of interest among Czechoslovak Bohemicists. It was their interest in technical terminology in particular that found further development in a number of studies, both theoretical and practical, that have appeared since the end of the second world war. (Cf. the contribution by J. Dubský to this volume).

The most important works in this field were written in the 'thirties by Z. Vančura, L. V. Kopeckij[1] and T. Krejčí.[2]

[1] L. V. Kopeckij. 'Funkční linguistika a metodika' (Functional Linguistics and Language Teaching Methodology) *Charisteria Guil. Mathesio* (Praha 1932) 141–2; 'Základní rysy moderní linguistiky a školní praxe' (Principal Features of Modern Linguistics and School Praxis) *ZÚOŠ* (1932) 8–10; 'O lexikálním plánu hospodářského jazyka' (On the Lexical Plane of the Language of Commerce) *SaS* 1 (1935) 120–2; Písemný *výcvik* při studiu cizího jazyka (The Teaching of the Written Language) (Praha 1941).

[2] T. Krejčí, 'Funkční linguistika a naše obchodní školství (Functional linguistics and our schools of commerce) *Naše doba* (Our Time) 40 (1932–33) 88–94; 'Funkce automatizovaných a aktualizujících jazykových prostředků v obchodní korespondenci' (The Function of Automatized and Foregrounding Means of Expression in Commercial Correspondence) *ZÚOŠ* (Praha 1935) 120–3; 'K syntaktickému plánu německého hospodářského jazyka' (On the Syntactic Plane of the German Language of Commerce) *SaS* (1936) 243–6.

J. Čada[1] actively propagated this new field of studies in his informative articles; in 1933 in his lecture on 'Les méthodes de la linguistique commercial et économique', delivered to the Third International Congress of Linguistics in Rome, he submitted a programme for the application of structural and functional principles in linguistic studies in the field of economy and commerce.

After World War II this work was pursued further by the late L. Cejp,[2] in his work *Structural Features of English Commercial Correspondence*. At the present time members of the staff of the Prague School of Economics, founded in 1953, are studying these matters: among them J. Dubský[3] in the Romance languages and V. Irgl[4] (mainly synonymy in economic texts) and the author of this chapter in English.[5]

II. Z. Vančura attempted a definition of 'the language of commerce' and defined the scope of research in this field in the work, mentioned above, *Economic Linguistics*. His study therefore serves as a starting point for this brief survey. In accordance with L. V. Kopeckij he conceived 'the language of commerce' as the result of the influence of the social environment (and the thematic basis given thereby) and the purpose for which the language is used. Vančura delimited the

[1] Josef Čada, 'Studium cizích jazyků na školách obchodních a jeho linguistický základ' (Foreign Language Learning at Schools of Commerce and its Linguistic Basis) *SaS* (1935) 54–5; 'Budování metodiky cizojazyčného studia na Vysoké škole obchodní v Praze' (Methodology of Foreign Language Studies at the Prague School of Commerce) *ZÚOŠ* 3 (1935) 100–3; (together with L. V. Kopeckij and Z. Vančura) *Teoretické základy studia cizích jazyků na obchodních školách* (Theoretical Foundations of Foreign Language Learning at Commercial Schools) (Praha 1935); *Commerce et terminologie commercial en France* (Praha 1938); (together with O. Dubský) *Struktura francouzského jazyka hospodářského* (Structure of the French Language of Commerce) (Praha 1946); and others.

[2] Ladislav Cejp, *Strukturální rysy anglické obchodní korespondence* (Structural Features of English Commercial Correspondence) (Praha 1947); *Úvod do hospodářské angličtiny* (Introduction to Commercial English) (Praha 1949).

[3] Josef Dubský studies the style of French and Spanish business letters in 'Konstantní a potencionální složky odborného jazykového projevu' (Constant and Potential Elements in the Technical Utterance) *CJvŠ* 7 (1962/63) 292–6; 'K frekvenčnímu rozboru potencionálního lexika odborného jazyka' (On the Frequency Analysis of the Potential Lexical Means in the Technical Style) *CJvŠ* 9 (1964/65) 385–9; and 'Las unidades estilísticas en las cartas comerciales españolas '(The Stylistic Units in Spanish Business Letters) *SJMP* (Praha 1965) 18–36; see also 'Hospodářský jazyk v cizojazyčném vyučování' (The Language of Economy in Foreign Language Teaching) *CJvŠ* 5 (1958) 216–2

[4] Vladimír Irgl, 'Několik poznámek k výuce obchodní korespondence' (Some Comments on the Teaching of Commercial Correspondence) *CJvŠ* (1962/63) 258–60; 'Místo obchodní korespondence ve vyučování cizím jazykům' (The Place of Commercial Correspondence in Foreign Language Teaching) *SJMP* (Praha 1965) 127–34; 'K synonymii v anglické obchodní korespondenci' (On Synonymy in English Commercial Correspondence) *SJvŠ* 9 (1965/66) 385–400.

[5] Josef Pytelka, 'Stylistic Tendencies in English Business Letters' *SJMP* (Praha 1965) 5–17.

language of commerce as the utilization of the language for the purposes of commercial life. He accepted Havránek's earlier differentiation into 'functional languages', but he increased this differentiation by defining the systematic character of the language on the basis of a purposefully conceived theme. To Havránek's stylistic viewpoint he added the thematic point of view. In regard to the delimitation of the thematic basis, Vančura pointed to Gutkind's chance enumeration,[1] which he criticized (commercial correspondence, the codified banking terminology and terminology of the trade with merchandise, the language of economics, stock exchange, advertisement, telegrams, advertising) and to examples given by L. V. Kopeckij (the language of scientific articles on economic life, of commercial and economic journals and papers, of commercial talks, contracts, commercial correspondence etc.), among others.

Another important contribution to research into the language of commerce and the language of science and technology in general was the demand that all language utterances should be considered the expression of the style in question. In the past, when the technical style was under examination, attention was centred on individual isolated phenomena, especially scientific and technical terms. The study of them was undertaken on the assumption that they were more or less heterogeneous elements in a given language, and an explanation was sought as to how and why they differed from ordinary usage, in other words, what their formal distinction from the common language was. In accordance with the theory of functional and structural linguistics it was suggested[2] that not only the form but also the function of lexical material should be considered. Whole passages or texts which are undeniably commercial in their purpose may contain no technical terms at all. Nevertheless their function is exclusively technical. Therefore the study should cover the whole area of linguistic material serving the needs of commercial and economic activities, and not merely isolated words and phrases.

In the case of the technical style some elements, i.e. the technical terms, and the automatized commercial phrases in the commercial style, are more prominent. They do not appear elsewhere, except as obvious borrowings. Vančura proposed calling them '*the constant elements*' of the functional style in question. These constant elements are built up into a connected whole by means of other elements,

[1] C. S. Gutkind, 'Bemerkungen zur Struktur der modernen französischen Wirtschaftssprache', *Neuphilologische Monatschrift* 2 (1931).

[2] Z. Vančura, 'The Study of the Language of Commerce', *TCLP* 6 (1936) 163.

common in form and meaning to the technical style and to some other functional style, usually the colloquial style or to standard (literary) language as a whole. He called them '*potential elements*' and considered them to be constituent parts of the functional style in question.

Vančura's distinction between constant—or as L. Cejp later called them 'real' or 'material'—and potential elements was generally adopted in further work on the functional style of the language of commerce, even though later modifications and more precise definitions were added.

Apart from the definition of the character of the language of commerce Vančura and his contemporaries paid particular attention to the character of *terms* and automatized commercial phrases, as basic elements. Even though it is impossible here to give the views of each individual research worker, the notion 'automatized commercial phrase' as a typical feature of commercial correspondence does need further explanation. By such a phrase we mean a more or less constant form of speech longer than one word, but not exceeding a sentence, by which the writer reacts to a given, often repeated situation. In the language of the commercial letter it has a stabilizing, economical function: e.g. *The goods leave much to be desired.—Would you please quote us for . . .* Such an automatized phrase should not be confused with a terminological phrase, which may often later become automatized. But certain utterances which do not contain technical terms must be qualified as an automatized phrase, e.g. *We refer to your letter of 10th March.—We look forward to your early reply.* At least this must be said about the terminological (constant) elements in the language of commerce.

Other linguists concentrated their attention on the non-terminological elements. J. Dubský[1] in his investigation of Spanish commercial letters recommended the method of including these elements in conceptual groups and fields. In this way he tried to determine the characteristic features of the composition of the vocabulary of commercial letters both from a qualitative viewpoint, i.e. by determining the variety of groups, and from a quantitative viewpoint, i.e. by determining the frequency of expressions belonging to each group and field. He then compared this frequency with the frequency of identical expressions in the non-technical language.

After determining the character of the language of commerce we shall try to explain, by analysing a concrete example of the language of commerce (the language of commercial letters) how it is possible to

[1] See fn. 3, p. 214.

obtain definite results in the field of methodology and stylistic characteristics.

In the practical part of his study Vančura applied his ideas and conclusions to accounting terminology. The work of his contemporaries likewise centred mainly on the lexical aspects, where the differences were most striking in comparison with, e.g. the colloquial style.

The book of the late Professor L. Cejp, *The Structural Features of English Commercial Correspondence*, published after the Second World War, was more systematic and more broadly based.

This interest in the language of the commercial letter[1] as found in a number of other post-war works[2] can be explained not only by the endeavour to work with strictly defined material but primarily by the attempt to help the teaching of commercial correspondence at specialized commercial schools. Suitable textbooks could not be produced without a thorough analysis of the language.[3]

L. Cejp deliberately continued in the pre-war tradition of the study of the language of commerce and that of the Prague School. His work was further inspired by studies undertaken by leading members of the Prague School, which had been published before 1947.

In the first place it was possible to make full use of the studies of the written language by J. Vachek,[4] especially as far as differences between the written (or printed) and the spoken norms of a language and distinctions in their norms are concerned.

Mukařovský's study of the dialogue[5] made its influence felt, since Cejp applied its conclusions to the commercial letter. He found in the letters the same antitheses as Mukařovský stipulated for the dialogue.

The influence of the Prague School can also be traced in his conception of a commercial letter as a sign in the sense of semiology. This sign is, of course, of a higher degree. The letter as a sign is the result of the interaction of linguistic and extra-linguistic factors, i.e. situation, intention and materialization of the intention by the letter.

[1] The point of transition from personal letters to commercial ones is not clearly marked, the border-lines between commercial, legal and official correspondence are likewise fluid. L. Cejp tried to find the dividing line, see op. cit. (15–23) fn. 2, p. 214.

[2] See fns. 3, 4, and 5, p. 214.

[3] All the above-mentioned linguists studying the language of commerce are authors of commercial correspondence textbooks or specialized readers.

[4] J. Vachek, 'Zum Problem der geschriebenen Sprache', *TCLP* 8 (1939) 94–104; reprinted in *PSRL* (1964) 441. 'Psaný jazyk a pravopis' (Written Language and Spelling), *Čtení o jazyce a poesii* (Reading about Language and Poetry) (Praha 1942) 229–306. Cf. V. Barnet's contribution to this volume, pp. 30–2.

[5] J. Mukařovský, *Kapitoly z české poetiky* (Chapters from Czech Poetics), especially 'Dvě studie o dialogu' (Two Studies of Dialogue) (Praha 1941) 129–56. German transl. *Kapitel aus der Poetik* (Frankfurt a.M. 1967). Cf. the contributions by J. Camutaliová and K. Koževniková to this volume.

Although his explanations are in places allusive and fragmentary, we cannot deny the theoretical part of his work and its stimulative value.

The theoretical part is substantiated in the concrete analysis of the style of the English commercial letter. In the lexical analysis he advanced research by turning attention to the creation of technical terms, and for the first time he presented a classification table of automatized commercial phrases. He took account of morphological peculiarities, as well as syntactical ones, but was mainly concerned with stylistic analysis. He dealt with nominal and passive tendencies which are characteristic of the language of commercial letters. Mention should also be made of other trends, which he called material tendencies, such as the tendency towards mechanical expression, abbreviation and dissimulation.

The studies of the language of commercial letters were continued on French and Spanish materials by Josef Dubský. He reached the conclusion that the differences between the use of syntactical means and the differences between the syntactical tendencies in the language system as a whole and the technical style as such are of a mere quantitative character, not a qualitative one. The language of commercial letters in different languages shows striking similarities in certain tendencies. In order to obtain more detailed characteristics of the style of commercial letters he confronted the Czech and the Spanish, or French materials. In this way he tried to discover how the potential (non-terminological) elements were functioning in more complex utterances. He distinguishes two basic forms of stylistic units characteristic of this style: one occurs on the level of grammar in the form of substitution of grammatical categories (e.g. the nominal construction in one language against the verbal in the language compared); the other units are of semantic character and J. Dubský calls them 'semantic modifications' such as, for instance, various forms of amplification, condensation, gradation, and stylistic inversion. By stressing the comparison of functional and structural similarities and differences he applies one of the important principles of the Prague School.

Some further efforts have been made to present stylistic characteristics of the commercial letter on the basis of comparison of contemporary usage and the language of commercial letters, and mutual comparison between individual languages, even though this comparison was not systematic. For this purpose the result of a frequency study[1] was also used.

[1] See fn. 5, p. 214 and also the author's unpublished thesis, 'Jazyk anglického obchodního dopisu a vyučování obchodní korespondenci' (The Language of English Commercial Letter and the Teaching of Business Correspondence) (Praha 1966). A frequency list based on 602 present-day letters is a part of it.

Thus in the language of commercial letters we can trace the influence of a complex of bi-polar tendencies that affect the selection and utilization of means of expression. Only the most typical can be mentioned here. (a) *The tendency towards automation* reveals itself, e.g. in the frequent use of standard lexical means, mainly ready-made automatized commercial phrases. It is particularly strong when the situation repeats itself frequently in a stereotyped manner, especially in letters with purely communicative function. Its clearest manifestation are different types of printed forms which are widely used in banking, insurance and transport.

Where, however, apart from communicative function, the function of appeal, the endeavour to influence the addressee takes first place, a contrary tendency manifests itself, namely *the tendency towards deautomation*. It is stronger in letters written by the seller than in those written by the buyer and is strongest in sales letters (unsolicited offers).[1]
(b) *The tendency towards clarity* is very strong in all commercial letters nowadays. But under certain circumstances the linguistic manifestation of the opposite tendency, i.e. *dissimulation*, may be functionally justified. This tendency was very strong in the past. At present it reveals itself, e.g. when there is an attempt to conceal the agent of a certain action (*the circles consulted are of the opinion . . .*), where there is no wish to give a firm promise (*the matter is under consideration*), etc.
(c) *The tendency towards conciseness*, which is also very strong nowadays, is encouraged by the use of modern means of telecommunication, where brevity is the primary requirement (see, e.g. abbreviations and elliptical expressions). Its antithesis is *the tendency towards amplification*. In spite of many critics we find its effect, e.g. in the use of a broader phrase in the place of a briefer one. We find, to give a few examples, instead of *to inquire—to make inquiries*, instead of *if—on condition that*, *in the event of*, *provided that* etc.
(d) *The influence of the tendency towards effectiveness*, i.e. the endeavour to achieve the best results can be found in modern business letters in the use of, e.g. commendatory expressions, expecially of adjectives expressing positive quality usually in the superlative form: *full/best/attention; excellent/superior/exceptional/outstanding/first-class quality*. The high frequency of such adjectives is matched by the very low frequency of their antonyms (comp. the ratio 71:1 for *good/better/best* x *bad/worse/worst*).

[1] Modern firms, especially in the U.S.A. encourage their employees to abandon stereotyped phrases and to use more individual style and also modern textbooks contain long lists of phrases typical of 'commercialese' and urge the learners to abandon them.

But whenever it becomes necessary to lessen negative or unpleasant facts or to weaken one's assertions, the effect of the opposite tendency is to be found.

(e) *The tendency towards impersonality* reveals itself in a wide range of passive and impersonal constructions and is very strong, especially in banking and payment correspondence.

Recently a contrary tendency to a more *personal and casual style* is strengthened by increasing personal contacts in international trade.

(f) *The tendency towards politeness* influences the selection of means of expression very considerably. It differs in intensity and form from language to language. While, e.g. French and Spanish use long polite phrases at the end of the letter, English is content with the simple 'Yours faithfully' or 'Yours truly'. Though this tendency reveals itself in all business letters, *the tendency towards terse matter-of-factness* can be traced in certain types of letters.

All these tendencies are partly the result of the need of the writer of the letter to adequately convey information to the addressee and partly the result of the opportunities the language provides in its written form. They are all mutually interrelated and in close relation to syntactical tendencies, especially the nominal and the passive. Together they reflect the inner tension of the style of business letters at a given time.

The analysis of contemporary commercial letters must necessarily be complemented by an analysis of letters written in the past.[1] Such a comparison shows that even at the beginning of this century the language of commercial correspondence was characterized by the tendency towards automatized expressions, dissimulation, tendency towards amplification, towards impersonality and the tendency towards politeness. All this has increased the exclusiveness and considerable difference of 'commercialese'[2] from common usage.

The present-day style, on the other hand, retains some standards of its own, utilizing certain features of technical usage, politeness, economy

[1] Cf. A. P. Herbert, *What a Word!* (London 1935) 64–87.

[2] An attempt to summarize the development of the style of German commercial letters was made by T. Krejčí who closely connected the study of the language with the study of economic life. Cf. 'Funkce automatizovaných a aktualizujících jazykových prostředků v obchodní korespondenci' (The Function of Automatized and Foregrounding Means of Expression in Commercial Correspondence) *ZÚOŠ* (1935) 120–3. See also H. Siebenschein, *Abhandlungen zur Wirtschaftsgermanistik* (Praha 1936) especially the chapter 'Die Industrialisierung als Faktor zur Umstaltung der deutschen Handelssprache', where he compares several textbooks of Commercial Correspondence from 1925–1931 to show the influence of industrialization on the language of commercial letters. The result is a more concise style, its depersonification and the increased resentment against foreign borrowings.

of expression, and the resulting automatized expressions. The trend, nevertheless, clearly moves towards deautomation (a whole series of formerly common commercial phrases are now considered archaic, obsolete or obsolescent) and emphasis is placed on simplicity, clarity, briefness, a personal style, a friendly and informal tone with stress on matter-of-factness. In this manner the style is approaching the principles required for 'good English' in general, i.e. clarity, simplicity, conciseness, precise and definite expressions with variety, impact, and relevance to the occasion.[1] In the United States this style of commercial correspondence is in common use and not merely a matter of textbooks. In Britain these trends are growing stronger, even though certain firms maintain their conservative ways and traditional forms remain strong in banking, insurance, etc.

In conclusion it should be stated that although today in the above-mentioned sets of bi-polar tendencies those features are growing stronger which correspond to present-day usage, a clear differentiation in style continues to exist in commercial correspondence.

III. The most eminent members of the Prague School have always shown a lively interest in the application of functional linguistics to foreign language teaching. And it can be said without exaggeration that it was the linguists who dealt with the language of commerce, who in a number of articles tried to apply to the fullest extent the principles of the Prague School, especially to the language teaching at commercial schools. The results of functionally directed research into the language of commerce provided a solid base for the study of languages at those schools. From the functional differentiation of the language they derived the demand for respect for the specific features of individual functional styles, both in laying down the teaching aims and in the selection of teaching material. As early as 1932 L. V. Kopeckij wrote: 'I consider it methodologically incorrect to base the teaching of a foreign language for practical purposes on passages from literature which serves an entirely different function. It is necessary to find a language we need, to choose its vocabulary and structures and teach that. That means limiting the study of a foreign language only to the

[1] Cf. e.g. E. Partridge, *English III, A Course for Human Beings* (London 1949); *Usage and Abusage, A Guide to Good English* (London, Penguin, 1964); G. H. Fowler, *A Dictionary of Modern English Usage* (Oxford 1963, 2) (revised by Sir Ernest Gowers); G. H. Vallins, *Good English, How to Write it* (London 1952); Sir Ernest Gowers, *Plain Words, A Guide to the Use of English* (London 1948); and many others. See also L. Dušková, 'Péče o styl v současné angličtině' (Remarks on How to Write Good English) *ČMF* 2 (1967) 105–13.

function that is most important for our purpose because mastery of the foreign language in all its functions is almost impossible.'[1]

It has been said that there are important differences between the individual functional styles, which affect all levels of language, in particular, vocabulary. Students have to realize the specific features of the individual styles. Overlooking these differences in norms, even though it does not prevent understanding, often leads to amusing mistakes. If in normal conversation we use the sentence 'I shall endeavour to do my best to meet all your requirements' it is just as unsuitable as beginning a commercial letter with the words 'Many thanks for dropping me a line'.

Further, since in individual styles there are differences also in the selection of linguistic means, it is important to draw attention in class to those features which are typical for one style or cause the students difficulties. In the language of commercial letters this may for instance be on the level of syntax and concern passive constructions, certain types of conditional clauses, final clauses, infinitive constructions, etc.

But in spite of their differences all functional styles have a common grammatical structure and common basic vocabulary. Any specialization in teaching must be based on this essential framework. The more thorough the command of this framework the easier, more successful and quicker the training in the specialized language.

The unity of terminological and non-terminological (constant and potential) elements means that the teaching of commercial correspondence should not be limited simply to the mechanical mastery of certain terms and phrases with the student unable to link them together with non-terminological elements. In other words, in teaching commercial correspondence the aim must be conscious language performance, not a mechanical study of individual elements or entire letters. This conscious mastery of the language can be helped by stress on the preparatory exercises in composition, especially exercises in synonymy limited not only to lexical elements but likewise to eatures of grammar, particularly syntactic ones.

The teaching must pay enough attention to the wording of commercial letters, i.e. to the selection of the most suitable lexical and syntactic variants. Textbooks of commercial correspondence in referring to style are usually content with laying down certain basic principles such as the necessity of politeness, brevity, clarity etc. and present them as static features not as a complex of developing bi-polar tendencies.

[1] L. V. Kopeckij, 'Základní rysy moderní linguistiky a školní praxe' (Principal Features of Modern Linguistics and School Praxis) *ZÚOŠ* (1932) 9.

The letters should be characterized from the point of view of these tendencies. Good letters should be compared with bad ones. Frequent comparison should be made of the presentation of the same matter in a letter and in colloquial style or in different languages. In this manner the student can acquire a good standard of stylistic ability and specialized training can contribute to his general mastery of the language.

14 The Frequency of Word Classes as a Function of Style and Linguistic Structure

Miroslav Rensky

It is almost a platitude to say that verbal predication is the main principle of organization of the sentence in Indo-European (IE) languages. That it is not the only and universal principle of expressing the substances and accidents of human thinking is shown not only by languages of other ethnic groups but even by occasional non-verbal constructions within the IE group. Nor do the IE languages utilize their main syntactic principle to its utmost theoretical capacity. There is no purely verbal language that would express, in every case, the whole predicated accident by a mere verb without further complementation. Such language is conceivable but its vast number of semantically differentiated verbal units would be utterly uneconomic. The actual structure of IE texts is the result of a flexible (and economic) equilibrium between syntax and lexis. Such structure not only makes it possible to depart from the primarily anthropocentric actor-action and actor-action-goal pattern of the sentence but also enables the speakers to express as accidents phenomena primarily conceived as substances and vice versa.

Within this broad frame of the basic pattern of the verbal clause, there is a good deal of variation in usage between individual languages and between various styles. It is reasonable to presume that on the level of word classes (parts of speech), this variability is reflected in the relative frequency of nouns and verbs, and of their respective concomitants, adjectives and adverbs. A great many authors have in fact touched on this question or dealt with it in a more or less systematic way, for the most part without any frequency count whatsoever.[1] While their occasional attempts at explanation of the motivation and of the causal mechanism of this variability are often conflicting, the

[1] For a survey of bibliography see M. Renský, 'Nominal Tendencies in English', *PP* 7 (1964) 135–50.

phenomenon itself has remained undisputed, so obvious is the impression even on a most fleeting comparison. It is characteristic that most observations of this sort are expressed in terms of nominal style, nominal tendencies, or even the nominal character of a language, i.e. predilection for nominal expression where other languages, other styles, or earlier stages of the same language, prefer a finite verb. This only proves how much the basic verbal character of IE languages is taken for granted.

Although some of the earliest studies concerning our problem deal with particular styles,[1] attention later shifted to the comparison of languages, and has only reverted back to style in the latter decades. (Several meanings of the term style are relevant to our subject. I employ it here mainly in the sense of the functional styles of the Prague School, i.e. in the sense roughly corresponding to the term register used by some authors.[2] For the most part, the discussion will be limited to the style of fiction and to that of scientific texts.) Little attention, however, has been paid to the mutual relation of the two variables, i.e. of the functional style and of linguistic structure. In the following paragraphs, I shall try to demonstrate on the basis of some simple word counts that the distribution of the four basic word classes is a function of the linguistic structure of a particular language on the one hand, and of the functional style on the other. I shall also try to estimate the mutual weight of the two variables, which I believe to be of some importance for language teaching.

In a study devoted chiefly to some methodological problems of word frequency counts, P. Guiraud[3] gives the results of a tentative word count for five literary genres (*prose abstraite*, *prose concrète*, *comédie en prose*, *tragédie en vers*, *poésie lyrique*) in the last five centuries, based on 1,000 words of French texts (10 samples of 100 words each) for each genre. In spite of the limited extent of Guiraud's samples (I shall come back to the length of the samples later), his data coincide to a surprising degree with the results of a much more extensive word count undertaken for Czech, which will here be called the Czech Frequency List (CzFL for short).[4] CzFL is a frequency count of lexical units, word classes, and inflectional forms based on 1,623,527 words yielded by total tabulation of 75 works belonging to eight different stylistic spheres.

[1] H. Jacobi, 'Über den nominalen Stil des wissenschaftlichen Sanskrits', *Indogermanische Forschungen* XIV (1903) 236 seq.
[2] W. F. Mackey, *Language Teaching Analysis* (London 1965).
[3] P. Guiraud, *Les caractères statistiques du vocabulaire* (Paris 1954).
[4] J. Jelínek, J. V. Bečka and M. Těšitelová, *Frekvence slov, slovních druhů a tvarů v českém jazyce* (The frequency of words, word classes and forms in Czech) (Praha 1961).

Such results of CzFL as are comparable with Guiraud's samples (and reduced to comparable percentages) give the following comparison:

	Fiction (*prose concrète*)		Science (*prose abstraite*)	
	Czech	French	Czech	French
Subst.	38·62	37·8	45·76	45
Adj.	13·50	13·2	22·60	16·5
Verb	31·01	35	19·68	28·2
Adv.	16·87	14	11·96	10

	Drama (*comédie en prose*)		Poetry (*poésie lyrique*)	
	Czech	French	Czech	French
Subst.	32·35	32·8	47·32	46
Adj.	9·85	13·4	14·33	17
Verb	37·06	38	25·44	28
Adv.	20·74	15·4	12·91	9

The confrontation not only confirms the presumption that some significant features of individual functional styles are shared by various languages but even shows that the differences between individual languages in the distribution of word classes are generally relatively small within the same stylistic sphere, whereas the differences between individual styles within a single language are far greater. (The only apparent deviation from this rule is the surprisingly high frequency of verbs in French scientific style. This can, however, be explained by the fact that Guiraud's samples of *prose abstraite* are probably not scientific literature as conceived nowadays but rather essayistic *belles-lettres*, and, not surprisingly, as some of the samples date from as early as the sixteenth and seventeenth centuries.)

It may seem premature to formulate rules on the basis of the evidence given so far. However, I shall be able to corroborate the rule with the results of yet another frequency count of yet another IE language, this time undertaken with the specific aim of examining the dependence of word class frequency on the interplay of functional style and linguistic structure.[1] The word count was based on 10 samples of 1,000 words each of contemporary English fiction and scientific literature. The English samples were compared both with existing Czech translations and with original Czech fiction and scientific texts. The amount of material analysed totalled almost 18,000 words. The results were

[1] M. Renský, 'The Noun-Verb Quotient in English and Czech', *PP* 8 (1965) 289–302.

also compared with those of the relevant parts of CzFL. For practical reasons and to permit comparison with CzFL, the words were classified under the ten traditional word classes (with articles as a separate class), all of which were included in the count.

In word counts of this kind, the length of the samples invariably presents some problems. Longer samples tend to eliminate the more variable factors of style (the chance influence of extra-linguistic reality, the stylistic aim of the author in a particular passage, etc.) and stress the more constant factors (the individual style of the author, the functional style, and the style of the language), and vice versa. Last but not least, there is the human factor—the amount of time and means available. In the circumstances, it seemed advisable to choose a sample length of 1,000 words, which made it possible to follow some of the more variable factors while having reasonable significance for the more constant ones, the more so as some consecutive samples could be simply added up to form larger ones. The presumption of a reasonable validity of the samples was based (besides some generally accepted formulae concerning the relation of the phenomena analyzed to the length of the sample) on the comparison of the 1,000-word samples with the results of CzFL. Thus for Čapek's novel *Život a dílo skladatele Foltýna* which, being a series of narrations, gives an intuitive impression of a fairly constant style, the results for the first 1,000 words as compared with the whole novel are as follows (in percentages):

	21,963 words (CzFL)	1,000 words
Substantives	20·87	19·1
Adjectives	7·84	9·1
Pronouns	15·72	13·7
Numerals	1·37	1·2
Verbs	21·83	21·8
Adverbs	12·46	13·6
Prepositions	8·40	9·0
Conjunctions	11·13	12·3
Interjections	0·38	0·2

Samples slightly longer than the 1,000-word ones chosen and substantially shorter than whole novels (e.g., samples of 2,000 to 5,000 words, which could still be handled by one individual) would not improve the results for the more constant factors in any significant way. This is evident from the comparison of two 2,000-word samples with their consecutive 1,000-word components.

Before reverting to our central problem, i.e. to the analysis of the more constant stylistic factors, it may be of some interest to dwell shortly on the more variable ones. The most influential and an easily traceable one is apparently the proportion of dialogue. In both English and Czech texts, the number of verbs tends to increase with the ratio of dialogue while the number of substantives tends to decrease. (This concerns chiefly the full verbs, while the ratio of copulas seems to be less influenced and the frequency of the nominalized forms of the verb hardly ever affected.) A dialogue in a literary work can be, of course, a highly stylized version of the colloquial style. It may be inferred, however, that what operates as a variable factor in literary style is a constant factor in colloquial style, i.e. that colloquial style is a less favourable medium for nominal expression than literary style. A convincing corroboration of this conclusion may be found in CzFL results for Czech drama.

In some samples, it is possible to trace a development of the noun-verb quotient in dependence on the subject-matter (other than the trivial case of enumeration of objects, which never occurred in our samples). Thus in the opening part of Priestley's novel, the noun/verb ratio develops from 2:1 for the first 100 words (description of a bar) through 7:5 for the first 500 words (thoughts of the barmaid) to 1:1 for the whole sample of 1,000 words, as the second half brings the swift development of action with some dialogue. This is certainly significant, and even if the 'static' character of the noun and the 'dynamic' character of the verb are often oversimplified, they cannot be entirely neglected. The fact that nouns and verbs usually denote notions normally conceived as objects and actions, respectively, does play a role in a word count in all IE languages alike, the slight differences in denomination (i.e. in lexis) between them being of hardly any statistical significance in this respect.

Of the more constant factors I can mention only marginally the samples giving some evidence for significant differences between the styles of individual authors. A statistically valid analysis of this factor, however, would require substantially longer samples to ensure safe elimination of the more variable factors discussed above. Another point I am obliged to ignore here are some phenomena characteristic of translations. It suffices to say that—as was to be expected for a highly inflected language—Czech translations are, on the average, 20 per cent shorter than their English originals. A more general point worth mentioning is the fact that even good translations reflect (to a certain extent at least) the linguistic structure of their originals.

Let us now return to our task of analyzing the structural and stylistic features of English and Czech literary and scientific texts as reflected in the frequency of the four word classes. To start with, I shall give here the data for the English texts in the same way as has been done above for Guiraud's French samples, i.e. reduced to 100 per cent for the four classes, and compared with the results of CzFL:

	Fiction		Science	
	Czech	English	Czech	English
Subst.	38·62	36·79	45·76	48·93
Adj.	13·50	14·26	22·60	25·31
Verb	31·01	34·38	19·68	17·70
Adv.	16·87	14·57	11·96	8·06

The pattern of the English samples follows that of Guiraud's French ones, except for the anomaly of *prose abstraite* already referred to. The comparison of English and Czech data corroborates our earlier conclusion, i.e. that the differences due to the two functional styles exceed those due to the linguistic structure of the two languages. In fact, the structural difference between English and Czech seems far too small for two languages that are supposed to be so different structurally as highly inflected Czech and analytic English. This applies particularly to fiction, where the ratio of nouns and verbs in the two languages is contrary to what may have been expected by some readers after all they have heard about the reputed nominal character of English and the reputedly verbal character of Czech. It is only the ratio of adjectives and adverbs that is true to the expected image. They also suggest the key to the solution of this apparent paradox.

The reason for the discrepancy is that our screen of word classes reproduced above is too coarse to reveal the actual differences in structural features. In order to accomplish this, it is necessary to break the class of verbs at least into the finite forms and the nominalized forms (or verbids, i.e. the infinitive and the two participles), as has been done both in our count and in that of CzFL. The results show that the apparent discrepancy is entirely due to the verbids; they are so frequent in English as to invert the total result for verbs to the advantage of English, whereas finite verbs in themselves are more numerous in Czech. (Another possible refinement of the count in this respect is a subdivision of the finite verb forms into the so-called full verbs and copulas, or empty verbs, which has been done for our samples. Within the finite verb forms, empty verbs are more numerous in English but here again, the full verbs are so numerous in Czech as to turn the scale to Czech for the total of the finite verbs.)

For our purpose, it is possible to regroup the data to obtain a 'corrected' frequency for the nominal and the verbal element:

	Fiction		Science	
	Czech	English	Czech	English
Subst.+verbids	38·97	44·23	48·31	54·79
Adj.	13·50	14·26	22·60	25·31
Verb—verbids	30·66	26·94	17·13	11·84
Adv.	16·87	14·57	11·96	8·06

These corrected data show that nouns plus verbids are now clearly more numerous in English than in Czech for both styles, whereas the proportion of finite verbs is higher in Czech. For the scientific style the figures demonstrate a fairly even increase in the nominal sphere for both languages, which entails a corresponding decrease in the verbal sphere. This trend, repeated in the two secondary components of the two spheres, is probably constant for scientific style in all IE languages. The shift of scientific style towards nominalization is undoubtedly due to the needs of highly developed and abstract thinking. The relation between thinking and the distribution of parts of speech, however, is not direct but mediate. The process of scientific thought puts specific demands on syntax and contextual organization. On the one hand, it connects into single relations the contents of two or more predications; on the other hand, it singles out specific parts of relations (usually expressed complexly in complemented predications) as nuclei of new utterances. Words must thus be incorporated into new or rare relations by the process of syntactic derivation; this is very often done by means of verbids, derivatives, or their synonyms of Latin and Greek origin.

The means of complying with these requirements of the scientific style, however, need not necessarily be the same in all languages; indeed, they are different in the two languages analyzed, as is obvious if the data of the two tables are compared. The proportion of verbids to nouns in English is almost the same for both styles, with the quotient of verbids slightly lower in scientific style (no doubt some Latin words in place of verbids account for that). In Czech, the nominal character of a scientific text is obtained by means of verbids to a higher degree than in English, since the proportion of verbids (infinitives are chiefly concerned), only slight in fiction, is increased almost three times in the scientific texts. This seems to confirm our hypothesis that the structure of a given text is primarily a function of linguistic structure and of functional style, and that the two components need not necessarily work in the same direction.

In answer to our second question, i.e. which of the two components is more powerful, our corrected frequency table attests that no matter how much the sum of nominals and nominalizations may differ in quality in individual languages and styles, the difference between the two styles is greater than that between the two languages where quantity of the nominal sphere is concerned. This is valid (for English and Czech at least) whether the sum of nominal elements is taken as comprising nouns only, nouns and verbids, or nouns, verbids and adjectives. In a more general form (insofar as it is possible to generalize on the strength of this limited evidence), our results seem to suggest that for phenomena on this level, the stylistic component is significantly stronger than the difference between the linguistic components of two IE languages.

This conclusion is of great importance for teaching a foreign language to adults, particularly to scientists. Of the various factors deciding the strategy and tactics of language teaching, the stylistic component of sentence structure is often neglected even in classes where the principal aim is the reading and comprehension of scientific texts. Yet, even students with short previous learning experience sometimes show surprisingly rapid progress in comprehension of unadapted texts in their own field, in spite of the difficulties in vocabulary and at a stage when they are still struggling with relatively elementary points of grammar in attempts at speaking. The above results explain to a great extent why this is so. Similarities in the sentence structure, the limited number of sentence patterns, the limited use of tenses, etc., all make the gap between the mother tongue and the second language smaller in scientific texts than in other styles, even in a simplified colloquial style of the language class.

I do not wish to suggest that reading-oriented classes for beginners should start with an analysis of unadapted scientific texts. Such an approach would be nearly tantamount to the mediaeval practice of memorizing pages of meaningless verse. It is, however, possible to start with simplified texts consisting of simple and frequent patterns with simple scientific vocabulary almost right away, and introduce unadapted scientific texts much earlier than is usually done, certainly not later than in the tenth lesson. The actual grading depends on the learner's familiarity with related foreign languages, which can be a great help with vocabulary. Grading according to extra-lingual difficulty takes the place of the 'cultural grading' usual for non-scientific texts. Besides the grade of complexity of the subject discussed, this grading should proceed from topics central to the particular field to interdisciplinary and generally scientific texts.

Apart from the selection and grading of texts, our statement about the relation of style and linguistic structure has some bearing on the selection and grading of grammar. It should induce prospective authors of textbooks not only to choose and order the grammatical phenomena according to their importance for the scientific style but also to devise their presentation as an explanation of grammatical differences on the basis of stylistic similarity. The practical application of this principle is largely governed by the character of the two languages concerned. For students whose mother tongue is highly inflected, such as Czech, the methodology of teaching has yet to provide an efficient means of learning how to break the code of sentences in English with its extremely limited and highly polysemantic system of endings. This is particularly true for the scientific style with its long sentences based on a limited number of sentence patterns but burdened with parentheses and clusters of modifiers. Decoding means running the sentence through an ordered set of rules, part of which may run somewhat like this:

	Yes	No
	(Proceed to rule No.:)	
1. See if you can find an unmistakable verb (*is*, *was*, *were*, etc.)!	31	2
2. See if you can find a word ending in *-s*!	3	51
3. Can you decide if this word is a verb?	19	4
4. Can you decide if the subsequent word is a verb?	23	5
⋮		
31. See if the subsequent word is a participle!	41	32
32. See if the next but one word is a participle!	41	33
⋮		

(Other rules lead the reader to disentangle nominal clusters starting with the last noun before *of*, etc. There are, of course, numerous short-cuts due to lexical content and previous experience with similar patterns.)

This is what the learner is actually learning (or rather left to pick up) while being made to concentrate on an entirely different (and usually much less productive) set of rules, such as the sequence of tenses, etc. It would be futile to expect that conscious learning of the whole set of rules as indicated above would help the learner any more than learning by heart the set of motions required for driving a car. A judicious selection of some central rules, however, may be of great help.

The same applies to contextual organization (functional sentence perspective), which is all the more important in scientific style because of the encumbered character of its sentence patterns. Yet in spite of its being interlocked with word order and with the means for determination, both of which function in an entirely different way in Slavonic languages, Czech learners of English get hardly any instruction on this interrelation apart from a brief mention of the 'existential *there*'.

Last but not least, there is selection and grading of exercises. A consciously and consistently style-oriented textbook can introduce many improvements in this field. In reading-and-comprehension classes, translation into the learner's mother tongue will no doubt keep its place (if only as a remedy against translation by guesswork, which can be annoyingly habit-forming with some learners). It is however, not nearly the only form, nor necessarily the best one at all stages, for exercise and testing. Many exercises can be based on some of the decoding rules mentioned above. Comprehension of texts can be tested (and practised) by sets of questions (different for scanning and for full comprehension), sentence completion, various quizzes, etc. In classes geared to encouraging competence in the spoken word many exercises can be grouped by the basic relations (and/or by the more specific formulas) frequently occurring in scientific texts (equivalence, implication, negation, admission, conclusion, etc.) rather than by the grammatical (and lexical) means of their expression.

It is not the intention of these marginal notes to give a prescription for a style-oriented textbook. They were meant to suggest that such a textbook is conceivable and useful, and to give another example of how language teaching can profit from the results of contrastive linguistic analysis.

Index of names

Index of subjects

In order to keep the index within the appropriate limits of this book, the items included in it are not exhaustive of the whole text (Editor).